Mark Twain's Last Years As a Writer

Mark Twain's Last Years
As a Writer

William R. Macnaughton

University of Missouri Press
Columbia & London, 1979

Acknowledgments

I would like to thank the University of Waterloo for granting me a sabbatical leave during which I was able to complete most of the research on this project. As well, I wish to express my deep appreciation for the financial aid given me by the Canada Council.

Almost all of my research was done at the Mark Twain Papers at the University of California, Berkeley. To the superbly capable, helpful, and friendly staff at the Papers, I am extremely grateful. I owe a particularly large debt to the director, Frederick Anderson. He not only convinced me of the project's value, but, as the project developed, he continually made available to me his knowledge, his tactful advice, and his kindness.

In addition to the individuals at the Mark Twain Papers, there are several other persons whose generosity I wish to acknowledge. Among Mark Twain scholars, I wish to thank Alan Gribben for his suggestions about Mark Twain's reading and Robert Regan for the ideas that my conversations with him helped me to generate when this project was in its early stages. I am particularly grateful to Louis Budd for his encouragement and for his willingness to read my manuscript and to make valuable criticisms of it.

Among my colleagues at the University of Waterloo, I wish to acknowledge an important debt to Ken Ledbetter, who perused the manuscript and made helpful suggestions about it. I wish also to thank Keith Thomas who made me feel welcome whenever I came to him seeking general information about how to prepare a long manuscript for publication. I am also grateful to Warren Ober, English department chairman, for encouraging me and for permitting me to structure my time so that I could complete this project. I wish as well to thank Maxine Bechtel for her skillful and dedicated secretarial assistance.

Finally, I wish to thank my wife for her enthusiastic interest, incisive suggestions, and patience.

To my sons, Paul and Eric
with thanks for their healthy skepticism

Contents

Library of Congress Cataloging in Publication Data

Macnaughton, William R., 1939–
    Mark Twain's Last Years As a Writer.

    Bibliography: p. 243
    Includes index.
    1. Clemens, Samuel Langhorne, 1835–1910.
2. Clemens, Samuel Langhorne, 1835–1910—Biography—
Last years and death.   I.   Title.
PS1332.M34   818'.4'09 [B]   78–19846
ISBN 0–8262–0264–0

Short References

MTP • The Mark Twain Papers, Bancroft Library, University of California, Berkeley

PS • Photostat

SLC • Samuel L. Clemens

TS • Typescript

Critical Heritage • *Mark Twain, The Critical Heritage,* ed. Frederick Anderson (London: Routledge & Kegan Paul, 1971)

damned human race • *Mark Twain on the damned human race,* ed. Janet Smith (New York: Hill and Wang, 1962)

F of M • *Mark Twain's Fables of Man,* ed. John S. Tuckey (Berkeley, Los Angeles, London: University of California Press, 1972)

God's Fool • Hamlin Hill, *Mark Twain, God's Fool* (New York, Evanston, San Francisco, London: Harper & Row, 1973)

HHR • *Mark Twain's Correspondence with Henry Huttleston Rogers, 1893–1909,* ed. Lewis Leary (Berkeley and Los Angeles: University of California Press, 1969)

HH and T • *Mark Twain's Hannibal, Huck and Tom,* ed. Walter Blair (Berkeley and Los Angeles: University of California Press, 1969)

LE • *Mark Twain's Letters from the Earth,* ed. Bernard De Voto (New York and Evanston: Harper & Row, 1962)

Mr. Clemens and Mark Twain • Justin Kaplan, *Mr. Clemens and Mark Twain* (New York: Simon and Schuster, 1966)

MSM • *Mark Twain's Mysterious Stranger Manuscripts,*
ed. William Gibson (Berkeley and Los Angeles:
University of California Press, 1969)

MTE • *Mark Twain in Eruption,* ed. Bernard De Voto
(New York: Harper & Row, 1940)

MTHL • *Mark Twain–Howells Letters,* ed. William
M. Gibson and Henry Nash Smith with the assistance
of Frederick Anderson, 2 vols. (Cambridge, Mass.:
Harvard University Press, 1960)

MTL • *Mark Twain's Letters,* arranged with comment
by Albert Bigelow Paine (New York and
London: Harper and Brothers, 1917)

MTLS • John Tuckey, *Mark Twain and Little Satan*
(West Lafayette: Purdue University Studies, 1963)

MTN • *Mark Twain's Notebook,* prepared for
publication with comments by Albert Bigelow Paine
(New York and London: Harper and Brothers, 1935)

MTW • Bernard De Voto, *Mark Twain at Work*
(Cambridge, Mass.: Harvard University Press, 1942)

WWD? • *Mark Twain's Which Was the Dream?,* ed.
John Tuckey (Berkeley and Los Angeles:
University of California Press, 1967)

What Is Man? • *What Is Man? and Other Philosophical
Writings.* Vol. 19 of *The Works of Mark Twain,* ed.
Paul Baender (Berkeley, Los Angeles, London:
Published for The Iowa Centre for Textual
Studies by the University of California Press, 1973)

Writings • *The Writings of Mark Twain, Definitive
Edition,* ed. Albert Bigelow Paine, 37 vols. (New York:
Gabriel Wells, 1922–1925)

Introduction

There was a time during the latter part of the 1880s, as he worked with sporadic enthusiasm on *A Connecticut Yankee in King Arthur's Court*, when Mark Twain felt that he was approaching the end of his writing career. The manuscript, he hoped, would be finished around the same time as the Paige typesetter, an invention in which he had invested heavily. Because the marvelous apparatus would make him a millionare and his publishing house would continue to prosper, he would no longer need to write; he could become Samuel Clemens, businessman.[1] Time proved, however, that his predictive powers were roughly commensurate with those of his Connecticut Yankee, whose dreams of a mechanized and democratized England were obliterated at the Battle of the Sand Belt. As Mark Twain continued to feed money to the omnivorous machine, it gradually became obvious that his predictions would be disastrously wrong. Words continued to pour from his pen: essays; short stories; sketches; longer fiction of inferior quality, like *The American Claimant*, *Tom Sawyer, Detective*, *Tom Sawyer Abroad*, and *Joan of Arc*; and one fascinating, flawed novella of generally superior quality called *The Tragedy of Pudd'nhead Wilson*, which was miraculously extracted from an unfunny farce, "Those Extraordinary Twins." More significantly, rather than becoming affluent, he subsided ingloriously into bankruptcy by the mid-1890s.

Primarily because of the urgings of his wife and of his friend and adviser H. H. Rogers of Standard Oil, the writer decided to pay his creditors one hundred cents on the dollar; then he (along with his wife, Livy, and his second daughter,

---

1. In his 24 August 1889 letter to Howells, written while he was awaiting the proofs of *Connecticut Yankee*, Mark Twain mentioned his hope that the novel would be his literary "swansong" (MTHL, 2:610–11). For abbreviations used in the footnotes, see "Short References," pp. ix–x.

Clara) began a world speaking tour in 1895, which was completed in the late summer of the next year. Twain then remained in England and, while waiting for the two women to return from America with his other two daughters, contemplated the book that would chronicle his travels. But his eldest daughter, Susy, did not return. She had died of spinal meningitis while her mother and sister were sailing for home. Livy, shattered, recrossed the Atlantic with Clara and her younger daughter, Jean (whose own condition was soon to be diagnosed as epilepsy). For approximately the next year the family secluded itself in London; Mark Twain labored on his travel book and fought with his grief. His career after he completed *Following the Equator* in the summer of 1897 will be the central concern of this study.

The consensus about Mark Twain as a writer during these last approximately thirteen years is that he was a failure—that although literally reports of his demise that circulated before he returned to America may have been greatly exaggerated, figuratively they were not. Critics have pointed to the abundant and pitiful array of manuscripts that he worked on so obsessively and never finished; have claimed that the ones he did complete are no longer worth reading; and have noted that the finished, posthumously published "Mysterious Stranger"—a narrative with a flair worthy of Mark Twain—was not completed by him, but was laundered and pasted together by Albert Bigelow Paine and Frederick A. Duneka. That this is the consensus is suggested primarily by two facts: first, practically all the general interpretative-evaluative works about the author either ignore this period or give it short shrift, typically including an extended discussion only of the Paine-Duneka "Mysterious Stranger" (with perhaps a nod in the direction of political writings such as "To The Person Sitting in Darkness" or short stories such as "The Man That Corrupted Hadleyburg"); second, despite the recent publication by the Mark Twain Papers of unfinished manuscripts written during these years, such as "Tom Sawyer's Conspiracy," "Which Was It?," and "The Refuge of the Derelicts," there is a dearth of journal articles devoted to the late literature.[2]

2. There has, however, been considerable interest shown in the

This, of course, is not to imply that any scholarly "establishment" conspiracy of silence exists in connection with these writings. My impression is that many admirers of Mark Twain either have not read this material (perhaps because they believe the consensus about it), have not read it recently, or have not read it with sufficient sympathy for the writer's purposes. What well may be the most formidable obstacle impeding an appreciation and understanding of many of the later writings is the continuing influence of the work of Mark Twain's second literary executor, Bernard De Voto. It is difficult, after reading in De Voto's *Mark Twain at Work* his remarkable essay "The Symbols of Despair," not to think of the words *despair* and *frustration* when pondering the

---

polemical writing that Mark Twain did during these years, although little of this work is critical, most of it being concerned either with explaining the history of certain political attitudes held by the humorist or with explaining the social context in which his pronouncements were made. My own study touches upon the polemical literature in several chapters and focuses upon it in Chapter 7. On all these occasions, I have attempted to acknowledge my debts to scholars such as Louis Budd and William Gibson, who have done excellent work in this area. My general understanding of Mark Twain's career as a whole has been aided immeasurably by my reading not only of the studies to which I often acknowledge specific indebtedness in these notes, but also of the work of scholars whose findings I have seldom used directly. In this latter category I would include such books as those by Pascal Covici, Jr., James Cox, and Kenneth Lynn on Mark Twain's humor; Roger Salomon's on the writer's attitude toward history; Albert Stone's on his use of childhood in his literature; and Gladys Bellamy's pioneering work on Mark Twain's literary techniques. Since one of my interests throughout my research was to discover whether significant continuities existed between the pre- and post-1897 writings, all of this scholarship and criticism proved valuable to me. On the other hand, with the exception of commentary on the fiction relating to little Satan (usually the Paine/Duneka "Mysterious Stranger"), there is little discussion of the other fiction that Mark Twain worked on during this late period. When I have discovered criticism relating to this fiction I have seized it eagerly, for example, Howard Baetzhold's comments on "The Double-Barreled Detective Story," Stanley Brodwin's discussion of the Adam and Eve material ("The Humor of the Absurd: Mark Twain's Adamic Diaries"); Arthur Pettit's remarks about "Which Was It?," and—most recently—Sholom Kahn's book on the "Mysterious Stranger" manuscripts.

manuscripts Mark Twain worked on after 1896.[3] It is hard
not to think of these words even if we remember that, from
De Voto's point of view, Mark Twain was able eventually
to transcend his problems; and even if we know from John
Tuckey's *Mark Twain and Little Satan* that DeVoto's guesses about the periods in which certain manuscripts were
written were generally incorrect. If, moreover, one has read
Justin Kaplan's *Mr. Clemens and Mark Twain* or Hamlin
Hill's *Mark Twain, God's Fool,* it is difficult not to be im-
pressed with the variations on the word *obsession* that both
writers use so effectively in explaining Clemens's activities
after he returned to America in October 1900.[4] As well, it is
incontrovertible that the writer was afflicted with many savagely bleak moods, that he did circle repeatedly over a few
ideas while attempting to give them fictional embodiment,
and that several of his manuscripts do provide only "the
thinnest kind of disguise for the author's own inner world,"
as John Gerber has written.[5] It is also true that many of his
projects aborted; that much of his finished work is not to the
contemporary taste; and that he wrote neither another *Huckleberry Finn*, nor a Menippian satire, nor even an attack on
the type of man that his "godfather," H. H. Rogers, is assumed really to have been. These are the works that many of
the writer's admirers—not only Van Wyck Brooks in *The
Ordeal of Mark Twain*—would have had him create.[6]

Despite these facts, the words *despair* and *obsession* will be
conscientiously avoided in this study, not only because they
have serious theological and psychological implications, but
also—and most significantly—because such abstractions are
misleading when used to explain complex states of mind.
It is the complexity of the problem—the reasons for Mark

3. *MTW*, pp. 105–30.
4. I will, of course, have more to say about both books later in
this study.
5. John Gerber, "Mark Twain," in *American Literary Scholarship, 1967,* ed. James Woodress (Durham: Duke University Press,
1969), p. 58.
6. Van Wyck Brooks, *The Ordeal of Mark Twain* (New York:
E. P. Dutton & Co., 1920). This work remains, it seems to me, the
most provocative book written about Mark Twain. It is filled with
oversimplifications, but these have enough truth in them to almost
compel that they be confronted.

Twain's inability to finish almost all his major projects—that will be examined in this book. Mark Twain started manuscripts, laid them aside, returned to them, shifted direction, then discarded them, all for a multitude of reasons: some, to the outsider, are picayune—he had a cold, he was moving to a new place of residence—some, from any point of view, are profound and are intimately related to his conception of himself as a man and a writer and to the problems of being a popular author for a large series of audiences in the late nineteenth and early twentieth centuries. When Mark Twain's hiatuses, his changes in direction, and his stops are examined closely, one comes to realize the wisdom of specificity, of focusing on a particular decision at a particular time. The only generalization that will be hazarded at this moment about the causes of his failure to complete several manuscripts is that Mark Twain had an unfortunate fondness for stories spun off from one idea—the idea of a man having a horrible dream of manifold disasters resulted in "The Great Dark," "Which Was the Dream?," and "Which Was It?," the narratives somewhat misleadingly referred to as the "despair group." On the other hand, it will be one of the purposes of this study to explain the reasons he was enamored of this concept.

I will devote a substantial amount of space to examining the writer's life during the approximately four years between Susy's death and his return to America in 1900. Within this period, Clemens and his family wandered through England, Switzerland, Austria, and Sweden for a variety of reasons: surcease; economy; the health of Livy Clemens and of the younger daughter, Jean; the musical aspirations of the older daughter, Clara. The links between the writer's life and his profession are crucial during this period, and not enough useful and revealing words have been written about them.[7] In discussing his last American years, the references to Clemens's

7. In addition to the biographies of Mark Twain by A. B. Paine (volumes 30–33 of *Writings*) and by Justin Kaplan (*Mr. Clemens and Mark Twain*), two books that contain useful information about this period are DeLancey Ferguson's *Mark Twain: Man and Legend* and Arthur Scott's *Mark Twain at Large*. Of the published information, the most important may be found in the volumes of correspondence between Clemens and Howells (*MTHL*) and, in particular, between Clemens and H. H. Rogers (*HHR*).

life will be shorter and less frequent, because much of the material is familiar. At times, however, I will suggest interpretations of Clemens's actions that differ from those offered, in particular, by Hamlin Hill in *God's Fool*. I should stress at this point both how much I have learned from Hill's book and also how substantially I disagree with the image that it projects of its subject. Having examined many of the same documents as Hill, I remain unconvinced that, as *God's Fool* suggests, Clemens was so frequently out of control.[8] Nor when I look do I see the unprincipled monster conjured up by some sections of this provocative, but I think sometimes misleading, study.

In addition to its detailed concern for the vicissitudes apparent in the Mark Twain manuscripts, my own work has a polemical purpose: to demonstrate the solid value of much of the literature that he wrote between 1897 and 1910 (in particular, between 1897 and 1906). Although a great deal of the Mark Twain writing was fragmentary, there exist some brilliant, memorable fragments. Moreover, many of the short pieces that he chose to publish during his lifetime were superb, not simply because they supported the right causes, but because they demonstrate great skill, particularly the essays,

---

8. In aligning myself (however uncomfortably) with the tradition established by Mark Twain's official biographer, Albert Bigelow Paine, I realize that I am not alone. In his reviews of *God's Fool*, for example, John Tuckey has indicated essential disagreement with some of its ideas, by saying, for example, "despite the tensions of his last years, he remained appreciably sane as well as creative" (*American Literature* 46 [1974]: 117). Also, in his "The Turn-of-the-Century Mark Twain: A Revisit," Bertram Mott asserts, "Surely there is copious evidence that the pessimism of the-turn-of-the-century Mark Twain, like the premature account of his death, has been somewhat exaggerated" (p. 16). And earlier, Edward Wagenknecht wrote, "Actually the contrast was not as clearcut as that, for Mark Twain knew a good deal of happiness even in his last period" (*Mark Twain: The Man and His Work*, p. 205). Most recently, Sholom Kahn has written a book whose central purpose is to convince readers that the "total effect" of many of Mark Twain's later writings—particularly "No. 44, the Mysterious Stranger"—is "one of mature mastery and control" (*Mark Twain's Mysterious Stranger: A Study of the Manuscript Texts*, p. 7).

like "King Leopold's Soliloquy," that are reputedly undisciplined.[9]

Before this introductory chapter is complete, a few idiosyncratic aspects of the following study should be explained—for example, its relative lack of lengthy references to the autobiographical dictations. On occasions, Mark Twain believed that his developing, sprawling, mammoth autobiography would outlive anything he had ever done. There is no doubt, however, that posterity will judge the writer to have been wrong, after difficult and inevitably controversial editorial decisions have been made about the corpus of the work and after responsible, scholarly editions of the autobiography have finally been published. Many of the entries published in the volumes edited by Albert Bigelow Paine and in *Mark Twain in Eruption* are pleasurable and fascinating, it is true. It is also true, however, that the majority of the autobiographical material is trivial, self-indulgent, and—what is most unfortunate coming from Mark Twain—dull. This is particularly true of the dictations that are still unpublished. Moreover, Hamlin Hill's *God's Fool* contains, scattered throughout the text, a number of intelligent comments about the dictations. For these reasons, therefore, I have not felt obliged to discuss the material at length, but only when it has suited my purposes.

Neither have I commented at length about the nonautobiographical pieces that Mark Twain worked on after *What Is Man?* was published in 1906. The scholarship already available seems to me to provide good and sufficient discussion of essentially insignificant (except for "Letters from the Earth") material.[10]

What may also strike the reader as idiosyncratic about the following study is the amount of space devoted in it to cer-

9. In reading Maxwell Geismar's enthusiastic *Mark Twain: An American Prophet,* one sometimes receives the impression that the only reason certain pieces are being praised is because their politics are, from Geismar's point of view, exemplary.

10. See, for example, the relevant sections in the several biographical works that discuss these years; the introductions and textual notes written for volumes such as *F of M* published by the Mark Twain Papers; and Stanley Brodwin's article, "Mark Twain's Masks of Satan: The Final Phase."

tain other works: several pages, for example, to an essay written in 1897 called "Stirring Times in Austria"; only a few pages to "No. 44, the Mysterious Stranger." In each of these instances, my justification is related to this book's primary focus, which is on Samuel Clemens neither as dismal drifting derelict, nor as Lear raging on the heath, nor as American prophet. It is instead on Mark Twain as professional writer. Any piece, therefore, that is particularly revealing about the man in this role will be deferred to.

1

A Man of Humor and Honor
August 1895 to July 1897

In late August 1895, as Samuel Clemens, Livy, and their daughter Clara prepared to embark from Vancouver on their world tour, a newspaper wrote,

> At the age of sixty years Mark Twain manfully faces four years of the hardest labor to provide money, not for his comforts nor for a heritage to descendants, but to pay debts contracted by a firm of which he was a member. . . .
>
> Without any appeal for sympathy or any suggestion of assistance, keeping away from pathos and avoiding pity, this man of stern honor begins in his old age the same struggle as he once before made.[1]

As the tour progressed, similar encomiums and continual loud applause greeted this "Man of Humor and Honor" (as the newspaper called him). A poem written by an ungifted but sincere South African admirer suggests the atmosphere in which Clemens and his family moved for much of their year's sojourn abroad:

> A famous man to Durban came—
> At least the papers said so;
> With praises oft, they spread his fame,
> And sweet is praise if true, oh.
>
> In this case, it seems rather strange,
> Where praise ran so unstinted,
> When tested, there's not one would change
> Its tone from what was printed.
>
> This gentleman was really Twain—
> Some called him Mister Clemens,

1. Clippings file, MTP, "1895–96, Around the World." For abbreviations used in the footnotes, see "Short References," pp. ix–x.

The Yankee humorist, whose vein
Could kill *delirium tremens*.

. . . . . .

As rarest flowers, or sparkling gems,
His humor's entrancing:
And, justly proud, all own the claims
That round dear Mark are dancing.

The *elite* and the non *elite*
Alike are moved to laughter;
Once seen, like the electric light,
He's prized forever after.

D. P. Carnegie[2]

Before leaving Clemens had remarked in a letter to a friend that, despite the bankruptcy, his family and he had tightened their belts and had "begun life on a new and not altogether unpromising basis."[3] From this modest beginning, the situation had improved considerably when, in late summer of 1896, he approached the tour's termination. He had lived a typically American story of poverty followed by wealth and then by bankruptcy; he would now be atypical by paying his creditors one hundred cents on the dollar and climbing toward wealth again. At sixty-one he would prepare for a new career, one that would undoubtedly be less flamboyant than those that preceded it, but that would probably be similar to the life he had led just after his marriage. Yet the outline of the future was still obscure and the answer to a large question was unprovided: how could he guarantee both security for his family and a modestly spectacular vocation for himself?

Letters and notebook entries from throughout this period portray a man uncertain about the direction of his next significant move, although not frightened by the prospect of mobility. Before beginning his trip, he doubted whether a long work could be derived from his experiences, at first guessing that only a series of articles would accrue. Then (and still before the tour had really begun), he predicted the launching of a lucrative subscription volume, with his ingenious publisher, Frank Bliss, at the editorial helm; writing for

2. Scrapbook 28, p. 81, MTP.
3. *HHR*, p. 100.

magazines, he confided, was more difficult than writing for subscription. Later, different plans sprang to mind. He was fascinated, for example, with the possibility of an "Affaire" involving the French Jewish army officer Alfred Dreyfus (it had not yet become *the* Dreyfus affair); and he wanted to publish a study of the situation. Then, on 12 January 1896, he talked of writing two books "before lecturing again." As his entourage followed the equator, flattering letters from his American impresario, Major Pond, tantalized him with prospects of future triumphant and profitable speaking engagements.[4] While in South Africa, he briefly pondered a nonliterary career as American consul to Johannesburg.[5] In general, however, Clemens saw himself as a man of letters; only the kind of letters remained undecided.

Yet one thing was almost certain: it would not be as a "mere" humorist that he would be regarded in the future. As many critics and newspapers had said, both in America before he left and in the countries that he took by storm, Mark Twain possessed a serious side that had been too long neglected. The conclusions reached by the prestigious critic Brander Matthews in his *Harper's Monthly* article of 1896 were ones now seemingly being formed by many readers:

> We have today here in the United States as a contemporary a great humorist, who is also one of the masters of English prose. He is one of the foremost story-tellers of the world, with the gift of swift narrative, with the certain grasp of human nature, with a rare power of presenting character at a passionate crisis. There is not in the fiction of our language and of our country anything finer of its kind than any one of half dozen chapters in *Tom Sawyer*, in *Huckleberry Finn*, in *Pudd'nhead Wilson*.[6]

4. SLC to Frank Bliss, 30 May 1895, PS, MTP; SLC to Andrew Chatto, 19 November 1895, MTP; *HHR*, p. 191 (he is probably referring to a book about Dreyfus and one based upon his tour); see, for example, James Pond to SLC, 3 July 1896, PS, MTP.

5. Clemens alludes to the possibility of a consulship in a letter to his wife on 8 June 1896 (MTP). He was writing to Livy at this time because, for several weeks, she and Clara were living in Durban, South Africa while he observed the political turmoil in the Transvaal. See Coleman O. Parsons, "Mark Twain: Traveler in South Africa."

6. "The Penalty of Humor." Matthews had been writing friendly comments about Mark Twain's work since the publication of

As if both to capitalize on and celebrate this kind of public recognition, Clemens asked Harper and Brother's at the trip's end to announce that the reverently written *Joan of Arc* was not merely edited by Mark Twain, but was actually his book (something that many readers already had been suspecting).[7]

The question of Mark Twain's flirtation with a reputation as an essentially "serious" writer is, of course, a complicated one, and one about which more will be said later in this study. But, judging from some of the comments that he made in interviews while on his world tour, an observer must conclude that Mark Twain was trying hard to gain general acceptance of this particular image of himself. In one interview, for example, he is quoted as saying, "I maintain that a man can never be a humorist, in thought or in deed, until he can feel the springs of pathos. . . . Trust me, he was never yet properly funny who was not capable at times of being very serious."[8]

Because of Clemens's later perspective on his world tour—his doleful memories of exhaustion, bronchitis, carbuncles, and longings for home—it may be worthwhile to stress at this point that in many ways his odyssey was exhilaratingly successful.[9] He loved to be lionized; he enjoyed the reports from

---

Huckleberry Finn, would write the introduction to the Uniform Edition of the author's works, and would continue to comment appreciatively about Mark Twain after his death in 1910.

7. SLC to Mr. Harper, 5 August 1896, PS, MTP. According to James Cox, Clemens had wanted to reveal the fact of his authorship of *Joan of Arc* a year before because "he thought it would help the lecturing tour by keeping his name before the public. He wrote later, however, that Olivia was troubled about the matter and wanted Harper to decide when the time was right. Harper decided that the time to capitalize on Mark Twain's name was when the book was to be published" (*Mark Twain: The Fate of Humor*, p. 251).

8. See Louis J. Budd, "Mark Twain Talks Mostly About Humor and Humorists," p. 11.

9. See, for example, his high-spirited letters to his nephew, Samuel Moffett, on 15 August 1895 (MTP); to Joseph Twichell on 24 May 1896 (MTP); and to H. H. Rogers on 26 May 1896 (*HHR*, p. 213). On the other hand, toward the end of the tour he complained occasionally of boredom and fatigue. On 10 June, for example, he exclaimed to Livy, "What *is* there so hateful as lecturing!" (MTP). And to Rogers on 22 July, he referred to the "slavery"

H. H. Rogers that " 'Mark Twain' is on the boom"; he had every reason to expect the success of the Uniform Edition of his work, the contract for which his cautious friend and adviser was negotiating; he could revel in the news that his debts were being paid. Moreover, even as he traveled and spoke he anticipated new literary projects: Tom Sawyer sketches, the Dreyfus satire, a Brigham Young farce.[10] In writing to Pond on 10 August while waiting alone for Livy to return from America with his daughters, he lamented that he never had been truly well on his trip; yet even as he rejected Pond's lure of further platform work, he made it clear that he was proud of his accomplishment.[11] In sum, despite his complaints, he had generally enjoyed the tour. More important, primarily because of it he could look forward to a promising future.

As the reader knows, however, a nightmare lay in wait. In England, Clemens waited impatiently for his family to arrive and began a diatribe, inspired by atrocities in Crete, entitled "The Lowest Animal."[12] In America, at the Clemens family home in Hartford, Susy—his favorite daughter—died on 18 August of spinal meningitis. The effect on the man was of course devastating, both immediately and from time to time for the rest of his life. During the next few months, he vacillated between blaming himself and finding many other causes—Charles Webster, the George Warners, Bryn Mawr College, doctors, mind curists, and God—for Susy's death. Several letters written within two months of the tragedy convey a genuine and terrible sense of loss. His well-known letter to William Dean Howells, for example, contains sincere, con-

---

of the platform (*HHR*, p. 227). His retrospective attitude is epitomized in his 2 April 1899 letter to William Dean Howells: "How I did loathe that journey around the world!—except the sea-part & India" (*MTHL*, 2:690).

10. See, for example, the lengthy entry concerning a possible Brigham Young farce in Notebook 30 (I), TS, pp. 27–30, MTP. Most of the material in the notebooks of this period refers to the trip, but on occasions Clemens jotted down ideas that might be useful in the future.

11. SLC to James Pond, 10 August 1896. PS, MTP.

12. Paul Baender argues that the piece was begun around 13 August and finished in October, before *Following the Equator* was begun. See "The Date of Mark Twain's 'The Lowest Animal.' "

ventionally expressed outpourings of grief as well as virulent, oblique references to a treacherous God:

> To me our loss is bitter, bitter, bitter. Then what must it be
> to my wife. It would bankrupt the vocabularies of all the lan-
> guages to put it into words. For the relation between Susy & her
> mother was not merely & only the relation of mother & child, but
> that of sweethearts, lovers also. "Do you love me, mamma?" "No,
> I don't love you, Susy, I worship you."
>
> What a ghastly tragedy it was; how cruel it was; how exactly
> & precisely it was planned; & how remorselessly every detail of the
> dispensation was carried out. Susy stood on the platform at Elmi-
> ra at half past ten on the 14th of July, 1895, in the glare of the
> electric lights, waving her good-byes as our train moved westward
> on the long trip; & she was brimming with life & the joy of it.
> That is what I saw; & it was what her mother saw through her
> tears. One year, one month, & one week later, Livy & Clara had
> completed the circuit of the globe, arriving at Elmira at the same
> hour in the evening, by the same train *& in the same car*—& Susy
> was there to meet them—lying white & fair in her coffin in the
> house she was born in.
>
> They were flying on the wings of steam & in the torture of
> dread & anxiety; & if three little days could have been spared
> them out of the rich hoard laid up for the building of the com-
> ing ages, poor Susy would have died in her mother's arms—& the
> poor three days were denied: they could not be afforded.
>
> (Blank to be filled some day.)
>
> We send our love to both of you. Mrs. Clemens asks me to
> thank Mr. Howells for his note, & to say that it was a comfort to
> her, coming as it did from a heart that had suffered the same
> bruise as her own.
>
> Good-bye. Will healing ever come, or life have value again?
>
> And shall we see Susy? Without doubt! without *shadow* of
> doubt, if it can furnish opportunity to break our hearts again.
>
> S L Clemens[13]

On the other hand—because so much attention has been
paid to the supposed effects on the writer of his daughter's
death—what must be emphasized at this point is that Clemens's bleak moods were not consistent. Nothing, in fact, is
more obvious in the surviving documents of this time than

13. *MTHL,* 2:663. See as well SLC to Edward Bunce, 26 October 1896, PS, MTP; and SLC to Mrs. Laurence Hutton, 26 November 1896, PS, MTP.

that Clemens was, remarkably, perhaps not even consciously, picking himself up again. Despite his occasional belief that "luck has turned his back on me for good, I reckon," almost as soon as he allowed his daughter's death to push his own feet into the grave, he began to scramble out again.[14] One thing that aided him was his marvelous sense of outrage: *"Sept. 26, 96.* The French have gone mad over the approaching visit of the Czar. Such an exhibition of boot-licking adulation has never been seen before. The wife of the Pres. of the Republic is not good enough to take part in the reception—by Russian command—and those lick spittles accept it & are not insulted. Is there anything that can insult a Frenchman?"

His superb sense of humor must also have been vitalizing:

Sept. 29. The Czar is to enter Paris Oct. 6. Following is the text of General Order No. 232, 964, 441, Series D, received by St. Peter late yesterday evening:

With all your experience it is apparent that you have not yet learned to exercise a politic discretion in important emergencies. I am amazed to find that you have appointed the 6th of October for My Son's Second Advent in the earth, and Paris the place. Do you wish it to go flat? Postpone it at once. I could not get the attention of the French Myself if *I* appeared in Paris on that date.

(Signed) God Almighty.[15]

The imaginatively irreverent concept, the bland bureaucratic language modulating into the angry, stentorian slang, and the signature combine to create a very funny sketch.

Along with this characteristic ebullience there was also the drive provided by his feeling of obligation to his wife and remaining two daughters. Thus, although he said in a January letter to a Hartford friend, the Reverend Joseph Twichell, that his work on the travel book will be primarily for surcease, another motive was certainly his desire to look after his family. He began also to peer beyond the travel book; the copyright on *The Innocents Abroad* was soon to

14. *HHR*, p. 236.

15. Notebook 31 (I), TS, pp. 3–4, MTP. One wonders if, in writing of French responses to the czar, he remembered a much earlier example of a similar sycophancy—that of himself and the other Quaker City pilgrims, thirty years before.

expire, and he reminded himself to renew the copyright so as not to permit this potential source of revenue to slip away. He showed keen interest in the details of the contract between Bliss and Harper for the Uniform Edition of his works, which the indefatigable Rogers was continuing to negotiate. And he looked beyond both the travel book and his old books toward future projects. On 1 November, he referred in a letter to Rogers to several literary ideas, one of which was his long considered and delayed autobiography. It is significant that he considered even this for subscription; until his debts were paid he was willing to think of practically any idea as the potential source of big sales.[16]

Several notebook entries written in December 1896 and January 1897 also suggest a man thinking, to a certain extent, of his literary future. He considered a story, for example, of a rich man who sends his daughter to live with paupers when she is two, planning to have her return to him when she is twenty-five so that she can enjoy a new and wonderful life. Because her early life has been so horrible, however, she refuses his offer and curses him for his hypocrisy.[17] Another idea concerned a picnic crowd of boys and girls who, after being lost in a forest, enter a mansion and encounter at midnight some old pilgrims from Canterbury. As the result of fairy enchantment, the groups exchange ages temporarily, the result being that while many pilgrims discover old lovers and resume their courtships, the erstwhile picnickers regret the years they have lost. Suddenly, both groups return to their previous ages, the pilgrims now feeling totally frustrated from their brief encounter with lost youth.[18] The notebook entries suggest a man preoccupied with grief. But they also suggest a writer who hopes to use dimensions of his experience—his guilt regarding his relationship with his daughter, his fears about old age, the frustration created by his

16. *MTL*, 2:641; see SLC to Frank Bliss, 21 October 1896, PS, MTP; see *HHR*, pp. 250–52; *HHR*, p. 243.

17. Notebook 31 (II), TS, pp. 37–39, MTP.

18. Ibid., pp. 41–43. Referring to this entry, Tony Tanner writes, "Age appears a terrible remorseless sentence; a punishment, a blight, an end of joy which is visited on the human race for no apparent reason" (*The Reign of Wonder: Naivety and Reality in American Literature*, p. 145).

memories of an irrecoverable past—as sources for a new kind of publishable fiction.

His moods during the months before leaving for Switzerland were often somber, but they were occasionally exuberant as well, as in this 4 January letter to Rogers celebrating the signing of contracts: "I've got a new book in my head—3 or 4 of them, for that matter. . . . I shall write *All* of them—a whole dam library. And I've struck an elegant new idea this morning for a lecture next winter in New York—a lecture that I can *enjoy*."[19] And notebook entries, even from the time he was writing the travel book, suggest an imagination neither dead not moribund, but vigorously alive, manipulating ideas both old and new, borrowed and original. He pondered, for example, an ironic romance in which a woman in heaven, after a long search for her daughter, discovers her in hell, where she herself decides to live. He thought of resurrecting an idea about which Edwin Booth had encouraged him twenty-five years before: a revamped *Hamlet* with a country cousin commenting on the action. From the London newspapers, he plucked a notorious murder case, which he proposed to fictionalize. He fantasized about a future in which Standard Oil, after gobbling up the world, prepares to gulp down the constellations.[20]

One thing to observe about each of these notations is that they were unrelated to his personal experience (except perhaps for the first, although it was related only in an indirect manner); the ideas about the rich man's daughter and the Canterbury pilgrims, on the other hand, had a definite, if somewhat veiled, relationship to his experiences. Taken to-

19. *HHR*, p. 259.
20. See Notebook 32a (I), TS, pp. 3–17, MTP. Among the several other ideas that he played with is one that he called a combined love, fashion, and adventure sketch in which even the adventures are ordered from the army and navy stores (p. 15); another idea was to lead to a love story about a promiscuous black grouse (p. 15). Still another plan was to revive an old idea of creating a "Skeleton Novelette"; either he would devise the plot and write all the stories himself or advertise the plot idea and ask for stories to be contributed to it, with five English pounds being awarded to each contributor. Typically, evinced in this plethora of ideas is both the fecundity of Mark Twain's imagination and the uncertainty of his taste.

gether, this complex is suggestive of a question that Clemens was compelled to answer while he was beginning again as a writer; how, or even whether, he was going to use his own life—particularly his most recent disasters—as an impetus for his art.

At times, his feelings overwhelmed him, the result being a letter such as the following to Joe Twichell:

> Dear Joe,—Do I want you to write to me? Indeed I do. I do not want most people to write, but I do want you to do it. The others break my heart, but you will not. You have a something divine in you that is not in other men. You have the touch that heals, not lacerates. And you know the secret places of our hearts. You know our life—the outside of it—as the others do—and the inside of it—which they do not. You have seen our whole voyage. You have seen us go to sea, a cloud of sail, and the flag at the peak; and you see us now, chartless, adrift—derelicts; battered, water-logged, our sails a ruck of rags, our pride gone. For it is gone. And there is nothing in its place. The vanity of life was all we had, and there is no more vanity left in us. We are even ashamed of that we had; ashamed that we trusted the promises of life and builded high—to come to this!
>
> I did know that Susy was part of us; I did *not* know that she could go away; I did not know that she could go away, and take our lives with her, yet leave our dull bodies behind. I did not know what she was. To me she was but treasure in the bank; the amount known, the need to look at it daily, handle it, weigh it, count it, *realize* it, not necessary; and now that I would do it, it is too late; they tell me it is not there, has vanished away in a night, the bank is broken, my fortune is gone, I am a pauper. How am I to comprehend this? How am I to *have* it? Why am I robbed, and who is benefited? [21]

Yet, even in the midst of such overt displays of grief, Clemens was prone to distort the truth: despite his assertions, he had not lost his pride, at least not consistently. He was enjoying the task of working on the still unnamed travel book and was proud of his work, as the following series of comments makes clear: "I mean to write a third more matter

21. *MTL*, 2:640–41. As has been pointed out by several critics, the imagery that Clemens employs to describe the situation of Livy and himself—particularly the references to drifting derelicts and chartless voyages—may have influenced aspects of fragments such as "The Great Dark" and "The Enchanted Sea Wilderness."

for the one volume than necessary, then weed out and leave one compact and satisfactory volume. . . . I am going to write with all my might on this book, and follow it with others as fast as I can, in the hope that within three years I can clear out the stuff that is in me waiting to be written, and that I shall then die in the promptest kind of way and no fooling around. But I want you and the rest of you to live as long as you would like to, and enjoy it all the time"; "I finished the book three weeks ago, then began the process of gutting. I gutted out one-third. I am revising and re-revising the remaining two-thirds, and am getting them into very satisfactory shape. Am very much pleased"; "The book improves every day. And I don't mind saying, now that I am getting to be most offensively proud of it and satisfied with it."[22] He was so satisfied with the developing manuscript, in fact, that he vowed to Frank Bliss that he would not be willing to trade it for any of his earlier books.[23]

He mentioned the care with which he had composed the book and complained (sounding surprisingly like Henry James) when he was asked to write material on South Africa, because "it is not easier to take a completed book apart than it is to take an Indian rug apart. Each figure would be spoiled—obliterated." Subsequently he relented; he prevented his aesthetic principles from subverting his desire to publish a best-seller and did as requested quickly, efficiently, and well. Moreover—and this is typical of practically all his work on the travel book—he had a good time doing it: "I have added 30,000 words. Part of it has been most enjoyable work to me—chaffing Rhodes and making fun of his Jameson raid. . . . It has taken me 7 months to write this book—and all of a sudden I feel tired."[24] In view of Clemens's later attitude toward his composition of *Following the Equator* (similar, of course, to his attitude toward the tour itself), it is easy to regard this period as one of unrelieved drudgery and to ignore the very real immediate and long-range bene-

22. *HHR*, pp. 214–15; ibid., p. 267; ibid., p. 269.

23. SLC to Frank Bliss, 26 March 1897, PS, MTP. For further examples of his pride in his travel book see SLC to Frank Fuller, 26 March 1897, TS, MTP; and SLC to Joseph Twichell, 10 April 1897, TS, MTP.

24. *HHR*, p. 225; ibid., pp. 276–77.

fits that accrued from the writer's "enslavement." The most tangible benefit was the money that publication produced; even more than the lecture tour, the travel book helped him escape bankruptcy.[25] Moreover, in addition to being enjoyable in itself, the activity of writing undoubtedly alleviated his grief when he otherwise might have been destroyed by it. Further, his ability to finish and publish the work must have made him more confident in his future as a professional writer.

There is something more to be said at this point, however, about the possible effects that Mark Twain's involvement with the travel book had upon his future as a writer, particularly if we conclude from the evidence that—despite his later remarks—he actually enjoyed the activity. When he wrote *Following the Equator* in 1896 and 1897, it had been many years since he had written a travel book; the last approximately two-thirds of *Life on the Mississippi* had been the most recent example, although sections of *Adventures of Huckleberry Finn*, *A Connecticut Yankee in King Arthur's Court*, and *Tom Sawyer Abroad* are in some ways analogous to travel literature. It therefore had been many years since he had savored some of the benefits that the form offered, as compared to the exigencies of fiction: the relative freedom from structural problems, which in fiction were caused primarily by the need for a plausible, carefully articulated plot; the relative ease with which his whims—a wish to write philosophically and openly about a man or a culture; a desire to compose gorgeous description; a need to create farce, satire, or burlesque—could be indulged. A final benefit was the relative lack of difficulty in finding enough material to fill a long subscription book. In other words, one of the reasons Mark Twain was unable to finish a long narrative after *Following the Equator* was that he was vexed by the contrast between the simplicity of travel writing and the problems involved in composing long fiction.

Whatever the long-range effects of his work on the travel book, in the spring of 1897 the financial success of *Following*

25. See Francis Madigan, Jr., "Mark Twain's Passage to India: A Genetic Study of *Following the Equator*," p. 220. Justin Kaplan states that the travel book sold thirty thousand copies almost immediately. See *Mark Twain and His World*, p. 176.

the Equator was anything but certain; and, during this period, Clemens's grasp on the future was not consistently firm, despite the optimistic financial bulletins from Rogers and the cheering letters from Twichell. Clemens worried about the lagging sales of his old books in an April letter to Rogers and speculated a bit fearfully about Bliss's failure to return to him the contract that he had signed so jubilantly on 4 January.[26] Then, Clemens revealed his insecurity—which continued even after Bliss visited London in May and signed the contracts—by diving headfirst into two schemes that easily could have blackened his heroic reputation with his American public. He described the first in a 27 May letter to Frank Fuller:

> Intimations have reached me a while back that friends of mine in New York and also in San Francisco would like to know if I would like to be invited to come next fall or winter and be treated to a "special benefit" lecture, at big prices for tickets and an auction of a dozen first-choice seats at Jenny Lind prices. I was not greatly taken with the idea and so I put it off and said I couldn't have time to weigh it in my mind until my book should be off my hands. . . .Lately the matter has come to me again. This time, with this suggestion: that a dozen men, each with influence over a millionaire, go each privately to his millionaire and get him to put up $1,000 and sign his name to an invitation to me to come and do a "benefit" lecture in the lecture-hall of the Waldorf hotel, and sell one seat privately at auction to the highest bidder—the highest bidder to agree beforehand as to the bid he would be willing to make—and that the rest of the tickets be put at $5 or $10 or $100 (privately sold) and if the boom failed to sell them, resort to papering the house . . . And that this private scheme be also worked by trusty men in Chicago and San Francisco—in which latter place it was believed that my old pal, Adolf Sutro would head the paper with $5,000.[27]

The second scheme, contemporary with the first, was even more fatuous and potentially humiliating. The *New York Herald*, according to a plan at first eagerly agreed to by Clemens, established a fund to rescue the pathetic bankrupt from his perils. Box scores were kept daily in the newspaper, listing the amount in the fund along with the name of each

26. *HHR,* pp. 273–75.
27. Quoted in ibid., pp. 287–88.

contributor and the amount of his donation. As soon as they heard about it, Livy and Rogers firmly quashed the scheme; by the time Clemens wrote to the newspaper manfully refusing the donations, it had already become clear, however, that the idea was going nowhere, despite one-thousand-dollar donations from the *Herald* and Andrew Carnegie.[28] In an attempt to protect his reputation from potential damage, Clemens asked Rogers on 23 June to donate forty thousand dollars (which would then be returned), so that the sum would not look so pitifully meager.[29] Despite the fact that Rogers refused, the writer withdrew from the fund smelling almost like a rose,[30] although a few people would undoubtedly have agreed with the editorialist in *Town Topics* who wrote:

> Whether or not "Mark Twain" is really in peril of abject poverty I do not know, for the *Herald*'s statements in the matter are worth nothing, but I am certain that Bennett's methods of relieving his alleged distress will do no more than to arouse widespread disgust and regret that one of the most brilliant lights in American letters has been made the victim either of rank ignorance or contemptible revenge.[31]

Finally, in early July, Livy scotched her husband's dreams of the big speech, prompting him to write wryly to Frank Fuller that henceforth he would stick to the legitimate, despite his

28. Justin Kaplan's biography of Mark Twain contains an accurate account of this fiasco. See *Mr. Clemens and Mark Twain*, p. 349.

29. *HHR*, p. 286.

30. Luckily for Clemens, the consensus regarding the episode is probably expressed in the following reminiscence: "In June, 1897, when he had circled the globe and had for a time settled in London, cablegrams came from that city announcing his mental and physical collapse. The English-speaking world was stricken with sympathy, and the New York *Herald* at once began a subscription fund for his relief. The report was contradicted at once, but the admiration for the author's strenuous effort seemed to grow, and the *Herald* fund was assuming generous proportions when the ... message declining to accept the relief came from the proposed beneficiary" (Edwin Watts Chubb, *Stories of Authors British and American*, p. 355).

31. See 1897 Clippings File, MTP.

distaste for this mode of operation.[32] What should be observed in these grotesque flounderings is how far this aging,
bankrupt writer was prepared to go to obtain money. Especially during the period before he returned to America in
1900, Clemens's financial insecurity influenced practically
all of his literary activities.

Significantly, almost immediately after he bowed ungrace-
fully out of the *Herald* fund, his notebook began to bulge
with new notions.[33] After the death of Susy, he often seemed
more than a bit reluctant to commit himself irrevocably to
the trade of writing, but he was running out of options; this
fact and his own genius were dragging him inevitably toward
authorship. He still had, however, one arrow left to shoot:
even while his notebook spoke of literature, he himself plied
Livy with blandishments about a Pond-managed lecture
tour.[34] Then, suddenly, in early July he was off to Switzerland, only just having been prevented by his wife from agree-
ing to a fall tour in which his daughter Clara was to have
been featured as a pianist! Perhaps it was best that he stay
out of the limelight, because of his debt to Susy's memory,
he wrote philosophically on 20 July, as he snuggled safely in
his Weggis mountain retreat.[35]

One of the most puzzling aspects of Clemens's life during
all of this period, from 1896 to 1910, was the effect his
daughter's death had on him. At times—as everyone at all
familiar with this period knows—he unleashed potent invec-
tives against a world lacking an Olivia Susan Clemens and
flagellated himself for his own responsibility in her death.
But occasionally much of this seems patently contrived,
false, and melodramatic, particularly when we compare such
outpourings with the mundane, often sunny utterances that
he was making in other contexts at practically the same time.
It is almost as if he was torturing himself because he believed

32. SLC to Frank Fuller, 2 July 1897, PS, MTP.
33. See Notebook 32a (II), TS, pp. 44–46, MTP. Among the
lengthy list of ideas are ones referring to Satan's boyhood, Ben
Franklin, Tom selling Huck for a slave, Coal-Oil Tommy, and a
new Stormfield in Heaven.
34. See SLC to Andrew Carnegie, 7 July 1897, TS, MTP.
35. SLC to James Pond, 20 July 1897, PS, MTP.

that this was how he should feel, if he hoped to be truly human. And undoubtedly he worked himself up into tantrums of grief in order to share—somehow—the suffering of his cherished wife, who lacked his resilience. It is also incontestable that the moods of this most mercurial of men led him into moments when his grief and guilt were excruciatingly, if evanescently, real.

Most of the time, however, even during the months following Susy's death, Clemens was vital and energetic, interested in the future, even while he viewed it with trepidation or occasionally yearned for the past. By the time he arrived in Switzerland, several factors had coalesced. For one thing, the travel book was finished satisfactorily (although proofs still had to be read) and its future was taken care of.[36] Moreover, the old books were promising to bring in new gold, his audience was eager to read his new work, and his market value was steadily appreciating. Finally, his "new" reputation (Andrew Lang had again called *Huckleberry Finn* the "great American novel" in a 10 June letter) seemed to provide possibilities for him to explore tones and subject matters that would have been difficult in the past.[37] Mark Twain was ready to work at being a writer.

36. In Madigan, "Mark Twain's Passage to India," it is suggested that Mark Twain's reconsideration of India as he composed *Following the Equator* would almost necessarily have had a beneficial effect on the writer, because the country was so much identified in his mind with the possibilities of rebirth. Sri 108, the 108-year-old Hindu, for example, was a "living personification of the rebirth process represented by the city of Benares, an individual made pure by abandoning the earth through religious ritual" (p. 313). And India, in general, Madigan argues, symbolized "transcendence of suffering through imagination, religion and art" (p. 328).

37. Andrew Lang to SLC, 10 June 1897, MTP. In an essay entitled "The Art of Mark Twain" written in 1891, Lang asserted, "The world appreciates it, no doubt, but 'cultural critics' are probably unaware of its singular value. A two-shilling novel by Mark Twain, with an ugly picture on the cover, 'has no show,' as Huck might say, and the great American novel has escaped the eyes of those who watch to see this new planet swim into their ken. And will Mark Twain never write such another? One is enough for him to live by, and for our gratitude, but not enough for our desire."

2

Beginning Again
July to September 1897

The Weggis environment was extremely salutary; here, as he wrote to a friend on 27 July, Clemens's spirit was beginning to heal.[1] The beauty of the mountains and lakes was something to which he devoted several ecstatic pages of notebook description. In the house above the lake there was a small den where he could read and smoke on stormy days and watch the lightning split the sky. When he wished to write, he could isolate himself in a room that he had rented in the Villa Tannen, and do so with no feelings of guilt regarding his wife and daughters, who had ample occupation with their visitors, Sue Crane and Julia Langdon, and with the magnificent Swiss terrain. In a 22 August letter he talked of working nine hours a day, seven days a week; yet, he had the time to enjoy a delightful brief visit with President Smith of Trinity College (whom Livy had met by accident in a boat on the lake) at the beginning of August and to be entranced by a performance of the Jubilee Singers later in the month.[2] He also encountered a peasant woman who prompted him to write a notebook entry combining laconic humor with frankly expressed admiration:

> Met a woman of 70 with a deep fruit-basket strapped on her back, and she stopped and remarked that the weather was very warm. I was of that opinion too—the perspiration was flowing from me, washing boulders down the hill. This was about a third of the way up the mountain. She asked if I was on my way to the summit. I said no, it was too much of a climb. She said she had been

1. See Notebook 32b (I), TS, pp. 11–13, MTP. See also SLC to Wayne MacVeigh, 27 July 1897, TS, MTP. For abbreviations used in the footnotes, see "Short References," pp. ix–x.
2. Notebook 32b (I), TS, pp. 14–15, MTP; SLC to Mr. Skrine, 22 August 1897, PS, MTP; see Notebook 32b (I), TS, p. 23, MTP; see Notebook 32b (I), TS, pp. 24–25, MTP.

up there to carry a load of peaches and pears, and was on her way down to get another load. I asked if she meant to carry that up, too. Yes, she said. Today? Oh yes, today. I tried to voice my admiration, but got tangled among the verbs and tenses and she bade me goodbye and resumed her brisk march down the slope without waiting to see where I was going to arrive with my speech. She was apparently not overheated, and was not perspiring. She was climbing 5000 feet, twice in the day, with a load of 100 lbs., descending the same distance twice, yet she seemed to think nothing of it. One ascent by itself would use me up.[3]

For a person who might have been tempted to luxuriate in grief or the pains of an imagined old age, examples like this had to be beneficial. The financial news was also good: Rogers had, as always, invested wisely and had informed his friend of the fruits of his wisdom at the beginning of August. On the other hand, 18 August was the first anniversary of Susy's death. On that date, Livy left her husband for the solitude of a private cabin, while he wrote an elegy to his daughter (soon to be published as "In Memoriam Susan Olivia Clemens").[4] He also composed a blasphemous private statement of rage and frustration with the revealing title "In My Bitterness":

In my bitterness I said, blaspheming, "Ah, my darling there you lie, rescued from life; fortunate for the first time in the years that you have lived; there you lie dumb and thankless, in this the first moment that ever you had anything to thank God for; there you lie poor abused slave, set free from the unspeakable insult of life, and by the same Hand that flung it in your face in the beginning. But I lie: you have still nothing to be thankful for; for you have not been freed out of pity for you, but to drive one more knife into my heart.

There—that is something which I have noticed before: He never does a kindness. When He seems to do one, it is a trap which He is setting; you will walk into it some day, then you will understand, and be ashamed to remember how stupidly grateful you had been. No, He gives you riches, merely as a trap; it is quadruple the bitterness of the poverty which He has planned for you. He gives you a healthy body and you are tricked into thanking Him for it; some day, when He has rotted it with

3. *MTN*, p. 335.
4. See *HHR*, pp. 295–96. Notebook 32b (I), TS, p. 27, MTP; *Writings*, 22:384–86.

disease and made it a hell of pains, you will know why He did it. He gives you a wife and children whom you adore, only that through the spectacle of the wanton shames and miseries which He will inflict upon them He may tear the palpitating heart out of your breast and slap you in the face with it. Ah yes, you are at peace, my pride, my joy, my solace. He has played the last and highest stake in His sorry game, and is defeated; for, for your sake, I will be glad—and am glad. You are out of His reach forever; and I am too; He can never hurt me any more.[5]

It would be personal feelings like these—here so nakedly revealed and melodramatically expressed—that would inform the most powerful sections of artful and relatively impersonal pieces such as "The Chronicle of Young Satan."

In a letter written during the next month, Clemens asserted that there had been no day in August when he had been in his right mind.[6] If we remember only "In My Bitterness," it would be difficult to disagree. Yet, that he was overstating is indicated by much of the previous evidence. As well, his ability to endure the pain of the anniversary and to turn it into literature was seemingly healthy for him; in a high-spirited 22 August letter to Twichell he wrote, "The 18th of August has come and gone Joe—and we still seem to live."[7] A letter written to Wayne MacVeigh also suggests a barely subdued exhilaration:

I have mapped out four books this morning, & will begin an emancipated life this afternoon & shift back & forth among them & make them furnish me recreation & entertainment for three or four years to come, if I last so long.

We live in a cottage on the grassy & woodsy Rhigi-side, overlooking the lake, a half hour by boat from Lucerne. Julia Langdon is staying with us, & she & our two girls bike 20 & 30 miles a day & row us old people about the lake in the evenings, & are tanned like a meerschaum, & wholesome to look at. . . .

Four days ago the anniversary of our unspeakable disaster came, & trailed its black shadow over us, & we went apart, each to himself, & sat in the gloom of that eclipse until the natural night came & the first part of our changed pilgrimage was behind us. I suppose it is still with you as with us—the calamity not a reality, but a dream, which will pass—*must* pass. . . .I am hoping

5. *F of M,* pp. 131–32.
6. SLC to Mr. Skrine, [?] September 1897, PS, MTP.
7. *Letters,* 2:646.

that the cold will hang back long enough to let us stay here till October. It promises very well. This is paradise.[8]

Mark Twain worked hard at a staggering number of literary projects during his two-month stay in the Swiss Eden. Whether this fact provides proof of his "obsessiveness," however, is another question. He had always worked diligently when the mood was on him, and he had always enjoyed juggling several literary balls at once. Moreover, during this period, which was so clearly a new beginning and perhaps an ending as well for him, he was not at all certain which of his projects would prove most profitable, both in a financial and a psychological sense. There is no doubt that on some days and at certain hours Samuel Clemens was out of control, as perhaps most people would have been who had suffered analogous experiences. On the other hand, his accomplishments during these months speak to me of commendable self-control and artistic discipline. When he arrived in Weggis in the middle of July, he spent several frustrating days reading proof for *More Tramps Abroad*, the English edition of *Following the Equator*; at the same time, since he still was unwilling to discard completely Pond's lecture-tour idea, he spent some time mulling over possible topics.

Probably near the beginning of the Weggis period, he wrote a sketch entitled "Letters to Satan," which was not published until *Europe and Elsewhere* in 1923. In this uneven, brief piece, one of Satan's deputies describes a tour to his master, hoping to entice him into visiting the earth, which he has not done for three hundred years. Around this premise, the author strings together a loose series of comments taken almost directly from the notebook jottings he made on his way to Switzerland. The narrator rambles on about Cook's tours (he's in favor), telephones (a nuisance, but useful), Scotch at a hotel (he takes it to "prevent toothaches," but it's costly), and a French "lift." Some of his remarks are amusing, but the usual level of commentary is that of an erratic comedian who specializes in one-liners. The writing helped, however, because (in addition to throwing him onto a train of thought that would lead to the "Mysterious Stranger" manuscripts) it started him again on

8. SLC to Wayne MacVeigh, 22 August 1897, MTP.

an exercise that had always provided him with pieces of small change: using practically any aspect of his immediate experience as the impetus for magazine pieces. One problem with "Letters to Satan" is that in it Mark Twain was unable to separate the modicum of wheat from the abundance of chaff, probably because at this point in his literary renaissance he was reluctant to throw any idea away—a tendency that was to also bother him in his more substantial enterprises. Yet, sections of the sketch are well done, particularly the one about Cecil Rhodes and the European Concert, with which the "Letters" conclude:

> But this letter is already too long. I will close it by saying that I was charmed with England and sorry to leave it. It is easy to do business there. I carried out all of Your Grace's instructions, and did it without difficulty. I doubted if it was needful to grease Mr. Cecil Rhodes's palm any further, for I think he would serve you just for the love of it; still, I obeyed your orders in the matter. I made him Permanent General Agent for South Africa, got him and his South Africa Company whitewashed by the Committee of Inquiry, and promised him a dukedom. I also continued the European Concert in office, without making any change in its material. In my opinion this is the best material for the purpose that exists outside of Your Grace's own personal Cabinet. It coddles the Sultan, it has defiled and degraded Greece, it has massacred a hundred thousand Christians in Armenia and a splendid multitude of them in Turkey, and has covered civilization and the Christian name with imperishable shame. If Your Grace would instruct me to add the Concert to the list of your publicly acknowledged servants, I think it would have a good effect. The Foreign Offices of the whole European world are now under your sovereignty, and little attentions like this would keep them so.[9]

Unfortunately, the tone of this section is almost totally at odds with the innocuous comedy of the rest. Mark Twain cannot decide whether he wants to be a genially humorous observer—content to allow the basic idea to satisfy his reputation for daring—or a penetrating black comedian, pushing the possibilities afforded by his choice of persona to the edge of unpublishability. Significantly, he does not seem to have sent this sketch to a publisher. Striking an effective—and

9. *Writings*, 29:219-20.

salable—balance between the two impulses was a problem with which he often had to contend. But primarily for two reasons the problem was particularly acute during this last part of his career. Both factors are well known, but are of sufficient importance to bear repeating. For one thing, after his embroilment with the Paige typesetter and his subsequent bankruptcy, after his world tour and his encounter with forms of evil and human misery that had not confronted him before, after Susy's death, his attitudes became, generally, more consistently heterodox than they had been earlier, particularly in those sensitive areas concerning human nature, God, the possibility of progress, and so on.

Secondly, there were the complications that derived from the increasing public and critical recognition of an aspect of his literary personality that he had been sporadically eager to have recognized since even before *The Innocents Abroad*: that he was much more than a "mere" humorist; that, in essence, he was a "serious" writer. After the publication of *Joan of Arc* and the revelation that it had been written by Mark Twain, and after the reissue of *Life on the Mississippi*, a number of reviewers began to acknowledge the writer's serious dimension. Robert Bridges, for example, in an article entitled, significantly, "Mark Twain Re-discovered" asserted that as a result of rereading *Life on the Mississippi* "you discover how much more there is to him than laughter" and "that he is a serious literary artist who has put into his style the thought and finish that give it permanent value as literature." And in a statement that Clemens saved, Walter Besant said, "First, we perceive that the writer has presented a Joan of Arc more noble, more spiritual, of a loftier type than we could have conceived possible in the author of *Huckleberry Finn*." The publication of *Following the Equator* helped to convince even more readers that Mark Twain could be a serious writer.[10]

This public recognition seemed to provide Mark Twain with more possibilities in tone and subject matter than had existed prior to this decade. Yet it is difficult now and it was

10. Robert Bridges, "Mark Twain Re-discovered"; Scrapbook 20, MTP. Not all reviewers of the new travel book were pleased, of course, about this serious dimension. See, in particular, the English reviews cited in *Critical Heritage*.

certainly difficult then to delineate the liberties created for him by his "new" reputation. In Brander Matthews's review, "The Penalty of Humor," the critic mentions his subject's "certain grasp of human nature." One wonders, however, how liberal Matthews would have been with his accolades if Mark Twain's "Gospel" had been published at that time, or even if ideas eventually expressed in that dialogue had penetrated consistently, undisguisedly, and deeply into his fiction. Clemens's ideas about selfishness and the importance of training and temperament had, of course, appeared occasionally in his writings for many years before this period (for example, there are the passages on "training" in *Connecticut Yankee*) and most recently in *Pudd'nhead Wilson*. But such ideas had neither been presented so consistently nor stressed so openly as to persuade readers that the writer was a "pessimist" or a "cynic"—terms still used to describe the Samuel Clemens of these last years. In *Pudd'nhead Wilson*, the theme of training is so obvious to most modern readers that it may be incomprehensible how Mark Twain's public could have ignored it. Of course, some readers did see the tale as an essentially serious study of the effects of training. Yet, when one remembers the farcical elements in the story, observes that several of the comments about training are made in Wilson's calendar in a semifacetious fashion, and learns that the American edition of the novella was published along with *Those Extraordinary Twins* and the author's self-depreciating comments about the composition of the story, it becomes easier to understand how the tale's original readers could have missed its implications concerning the skeptical—even cynical—nature of its creator.[11]

11. In this connection, Douglas Grant's comments are also relevant: "Twain's message in these later stories may seem so hopeless and intolerable that it is surprising his public did not turn from him. But the popular image of him as a humorist and sentimentalist was not to be shaken by the solemn or astringent meditations of the scarcely recognized S. L. Clemens. They had to contend for their effect not only with the irresistible weight of his earlier writings, . . . but by the context in which they were presented. The observations in Pudd'nhead Wilson's Calendar are often vitriolic enough . . . but taken altogether, they are delivered with too much of the air of the cracker-barrel philosopher to lodge permanently in the reader" (*Twain*, p. 102).

One wonders, however, what might have happened to
Mark Twain's reputation if readers had begun to feel the
skepticism in his books. One wonders also how those critics
who were beginning to speak of Mark Twain as a moralist
would have reacted if the moralizing had implied to them
a clearly and unmistakably pessimistic view of human life.
Despite the emergence of European giants such as Émile
Zola and Thomas Hardy prior to 1890 and the appearance
of American writers such as Stephen Crane, Hamlin Garland, Frank Norris, Theodore Dreiser, and Upton Sinclair
during the last two decades of Samuel Clemens's life, one
must remember that the genteel tradition remained alive
and well in America.

Consider the following 1895 *Atlantic Monthly* review of
George Moore's *Celibates*: "[Moore] is one of those persons
who imagines that ugliness is tragedy, who never shrink
from the revolting, who confound manliness with brutality,
and, because they have forgotten delicacy themselves, fancy
that sweetness and wonder have departed from the earth.
And their ghastly inventions are condoned in the sacred
name of art." Or scan the following 1896 reference in the
same journal to *Jude the Obscure*: "It is melancholy to see
how Mr. Hardy has allowed himself to brood over unwholesome scenes." Or the 1897 reference to Edward Bellamy's
Equality made by Mark Twain's friend Charles Dudley
Warner in *Harper's Monthly*: "[Bellamy] seems to forget
that there is any design in the universe and any overruling
Providence." Given such widely held beliefs, and given the
attitude expressed in William Dean Howells's 1897 article
entitled "The Modern American Mood" that it was legitimate to criticize America as long as one's tone was not too
condemnatory nor one's purpose devoid of positive implications (Howells speaks of the "quiet of our patriotism"), it
should be possible to appreciate Mark Twain's quandry.[12] If
his fiction was to honestly reflect his experience, he would
have to assault subjects and adopt tones that would probably make such fiction unpublishable. But the word *probably*
suggests another dimension. Times were changing. Zola and

12. *Atlantic Monthly* 76 (1895): 707; *Atlantic Monthly,* 77
(1896): 279; *Harper's New Monthly Magazine* 95 (1897): 799; *Harper's New Monthly Magazine* 95 (1897): 199–204.

Hardy were being defended in the same journals in which they were being attacked, Howells was encouraging the young naturalists and preparing to savage American imperialism.[13] Thus, Mark Twain's uncertainty regarding— to put it crudely—what he could get away with is understandable.

Moreover, there are additional complicating factors: Mark Twain was read by several audiences ("the *elite* and the non *elite* / Alike are moved to laughter") and, although he enjoyed being an author with universal appeal, he was tempted to treat subjects (religion, theories of human nature, politics) in manners that would antagonize one or more of his audiences; in addition, the writer did not know consistently what he *wanted* to get away with. One of the inadequacies of terms such as *pessimist* in relation to this man is that they imply more or less continuous states of being. The essence of the Clemens identity, on the other hand, was mobility, although he tended toward pessimism in his last years. His attitudes changed frequently concerning God, human capacity for goodness, and so on. Therefore, his difficulty in deciding what he wanted to say and how he wanted to say it seems only natural. All these factors—and more that will be discussed later—help to explain his inability to complete major projects. They also explain why he changed his mind so often concerning the present and future potential publishability of his manuscripts, despite his tidy attempts to compartmentalize them. To risk a word that seems to me to be more useful than *despairing* or *obsessed* or *frustrated* as an epitome of the writer's problems during these last years, Mark Twain was frequently *confused*, and for good reason.

Two manuscripts that he began at Weggis—"Villagers" and "Tom Sawyer's Conspiracy"—are closely connected with, and illustrative of, these problems. Both, moreover, center upon the aspect of his past—what Henry Nash Smith has called the "Matter of Hannibal"—that during his most successful years had provided him with his best material. It is

13. See, for example, Enrico Ferri, "The Delinquent in Art and Literature." Ferri's article includes high praise of Émile Zola and Henrik Ibsen, although he believes that both writers tend to glorify criminals at the expense of the people who remain honest.

not surprising, therefore, that when he was beginning again at Weggis he attempted to mine his Hannibal past. "Villagers"—as many readers have conceded since it was first published by the Mark Twain Papers—is a remarkable document, both for the proof it provides of the comprehensiveness and accuracy of Clemens's memory and for its penetrating picture of the seamy underside of the St. Petersburg idyll.[14] The following excerpts are typical:

> *Russell Moss.* Pork-house. Rich. Mary, very sweet and pretty at 16 and 17. Wanted to marry George Robards. Lawyer Lakenan the rising stranger, held to be the better match by the parents, who were looking higher than commerce. They made her engage herself to L. L. made her study hard a year to fit herself to be his intellectual company; then married her, shut her up, the docile and heart-hurt young beauty, and continued her education rigorously. When he was ready to trot her out in society 2 years later and exhibit her, she had become wedded to her seclusion and her melancholy broodings, and begged to be left alone. He compelled her—that is, commanded. She obeyed. Her first exit was her last. The sleigh was overturned, her thigh was broken; it was badly set. She got well with a terrible limp, and forever stayed in the house and produced children. Saw no company, not even the mates of her girlhood. (p. 29)
>
> *Neil Moss.* The envied rich boy of the Meth. S.S. Spoiled and of small account. Dawson's. Was sent to Yale—a mighty journey and an incomparable distinction. Came back in swell eastern clothes, and the young men dressed up the warped negro bell ringer in a travesty of him—which made him descend to village fashions. At 30 he was a graceless tramp in Nevada, living by mendicancy and borrowed money. Disappeared. The parents died after the war. Mary Lakenan's husband got the property. (p. 29)
>
> *Jesse Armstrong.* Clerk for *Selmes.* Married ———. After many years she fell in love with her physician. One night somebody entered the back door— A. jumped out of bed to see about it and was chopped to pieces with an axe brought from his own woodpile. The widow and the physician tried for the murder.

14. In his introduction to "Villagers," Walter Blair discusses the relationship between Mark Twain's memories of Hannibal and the facts. See *HH and T*, pp. 23–27. Henceforth, references to *HH and T*, which includes both "Villagers" and "Tom Sawyer's Conspiracy," will be made in the text.

Evidence insufficient. Acquitted, but Judge, jury and all the town believed them guilty. Before the year was out they married, and were at once and rigorously ostracised. The physician's practice shrunk to nothing, but Armstrong left wealth, so it was no matter. (p. 30)

   Sam. Pilot. Slept with the rich baker's daughter, telling the adoptive parents they were married. The baker died and left all his wealth to "Mr. and Mrs. S. Bowen." They rushed off to a Carondolet magistrate, got married, and bribed him to antedate the marriage. Heirs from Germany proved the fraud and took the wealth. Sam no account and a pauper. Neglected his wife; she took up with another man. Sam a drinker. Dropped pretty low. Died of yellow fever and whiskey on a little boat with Bill Kribben the defaulting secretary. Both buried at the head of 82. In 5 years 82 got washed away. (p. 32)

Although it is impossible to draw definite conclusions about Mark Twain's motives in composing these at times almost garish jottings, one plausible surmise is that through them he was preparing to take advantage of his new reputation and the growing willingness of the middle-class audience to widen its definition of "serious" literature. Apparently, he hoped to write—for publication—a critical novel about the rural antebellum South portraying aspects of that environment that he had never before dealt with so directly and openly, even in *Huckleberry Finn* and *Pudd'nhead Wilson.* Certainly some of the notes relevant to "Tom Sawyer's Conspiracy" indicate a Tom Sawyer book that might have differed significantly from anything he previously had attempted. There is the reference, for example, to the "tale of scaring the women into insanity by skull and dough face" written just prior to leaving London; this provided the plot of a short Huck story written around this time but was never used in a longer narrative.[15] A notebook entry penned upon his arrival in Weggis is even more startling:

   Killing the negro man with a chunk of coal . . . Negro (brought) smuggled from Va. in featherbed when lynchers were after him. In Mo. he raped a girl of 13 & killed her & her brother in the woods & before being hanged confessed to many rapes of white

15. Notebook 32a. TS, p. 36, MTP. See also *HH and T,* pp. 141–42.

married women who kept it quiet partly from fear of him &
partly to escape the scandal.

Whites seized the slave nurse & hanged her for poisoning the
baby while another party were scouring the woods & discovered
the baby's uncle in suspicious circumstances, hiding something,
& charged him (Tom or Huck discovered him) & he confessed; &
he arrived in custody just after the innocent slave girl had been
lynched—or (shan't) Tom and Huck shall *save* her.[16]

The emphasis in both the Tom Sawyer and "Villagers"
notes upon animalistic behavior in squalid circumstances
suggests books that, on the surface, might have resembled
the growing number of volumes being published by naturalistic writers in Europe and the United States. Yet—unlike
Garland's *Main-Travelled Roads*, for example—what is noticeably absent from these quasi-naturalistic notes is any
sense of the writer's moral outrage over the debilitating
effects of environment. In "Villagers," the narrator's attitude toward his material changes often. At times, as in his
cool description of Jesse Armstrong's violent ax murder, he
is almost clinically detached; at others, he is sympathetic, as
in his pitying comments about Mary Moss, that "docile and
heart-hurt young beauty," ruined by her husband's cruel
education and a horrible accident; at others, almost vindic-
tively accusing, as in his references to Neil Moss, who is
"spoiled and of small account." There is a certain consis-
tency of tone in many of these sketches because they are
generally cynical about human motivation, action, and destiny. But, seemingly as soon as the narrator begins to recognize how cynical he has been, he writes, "No young girl was
ever insulted, or seduced, or even scandalously gossiped
about. Such things were not even dreamed of in that society,
much less spoke of and referred to as possibilities" (p. 35).

16. Notebook 32a (II), TS, p. 57, MTP. Quoted in Arthur
Pettit, *Mark Twain & the South*, p. 166. About this entry, Pettit
comments, "The business about killing the negro man with a
'chunk of coal' shows how vividly he remembered the slave who
was struck and killed with a slag of coal in the main street of Hannibal when Sam Clemens was nine years old. And the notes about
black rape—and about polluted white women who keep quiet 'to
escape the scandal'—imply that Mark Twain was interested in exploring a subject which would haunt the generation of Southern
writers who followed him" (p. 166).

Clemens's motive for making such a maudlin assertion is not at all clear. Perhaps he consciously realized that his notes were becoming too bleak to inspire publishable fiction and he wanted to counteract their tenor dramatically; perhaps, unconsciously, he wanted to reject unequivocally a flow of memories that was beginning to threaten a healthy and substantial part of his being. In any event, one of the major reasons he was unable to use these notes to inspire a prose *Children of the Night* (most of the poems from which, coincidentally, E. A. Robinson had privately published in 1896 in *The Torrent and the Night Before*) was that his perspective on this dimension of his past was too uncertain.

A similar uncertainty is suggested by the notes for the new Tom Sawyer book. After talk of rapes, murders, and lynchings, the entry continues for several pages. As it does, episodes suggestive of farce and burlesque—for example, a ridiculous duel involving Clemens's brother Orion, with Colonel Sellers as his second—alternate with other ideas that the writer would return to repeatedly as he tried to decide how they should be embodied in fiction.[17] The entries constitute an incredible mishmash; they are seemingly written by a man who either wished to exorcise personal ghosts or to flush out his mind for fear of leaving within any idea that might provoke a plot. Entries such as these point to another problem that he would grapple with during the weeks when he was beginning again: where—not only in what story but often in what medium—he should embody these concepts. Constantly, his imagination played with ideas relating to Huck and Tom, to Orion, to Susy, to a relative of Satan; all the ideas centered around Hannibal. Should he use them in fiction, in his autobiography, in lectures, or even in plays?

Despite these difficulties—caused not by a paucity, but by a plethora of options—"Tom Sawyer's Conspiracy" is quite tautly plotted and not at all the baggy monster threatened by the notebook entries.[18] Tom hopes to enliven a boring

17. Mark Twain, for example, yearned often to use a character whom he referred to as "the Spanish grandee barber."
18. The critical consensus about the story is that it is poorly written. In *MTW,* for example, Bernard De Voto referred to "Tom Sawyer's Conspiracy" as a badly botched job. Pettit refers to the story's promising beginning and then writes, "but the story soon

summer by concocting an abolitionist conspiracy scare; when the town has been nicely worked up, Huck and Jim will steal a slave (Tom in disguise) from Bat Bradish, the "nigger" trader. After this, the boys and Jim will amuse themselves pretending to chase the escapee, everything climaxing in a torchlight parade. So that their machinations will not be discovered, Tom's good brother, Sid, must be disposed of; Tom purposely contracts measles (which "fortunately" turn out to be scarlet fever), and Tom's sister and Sid are trundled off to the country while Tom undergoes a harrowing convalescence. Huck and Jim begin to advertise the conspiracy, Tom contributing in the last days of his illness by creating a couple of oafish—but to the town, menacing—posters. The plot thickens just as the team prepares to launch its trick, when Tom discovers that another slave at Bradish's is only pretending to be black; and, overhearing a conversation at the haunted house, Tom discovers further that they are not the only ones preparing to steal a "black man" out of slavery. At this point, the Weggis version halts, not because the writer has run out of ideas, but probably because he was working on other things prior to leaving for Vienna; thus, this section of the manuscript gives a strong sense that it will be "continued next week." Early on (p. 168), the appearance of the Duke and King is foreshadowed; later, Tom alludes to something that he discovers about the fake black, which he refuses to divulge and which becomes important when the story is resumed.

In his generally critical introduction to "Tom Sawyer's Conspiracy," Walter Blair refers to the implausibility of the doubling of the essential plot mechanism;[19] yet, even Mark Twain's best books contain implausible episodes (despite

---

bogs down in the same jailbreak shenanigans that ruined the last part of *Huckleberry Finn*" (*Mark Twain & the South*, p. 164). And in George Carrington's new study, the critic does not seem to be aware of the "Conspiracy's" existence. Commenting on Mark Twain's further uses of Huck after *Huckleberry Finn*, Carrington writes, "Twain tried to use Huck in the unfinished 'prairie-manuscript,' and did use him in *Tom Sawyer, Detective* and *Tom Sawyer Abroad*, neither of which add any dimensions to Huck or indeed have much literary quality" (*The Dramatic Unity of Huckleberry Finn*, n. 1, p. 148).

19. *HH and T*, p. 162.

his attacks on James Fenimore Cooper for the same offense), which the reader accepts because of what the writer makes of them. Moreover, here his concern for verisimilitude in other areas helps to create a suspension of disbelief; thus, plot details such as the doubling are not bothersome. Twain is careful to explain why, for example, the boys may wander around at night during the scare while others are kept off the street: their escapades in *Tom Sawyer, Detective* have gained them respect. Bat Bradish cannot discern that the "slave" he buys is white because of his weak eyes. Any writer suggests to his reader a kind of plausibility boundary, which he violates at his peril. Episodes in a typical Mark Twain novel would seem implausible in a Howellsian or Jamesian world, but not in the world that Mark Twain creates. Elements such as the double plot in "Tom Sawyer's Conspiracy" should therefore not imply a failure on the part of the writer; the first section of this story is well plotted, and the writer's care is everywhere in evidence.

The most commendable thing about the initial section of this manuscript, however, is the way in which it avoids the savagely cynical and sentimental extremes of "Villagers" and the analogous heterogeneity of the notes. Such potential problems became considerably less acute, of course, as soon as Mark Twain began to narrate his book from the perspective of Huckleberry Finn. For one thing, it was impossible to be cynical or blackly pessimistic when viewing the world through the eyes of someone—like Huck—who is so tolerant of white individuals, so sympathetic to their difficulties, and so marvelously appreciative of the specifics of his physical environment. Consider, for example, Huck's explanation of Tom's fondness for words: one is used "becuz it tasted good in his mouth." Or his description of sitting down "frog-fashion, very gentle and soft" (p. 18). Or his portrait of a night storm:

> It come on to storm about one in the morning, and the thunder and lightning woke us up. The rain come down in floods and floods; and ripped and raced along the shingles enough to deefen you, and would come slashing and thrashing against the windows, and make you feel so snug and cosy in the bed, and the wind was a howling around the eaves in a hoarse voice, and then it would die down a little and pretty soon come in a boom-

ing gust, and sing, and then wheeze, and then scream, and then
shriek, and rock the house and make it shiver, and you would
hear the shutters slamming all down the street, and then there'd
be a glare like the world afire, and the thunder would crash
down, right at your head and seem to tear everything to rags,
and it was just good to be alive and tucked up comfortable to
enjoy it; but Tom shouts "Turn out, Huck, we can't ever have
it righter than this," and although he shouted it I hardly hear
him through the rattle and bang and roar and racket. (p. 180)

In the description of the storm, Mark Twain is not breaking
any new ground as a writer; in fact, the rhythm of the passage
("ripped and raced," "slashing and thrashing"), along with
the obvious onomatopoeic effects, may remind the reader so
insistently of passages in *Huckleberry Finn* as to seem almost
trite. Yet, the similarity may be intentional: the writer seems
to know that this perspective and this prose, combining as
they do expansiveness and focus, will help him to avoid the
destructive extremes of "Villagers."

But Huck is no Pollyanna: he is occasionally a skeptical
observer of human weakness, as when he remarks about the
obtuse detective, Jake Bleeker (whom the townspeople wor-
ship), that "he don't know enough to follow the fence and
find the corner." Or when he observes of Aunt Polly that
"she was out getting her share of the scare." For this reason
Huck is an effective means of avoiding the maudlin. Sometimes, his combination of naive appreciativeness and obser-
vant common sense helps Mark Twain create memorable
comedy, as in the following description of Mr. Baxter:

He was the foreman of the printing office, and had Mr. Day
and a boy under him and was one of the most principal men in
the town, and looked up to by everybody. There warn't nothing
agoing for the highsting up of the human race but he was under
it and a-shoving up the best he could—being a pillow of the
church and taking up the collection, Sundays, and doing it wide
open and square, with a plate, and setting it on the table when
he got done where everybody could see, and never putting his
hand anear it, never pawing around in it the way old Paxton always done, letting on to see how much they had pulled in; and
he was Inside Sentinel of the Masons, and Outside Sentinel of
the Odd Fellows, and a kind a head bung-starter or something
of the Foes of the Flowing Bowl, and something or other to the
Daughters of Rebecca, and something like it to the King's Daugh-

ters, and Royal Grand Warden to the Knights of Morality, and Sublime Grand Marshal of the Good Templars, and there warn't no fancy apron agoing but he had a sample, and no turnout but he was in the procession, with his banner, or his sword, or toting a bible on a tray, and looking awful serious and responsible, and yet not getting a cent. A good man, he was, they don't make no better. (pp. 188–89)

The effect of such passages depends upon Huck's precarious relationship with St. Petersburg's respectable society: he is both outside and inside it. Because he is outside it, he can see, appreciate, and criticize aspects of this world that others could not; the criticism is usually tacit, because, as in *Huckleberry Finn*, he possesses neither the self-confidence nor the clearly articulated value system that would enable him to attack openly. More importantly, because he is also inside society, he can accept with relative equanimity actions and principles that the implied author wants his reader to examine. In a notebook entry, for example, Clemens wrote, "There are many scape-goats for our sins, but the most popular is Providence."[20] "Tom Sawyer's Conspiracy" is full of sections in which this attitude is satirized, as in the following passage (redolent of Jim Blaine and his ram), where Huck's ambiguous position is used delightfully:

We had to have a basket . . . ; so we went down stairs and got it while she was pricing a catfish that a nigger had to sell, and fetched it up and put the outfit in it, and then had to wait nearly an hour before we could get away, becuz Sid and Mary was gone somewheres and there wasn't anybody but us to help her hunt for the basket. But at last she had suspicions of the nigger that sold her the catfish, and went out to hunt for him, so then we got away. Tom allowed the hand of Providence was plain in it, and I reckoned it was, too, for it did look like it, as far as we was concerned, but I couldn't see where the nigger's share come in, but Tom said wait and I would see that the nigger would be took care of in some mysterious inscrutable way and not overlooked; and it turned out just so, for when aunt Polly give the nigger a raking over and then he proved he hadn't took the basket she was sorry and asked him to forgive her, and bought another catfish. And we found it in the cubberd that night and traded it off for a box of sardines to take over to the island, and the cat got into trouble about it; and when I said, now then the

20. Notebook 32b (I), TS, p. 22, MTP.

nigger is rectified but the cat is overlooked, Tom said again wait
and I would see that the cat would be took care of in some mysterious inscrutable way; and it was so, for while aunt Polly was
gone to get her switch to whip her with she got the other fish
and et it up. So Tom was right, all the way through, and it shows
that every one *is* watched over, and all you have to do is to
be trustful and everything will come out right, and everybody
helped. (pp. 178–79)

Here the satiric point is obvious, as is the way in which the
satire is aided by Huck's perspective. An instance, however,
in which the implied author's point is not so immediately
patent and in which the contribution of Huck's perspective
is somewhat different occurs in the story's first paragraph:

Well, we was back home and I was at the Widow Douglas's
up on Cardiff Hill again getting sivilised some more along of
her and old Miss Watson all the winter and spring, and the
Widow was hiring Jim for wages so he could buy his wife and
children's freedom some time or other, and the summer days was
coming, now, and the new leaves and the wind-flowers was out,
and marbles and hoops and kites was coming in, and it was already barefoot time and ever so bammy and soft and pleasant,
and the damp a-stewing out of the ground and the birds a-carry-
ing on in the woods, and everybody taking down the parlor stoves
and stowing them up garret, and speckled straw hats and fish-
hooks beginning to show up for sale, and the early girls out in
white frocks and blue ribbons, and schoolboys getting restless
and fidgetty, and anybody could see that the derned winter was
over. Winter is plenty lovely enough when it is winter and the
river is froze over and there's hail and sleet and bitter cold and
booming storms and all that, but spring is not good—just rainy
and slushy and sloppy and dismal and ornery and uncomfortable, and ought to be stopped. Tom Sawyer he says the same.
(p. 163)

Upon reading this passage, one's first impression is of the
sense of freedom and oneness with the physical universe
conveyed by Huck's language, qualities pleasurably reminiscent of *Huckleberry Finn*. It is only upon a second reading,
after having noticed later examples of a similar tendency,
that one observes Huck's comfortable unselfconscious juxtaposition of gorgeous natural descriptions and references to
black enslavement. On the question of slavery, Huck remains
very much inside the St. Petersburg world. Thus it may take

accumulated examples of his insouciance for the reader to discover that one of Mark Twain's concerns in "Tom Sawyer's Conspiracy" is this institution, although the writer's attitude does become more evident in the portion of the manuscript written after he left Weggis.

One thing to stress about Huck as narrator is that, for the first time in any of "his" books, his retrospective relationship to the events that he describes is made clear. Several references in the text indicate that he is an adult living after the Civil War describing a pre–Civil War experience. The following passage is the best example:

> But he give up the civil war, and it is one of the brightest things to his credit. And he could a had it easy enough if he had sejested it, anybody can see it now. And it don't seem right and fair that Harriet Beacher Stow and all them other second-handers gets all the credit of starting that war and you never hear Tom Sawyer mentioned in the histories ransack them how you will, and yet he was the first one that thought of it. Yes, and years and years before ever they had the idea. And it was all his own, too, and come out of his own head, and was a bigger one than theirs, and would a cost forty times as much, and if it hadn't been for Jim he would a been in ahead and got the glory. I know, becuz I was there, and I could go this day and point out the very place on Jackson's island, there on the sand-bar up at the head where it begins to shoal off. And where is Tom Sawyer's monument, I would like to know? There ain't any. And there ain't ever going to be any. It's just the way, in this world. One person *does* the thing, and the other one gets the monument. (p. 167)

Noteworthy about the post–Civil War Huck is that his attitude toward blacks remains unchanged:

> Jim knowed it wouldn't do for him to chip in any more for a spell, but he went on mumbling to himself, the way a nigger does. . . .But Tom didn't let on to hear; and it's the best way, to let a nigger or a child go on and grumble itself out, then it's satisfied. (p. 171)

> It was natural for him to think that, you know, becuz he knowed that if you wanted to start a saloon, or peddle things, or trade in niggers, or drive a dray, or give a show, or own a dog, or do most any blame thing you could think of, you had to take out a licence, and so he reckoned it would be the same with a conspiracy, and would be sinful to run it without one, becuz it

would be cheating the gover'ment. He was troubled about it, and said he had been praying for light. And then he says, in that kind of pitiful way a nigger has that is feeling ignorant and distressed—

"De prar hain't ben answered straight en squah, but as fur as I can make out fum de symptoms, hit's agin de conspiracy onless we git de licence."

Well, I could see Jim's side, and knowed I oughtn't to fret at a poor nigger that didn't mean no harm, but was only going according to his lights the best he could. (p. 175)

"Tom Sawyer, that's a five-hundred-dollar nigger; you ain't a five-hundred-dollar nigger, I don't care *how* you dress up."

He couldn't get around that, you know; there warn't any way. But he didn't like to let on that I had laid him out; so he talked random a minute, trying to work out, then he said we couldn't tell anything about it till we had *seen* the nigger. And said, come along.

I didn't think there was any sense in it, but I was willing to let him down as easy as I could, so we struck out up the hollow. It was dark, now, but we knowed the way well enough. It was a log house, and no light in it; but there was a light in the lean-to, and we could see through the chinks. Sure enough it was a man, and a hearty good strong one—a thousand dollar nigger, and worth it anywhere. He was stretched out on the ground, chained, and snoring hard. (p. 202)

In no other book—with the possible exception of *Huckleberry Finn*—does the word *nigger* seem to appear so often in so few pages; moreover, Huck's condescending and disparaging attitude toward blacks in general takes on added significance because Huck is an adult narrator who has lived through the holocaust of the Civil War.

Jim's attitudes are also revealing. Arthur Pettit, in his comments on "Tom Sawyer's Conspiracy," discusses the "deterioration of Nigger Jim" and laments that "At the end of his career Jim has become a banjo-plucking, cakewalk nigger, virtually indistinguishable from the slaphappy slaves of James Kirke Paulding's ante-bellum novels." Professor Pettit goes on to contrast Jim with another black character created by Mark Twain during these years: Jasper in "Which Was It?" The critic refers to Jasper as a "Mulatto Superman," who for Mark Twain "*was* a black power. Nigger Jim may have been blacker, but the mulatto Jasper, wandering through the wind and snow of nighttime Indiantown plotting revenge, is the white man's very image of a black Satan."[21]

More will be said about Jasper later in this study, but the point to be emphasized here is that Jim is not this kind of character. Instead, Mark Twain is interested in him as an example of someone whose legal freedom is less important than his psychological enslavement. This outcome is of course prefigured in *Huckleberry Finn*, although in *Tom Sawyer Abroad*, Jim's status as a freed slave is not important and in *Tom Sawyer, Detective* he appears only briefly. Here, however, there are significant references to Jim's enslaved wife and children at the beginning of the manuscript. Moreover, even though Mark Twain was only halfway into his story when he put it aside, he included enough of Jim's trusting comments about providence, about the necessity of licenses, and about the criminality of stealing another man's slave, to portray a pleasant man-child socialized to such an extent that technical freedom is a potential weakness rather than a strength. These points are not belabored. The reader, in fact, is invited to accept Jim's evaluation of himself and Huck's of blacks in general and to miss the implications of these attitudes; the reader is also invited to laugh at the boys' antics. But readers (and many for whom the manuscript was intended would have prided themselves on their tolerance) lured by Huck's voice and their own unacknowledged ignorance and prejudice should be shocked—perhaps into guilt— by the story's next section: the games of Tom and Huck involve them in murder; the attitudes of Jim and the boys threaten the black man with mob revenge and legal execution. It is, therefore, through his handling of a narrator who is often unconscious of significances that Mark Twain begins a book that solves the problem of tone anticipated by the notes for it and by "Villagers" and that successfully blends humor and seriousness.

It is not at all certain when "Tom Sawyer's Conspiracy" was begun; perhaps on 22 August, for Clemens mentions in a letter that he has mapped out several books that he plans to alternate between for the sake of recreation and entertainment. We know from his notebook entries, on the other

21. Pettit, *Mark Twain & the South*, pp. 164–73.

hand, that he began "Hellfire Hotchkiss" on 4 August.[22] Franklin Rogers traces the genesis of this story to the writer's early attempt to use his brother Orion as literary material— in "The Autobiography of a Damned Fool"— and his subsequent attempts to resuscitate this character.[23] The version that he began in Weggis departs in important ways from the earlier versions. For one thing—as the title suggests—the focus has shifted at least partially from the Orion character to the female lead—the intelligent, dangerously competent, daring tomboy who tries uncomfortably to reconcile the dictates of her own free spirit with the stodgy but useful ways of the town. Hellfire is an interesting creation, explained in the story's almost naturalistic third chapter as being a product of her inherited drives, uncertain paternal guidance, and the restricted personalities of her female peers, whom she shuns because they are so dull. One cannot help but speculate that Hellfire is Clemens's version of Susy as she might have become—given her inherited qualities—in a different kind of family and environment. Certainly the verve and talent that Hellfire exhibits are traits that Clemens stresses in his notebook entries relating to his daughter. Paine tells us that the writer had been contemplating a memorial volume to Susy but had eventually discarded the notion.[24] Perhaps this story became his substitute (or would have, if he had finished it), as did the elegy written on the anniversary of her death.

Given Mark Twain's admiring portrait of his female protagonist, the Orion character—Oscar, or "Thug"—could not remain the hilariously pompous, stupid prig of "The Autobiography of a Damned Fool." Mark Twain began the story in all probability with publication in mind, so when he imagined a quasi-romantic relationship for Hellfire, it could not be with a man as doltishly unattractive as the narrator of the earlier manuscript. And there is evidence that the writer was trying to shape someone who might pass as a rather unconventional romantic lead, seemingly still another example

22. SLC to Wayne MacVeigh, 22 August 1897, PS, MTP; Notebook 32b (I), TS, p. 24, MTP.

23. Franklin R. Rogers, ed., *Mark Twain's Satires & Burlesques*, pp. 134–35, 165–69, 172–74. Henceforth, references to "Hellfire Hotchkiss" will be made in the text.

24. *MTN*, pp. 314–22.

of the "unpromising hero" type that, according to Robert Regan, was so congenial to Clemens's imagination.[25] Oscar's father grudgingly refers to him as being "very much brighter than the average, indeed; he is honest, upright, honorable, his impulses are always high, never otherwise" (p. 183). As well, "Pudd'nhead Wilson says Thug's got the rightest heart and the best disposition of any person in this town, and pretty near the quickest brains, too" (pp. 187–88). Yet, what Mark Twain gives with one hand, he soon takes back; Thug is also an effeminate, totally unpredictable coward. Clemens seems to have been so enamored of the humorous fictional possibilities of Orion's weather-vane approach to principles that—at least until his brother's death—he was unable to relinquish this conception of his character. There was also something in the personalities of Hellfire and Oscar—the male soul in the female body, and the female soul in the male body—that appealed to him, fascinated as he was with the mysteries of identity:

> "And they are talking about me—like that. Who would ever have dreamed it? Aunt Betsy is right. It *is* time to call a halt. It is a pity, too. The boys are such good company, and it is going to be so so dull without them. Oh, everything seems to be made wrong, nothing seems to [be] the way it ought to be. Thug Carpenter is out of his sphere, I am out of mine. Neither of us can arrive at any success in life, we shall always be hampered and fretted and kept back by our misplaced sexes, and in the end defeated by them, whereas if we could change we should stand as good a chance as any of the young people in the town. I wonder which case is the hardest. I am sorry for him, and yet I do not see that he is any more entitled to pity than I am." (p. 199)

Despite the confusion in the writer's attitude toward his male protagonist, "Hellfire Hotchkiss" begins quite well. The opening—a conversation between Thug's parents about their son—is almost completely scenic, sketching economically and entertainingly the pertinent information about the character. He is a "creature of enthusiasms. Burning enthusiasms. . . .Then they go out and he catches fire in another place" (p. 177), to quote his skeptical father; but he is also

25. Robert Regan, *Unpromising Heroes: Mark Twain and His Characters.*

one with splendid potential, according to his doting mother. The story has been underway for several pages before there is any authorial comment, which suggests that—originally at least—Mark Twain might have wanted to turn the story into a play, as he had hoped to do, through the help of William Dean Howells, with "The Autobiography of a Damned Fool." Having introduced the question of Thug's potential, the narrator also suggests that it may remain unrealized, because as the chapter closes word is shouted that the boy is "drownded" (p. 184). The second chapter is exciting as well as humorous; it dramatizes Thug's rescue by Hellfire, who revives him by feeding him alcohol while pretending it is milk (because he is at present a teetotaler). In this scene, the townspeople function as a chorus, cheering on the young girl, talking about the characters, expressing their reactions to developments. The primary character in the "chorus" is Pudd'nhead Wilson, as the writer prepares to pull out all stops in order to guarantee the popular success of his new tale. Once Thug has been rescued and interest in Mark Twain's heroine has been aroused, chapter 3 contains lengthy comments on her character. Here, the tale moves totally away from drama; although, if the writer eventually had decided to stage the story, he could have devised a method of introducing such expository material. Important in the narrative at this point is Hellfire's relationship with her family and community; and here, the ideas about heredity and environment that eventually inform *What Is Man?* become evident—ideas that his notebooks of the time tell us he was contemplating; Mark Twain's technique here is almost Dreiserian in its concern for place and time. In sum, this abortive novel is very revealing from a technical point of view, because it evinces the author's skill in composing what James called scene and picture.

Thematically, the writer was beginning to explore, really for the first time—although *Joan of Arc* and the Laura Hawkins subplot of *The Gilded Age* certainly touch upon it—the problem of the relationship between an unconventional female and her community, a relationship perhaps suggested by his memories, in "Villagers," of the plight of some women in Hannibal. His analysis of Hellfire's situation is certainly more balanced than his treatment of the women in

"Villagers," who are generally viewed either as pathetic victims or admired vestal virgins: his sympathy for Hellfire's situation is obvious, but by the end of the incomplete chapter 3 he suggests that the conservative influence of the community is beneficial. In this work, in fact, the community is seen as watching over its aberrant individuals with primarily benign concern, applying necessary corrective pressure when they threaten to go too far. As Aunt Betsy remarks and Rachel (Hellfire) reluctantly agrees, "Take it all around, this is a fair town, and a just town, and it has been good to you—very good to you, everything considered, for you *have* led it a dance, and you know it" (p. 198). Mark Twain's view of community influence was certainly not always so sanguine, but his attitude here may be viewed as a natural result of his attempt to recapture and in a sense reevaluate his past. It was a result, as well, of his having been absent from any real community for several years and of his occasional longing for one.[26]

After the story had begun so well, something happened, something that points to one of the crucial difficulties that the writer constantly had to overcome during this last period. Aspects of his own life began to impinge so insistently upon his fiction that they destroyed it. Up until this point, he has had things fairly well under control. Characters resemble real people, but not so photographically as to distort the fabric of the story. Real episodes contribute to the portrayal of fictional characters, as in the episode where Hellfire defeats the cruel Stover brothers, the pistol of one having misfired while

26. Although Thomas Blues does not refer to "Hellfire Hotchkiss" in his *Mark Twain & The Community*, it seems to me that this fragment would afford additional evidence for Blues's thesis that "at the center of Mark Twain's consciousness as a novelist was a vision of an idealized relation between the individual and the community, in which an independent individual could freely challenge the community's values, disrupt its sense of order, and yet somehow retain his identity as a conventional member of it" (p. ix). The fragment also suggests that this ideal persisted well after *A Connecticut Yankee*, something that Blues does not believe to be the case: "Mark Twain was not reconciled to the breakdown of the ideal relation he had so heavily relied upon, a fact which accounts not only for the total collapse of *A Connecticut Yankee*, but also in large part for the bitter, cynical fiction of the last two decades of his life" (p. xi).

leveled at an enemy's head; in "Villagers," Ed and Dick Hyde fail to kill their uncle when their pistol misfires. Then, in notes seemingly composed at Weggis and upon which he had written "rejected manuscript that may come good," the story flies out of control. Thug Carpenter becomes "Parson Snivel" and metamorphoses again into the prig of "The Autobiography of a Damned Fool," "All of which pleased him, and made him a hero to himself: for he was turning his other cheek, as commanded, he was being reviled and persecuted for righteousness' sake, and all that" (p. 200). Moreover, Thug's mother, who had been treated from a controlled, cool distance in chapter 1—entering the action only through dialogue—begins to dominate the story:

> She had to do all the encouraging herself; the rest of the family were indifferent, and this wounded her, and brought gentle reproaches out of her that were strangely eloquent and moving, considering how simple and unaffected her language was, and how effortless and unconscious. But there was a subtle something in her voice and her manner that was irresistibly pathetic, and perhaps that was where a great part of the power lay; in that and in her moist eyes and trembling lip. (p. 201)

As well, the effaced narrator of the earlier episodes moves suspiciously close to the real Samuel Clemens when he writes,

> I know now that she was the most eloquent person whom I have met in all my days, but I did not know it then, and I suppose that no one in all the village suspected that she was a marvel, or indeed that she was in any degree above the common. I had been abroad in the world for twenty years . . . before it at last dawned on me that in the matter of moving and pathetic eloquence none of them was the equal of that . . . obscure little woman with the beautiful spirit and the great heart and the enchanted tongue. (pp. 201–2)

What seems to happen is that Clemens's increasingly sentimental memories of his dead mother either combine with or trigger a nasty hostility toward his brother, who, although inept, had remained close to, and had been defended by, the deeply admired parent; Mark Twain's fiction is inundated with versions of fact, and the story disintegrates. He apparently looked at the manuscript again in Vienna, but then discarded it, probably deciding to deal with his Orion and

Susy figures in different ways and in other narratives. During this Weggis period, memories of both his distant and relatively immediate past sometimes flooded his mind—usually to the detriment of his fiction.

And it is really the disasters of his immediate past that were a crucial source of the manuscript entitled "Which Was the Dream?," which he may have worked on after the experience of Susy's anniversary had been endured and after he had lived in a mental world of frustration and bitterness for several days. As John Tuckey points out in his excellent introduction to *Mark Twain's Which Was the Dream?*, the author had contemplated, as early as 1891, a tale in which a man living happily with his wife and daughters has a frightening dream centering around personal disasters and seeming to last several years; on awakening, he discovers that the dream was momentary and that his life remains unchanged. When Mark Twain returned to the idea after finishing his travel book on 10 May 1897, "the narrator's terrible dream . . . was to make him a stranger in his own household at the moment of awakening." An important addition to the conception at this time was the idea of a voyage, in which characters modeled on James C. Paige, the inventor; Clemens's nephew Charles Webster; Frank Whitmore, Clemens's Hartford business agent; Orion; and Clemens's old Nevada friend, Joe Goodman, would somehow figure.

He said in his 23 May notebook entry that he wrote the first chapter on that day. When he returned to the narrative in August at Weggis he made a few revisions and then finished the manuscript entitled "Which Was the Dream?"[27] In it, the wife talks of her eldest daughter's birthday party to be held that evening, mentions her husband's plan to write his autobiography for his children, and then points to her husband nodding sleepily over the manuscript. The youthful "Major General X" next speaks, describing his humble childhood, his early military and political success (he is on the verge of the presidency), and his happy home life. Then, the disaster dream begins, although the reader is not told this: there is a fire that leads to total financial loss because the insurance has expired; the discovery that a trusted relative and

27. For information on the dating of "Which Was the Dream?" see *WWD?*, pp. 10, 11, 38.

financial adviser is a thief; bankruptcy; a charge of forgery, which shocks the general into unconsciousness; and, finally, his "awakening" over a year later to a new environment—a log cabin—where his faithful family has been nursing him. This last detail should be observed carefully: despite the disasters, the major's most cherished value—the love of his family—survives. Even this fragment could therefore be interpreted as a not particularly pessimistic one. Worth observing as well are Clemens's attempts to distance himself from the story; if it had been published, the historical character whom most readers would have been reminded of by the protagonist was Ulysses S. Grant, not Samuel Clemens. Mark Twain was trying to write fiction, not autobiography.

At this point, the narrative breaks off and an elaborate, detailed description of the major's voyage toward Australia is included in the notebook, as Mark Twain begins to view his idea as the basis for—among other things—a kind of universal satire. The voyage setting, of course, would provide a conventional and appropriate microcosm for such a work. Moreover, Mark Twain may have hoped that the sea environment, which he knew well because of his travels, could provide for his imagination a new stimulus, one that could alternate with his Hannibal past as the source of new fictional projects. Unfortunately, to read this proposed plot continuation is to become almost exhausted; if Mark Twain had actually written a novel that approximated the outline, it would have contained the following: an embittered Faustian narrator fleeing, with his wife and two daughters, from a crime of perhaps murder, although it is impossible to determine if he is actually guilty—he has, however, lost his self-respect; a plot spiced with sex (a bastard child and an affair between a young married man and woman traveling to meet their spouses) and replete with violence (murder, and then a hanging after the villain has been captured by an old sailor resembling Ned Wakeman; suicides after the ship enters the "Devil's Race Track"); religious debates; farcical high jinks—in short, almost every conceivable kind of action. The cast of characters includes such disparate types as a prince in line for the czardom, religious figures modeled on real people (Twichell, Robert Ingersoll), a ballet troupe, an agent for Colt revolvers, an Englishman who has struck it rich in Australia and is now returning to the country ("Coal-oil Tommy"), ambitious young men who gamble, and so on.[28] Episodes and characters are drawn from a wide variety of sources: Clemens's Hannibal and Hartford past, his world trip, contemporary figures whom he either knew slightly or had read about, pulp fiction, his own family.[29] Given the plentiful possibilities, it is not surprising that he did not immediately begin work on the book, especially since he was preparing to move to Vienna. Nor is it really surprising that he never developed this particular voyage idea beyond the notebook stage, although he had made fictional coherence out of similar jumbles before.

What is most interesting about this potpourri—and about several other manuscripts that he wrote in the Weggis/Vienna period—is the insight that it provides into problems that he often had to overcome throughout this final epoch of his career. The biggest problem seems to have been his desire—almost his need—to write a long book and, judging from several references, one that could be sold by subscription.[30] A successful subscription book would have had tremendous actual and symbolic importance to Clemens: in his glory years, subscription publication had been his form (it had, of course, been largely as a result of his efforts that this "inferior" type of publication had attained a modicum of re-

28. In a recent article, Thomas D. Schwartz suggests that Mark Twain admired the freethinker Robert Ingersoll for expressing ideas with which he was in basic agreement, but which he did not have the courage to express openly. See "Mark Twain and Robert Ingersoll: The Free Thought Connection." Perhaps in contemplating the use of the Ingersoll figure, Mark Twain was considering a means of smuggling in religious ideas that he would otherwise have had difficulty including.

29. See Notebook 32b (I), TS, MTP, pp. 28–34. John Tuckey points out how Mark Twain's proposed continuation of "Which Was the Dream?" was linked to a discarded section of *Following the Equator* entitled "The Enchanted Sea Wilderness": the passengers of the ship were to find themselves in the Devil's Race Track and eventually were to be led into the trap of the hideous becalming called Everlasting Sunday. See *WWD?*, pp. 8, 12.

30. At various times, he hoped to publish by subscription—in addition to more conventional projects—his autobiography, a translation of the trials of Joan of Arc, and a book about lynching in the United States.

spectability); a new triumph would therefore prove to the world and to himself that he really was all the way back as a writer. And as a businessman. This last point should not be overlooked, for it had been primarily as a businessman—with all that this implied to a middle-class man like Clemens—that he had failed in the past—a failure that had compelled him to depend so absolutely on the advice of H. H. Rogers. On several occasions when Mark Twain had run out of literary inspiration—particularly before he returned to America as a hero—he would catapult himself into investment schemes, sometimes trying to involve Rogers, sometimes not seeking his advice, sometimes acting against it. Such evidence reveals clearly how crucial business success was to Clemens, occasionally much more important than achievement as a writer.[31] A popular subscription book, since it would have been read by a large, heterogeneous audience, would have satisfied not only the "artistic" but also the business side of his temperament.

Combined with his desire to write a subscription book was his ostensible fear that he could not create one without many characters and many incidents. Writing to Howells on 19 October 1899, Clemens complained, "Ah, if I could look into the insides of people as you do and say, and tell *how* they said it, I could write a fine and readable book now, for I've got a prime subject."[32] The letter was written two years after the period that I am now discussing, but the inadequacy that it describes is one that he felt consistently: he knew—or thought he knew, which created the same effect—that he could not write a long book with a relatively small, homogeneous cast of characters and a relatively small number of exciting incidents. He was seldom good at creating adult characters or delineating adult relationships in depth. Thus,

31. In connection with this idea—the importance of business success to the writer, in particular the links between success and failure in the worlds of business and literature—see James Cox's discussion of the years in which Clemens fought to avoid bankruptcy. Cox's remarks about Joan of Arc are particularly interesting; he says, for example, "Here again there is every indication that Mark Twain did not lose sight of the commercial possibilities of his great, pure project" (*Mark Twain: The Fate of Humor*, p. 251).

32. *MTHL*, 2:710.

he attempted to write a big book by substituting quantity for narrow focus and thorough development. Thus, he occasionally felt an acute difficulty in finding many incidents and characters that could exist together in a believable fictional world, particularly, as in the present instance, in a book where—despite the dream premise—he wanted to treat the materials more or less realistically.

Intensifying the problem was the fact that, in his best work, Mark Twain truly was the "most autobiographical of writers"; and his own life had been unusually varied, involving people and experiences not easily compressible into the same fictional world. The problem I describe is in essence a structural one—the need for both length and coherence—and one that Mark Twain always wrestled with. At times, the freedom permitted by the travel format alleviated the problem (*The Innocents Abroad, Roughing It, A Tramp Abroad*, the major portion of *Life on the Mississippi, Following the Equator*); at times, it was alleviated by the need to adhere, at least approximately, to extremely rich sources (*Connecticut Yankee, Joan of Arc*), to a world that could be seen by a child (the Tom Sawyer books), and so on. The reference to the Tom Sawyer books brings me to another point: *Tom Sawyer, Detective*—the most recently published Tom Sawyer book—had been only a novelette; the volume containing it was padded into a subscription book by the inclusion of previously published material.[33] *Pudd'nhead Wilson* was also relatively short, and it also became part of a subscription book in America only through the inclusion of additional material: "Those Incredible Twins" plus Mark Twain's facetious comments about himself as a "jackleg novelist." *Joan of Arc* and *Following the Equator* were certainly long enough and, at least from Mark Twain's perspective, coherent enough, but both length and structure were imposed from without by history and the actual events of the world tour. Now he was forced to depend to a large extent on memory and imagination.

33. *Tom Sawyer, Detective* was published in a volume also containing other previously published material: *Tom Sawyer Abroad* and stories from *The Stolen White Elephant*. The volume, published in America by Harper and Brothers in 1896, was entitled *Tom Sawyer Abroad, Tom Sawyer, Detective and Other Stories*.

Judging from documents like "Villagers," even the writer's Hannibal world contained enough variety to form the basis of several different types of fiction. Yet, either his fear of not being able to write enough pages, or his desire to tell the whole truth, or the pleasure he derived from the contemplation of many possibilities, or all these motives almost compelled him to consider using characters and incidents that did not belong together—fictionally, that is. Writing of James Lampton—the prototype of Colonel Sellers—in the *Autobiography*, he vowed that Sellers was "real," even the incident of the turnips. In Sellers's book, however, this character's reality is so marvelously different from that of the other characters that he helps to destroy whatever suggestion of fictional integrity *The Gilded Age* might have had. Any number of characters and situations, all real, that Mark Twain thought of using during this last period would have enabled him to write a long book, but also one very difficult to unify, although a shipboard setting would have helped to alleviate the difficulties.

Complicating things further is the fact that his perspective varied concerning the shape of the actions that he would require these characters and incidents to trace. To oversimplify in order to be succinct: sometimes life seemed comic, sometimes tragic, sometimes wonderful, sometimes terrible.[34] For all these reasons, and more, Mark Twain found it difficult to finish novels. And yet his stay at Weggis had been extremely beneficial: Susy's anniversary had been faced down, *Following the Equator* had been finished, projects had been begun related to his own distant and immediate past. He had even written the first few pages to a narrative that, if it had been continued, would have been divorced totally from his personal life—a historical novel about Wilhelmina of Prussia entitled "Fragment of Prussian History."[35] Despite

34. Writing of Mark Twain's late fiction, Richard Hauck asserts, "They represent a final vision of ambivalence. The total absurd view includes the awareness that endings are arbitrarily and illogically happy or sad" (*A Cheerful Nihilism: Confidence and the Absurd in American Humorous Fiction*, p. 157).

35. "Fragment of Prussian History" may be found in Paine 212, MTP. The twenty-four manuscript pages and thirteen pages of notes are written on the distinctive cross-barred paper of the Weggis period. According to Alan Gribben, who is writing a book

his problems, he had recommenced in a remarkably promising fashion as a professional writer.

---

about Mark Twain's reading and who was kind enough to provide me with background information about the writer's interest in Wilhelmina, Howells had edited the memoirs of the princess in 1877 and a new translation and edition had been published in 1877 by Princess Christian. Mark Twain had considered using episodes from the latter work in his proposed appendix to *A Connecticut Yankee in King Arthur's Court*. This appendix would also have contained anecdotes from works such as Rousseau's *Confessions* and Taine's *L'Ancien Régime*, all "in support of the assertion that there were not real ladies and gentlemen before our century." See Howard Baetzhold, "The Course of Composition of *A Connecticut Yankee*: A Reinterpretation," p. 200. Then, in 1891, according to Gribben, Clemens told Henry Fisher that he adored Wilhelmina and ranked her memoirs with the autobiography of Benvenuto Cellini. The writer seems to have admired several qualities possessed by Wilhelmina, all of which are suggested in the story that he began about her: frankness, independence, ambition, a sense of humor. After describing her amusing first impressions of the extremely provincial court of her new husband, Henry of Bayreuth, and after deliberating unsuccessfully about how to introduce background information about his central character, Mark Twain seems to have dropped the project. Two manuscripts focusing on unconventional females—this one and "Hellfire Hotchkiss"—had been begun during the Weggis months. It would not be until his articles about Mary Baker Eddy, however, that the humorist would begin a successful involvement with this type of character.

3

Vienna
October 1897 to April 1898

By 3 October 1897, after rejecting at least seven hotels, Clemens and his family were ensconced in the Hotel Metropole in Vienna, preparing to begin several months in this Austrian city, which would prove to be occasionally debilitating and frustrating, often exhilarating, and continually perplexing. On the one hand, Samuel Clemens in Vienna was a splendidly free, magnificently courted, royally treated man. Everywhere, doors opened wide to him, people deferred to him, groups clamored for the presence of the "great American humorist." An affair that he attended with Clara in December is typical:

> Dec. 1. Night before last, Madame Leschetizky came and took Clara and me to Ritter von Dutschka's to dine. Twenty persons at dinner; Count von Eulenberg (German Ambassador) and others came in after dinner. A remarkable gathering—no commonplace people present, no leatherheads. Princes and other titled people there, not *because* of their titles, but for their distinction in achievement. It was like a Salon of old time Paris. Madame Dutschka is large and stately and beautiful, cordial and full of all kinds of charms of manner, and ways and speech. She is Russian; appears to be about 30, but is really 52, and has a son 28. Count Kilmansegge, Governor of Upper Austria, and wife, and—but I cannot remember the name. The new baritone from Beyreut (von Rooy) sang—a wonderful voice. He is but 26 and has a future before him. Leschetizky played. A marvelous performance. He never plays except in that house, she says. He sacrificed himself for his first wife—believed she would be the greatest pianist of all time—and now they have been many years separated. If he had developed himself instead of her he would have been the world's wonder himself.[1]

1. *MTN,* p. 342. For abbreviations used in the footnotes, see "Short References," pp. ix–x.

On the other hand, there was Clemens's continual awareness of Susy's death, Jean's ill health, and Livy's despondency. Thus, when he talked of his "deadness" in a letter to Howells on 22 January or referred to Livy and himself as a "pair of old derelicts," he was probably not being hyperbolic.[2] At times—despite his remarkable energy—he undoubtedly felt that way, or thought he did, or thought he should have. As I have mentioned before, Clemens's desire to empathize with Livy doubtlessly affected his analysis of his own feelings. Even though he would have loved to revel in his adventures with royalty or in the regal treatment that he himself was afforded, his sense of decorum either kept him from fully enjoying his situation or created feelings of guilt when he did.

There was a further complication. During the fall of 1897 and the winter and spring of 1898 he became more and more solvent: Rogers was investing well, *Following the Equator* was selling, the Bliss/Harper contract was crawling to a conclusion and would probably guarantee him a solid sum for life. At the same time, however, his conception of the amount of money that he should have and that he might obtain was inflating. Causing this inflation were such factors as Clara's music lessons and Jean's and Livy's medical expenses. Causing it as well was his own need to make a spectacular escape from the stigma of past financial failure. For these reasons, at certain times he talked confidently about his economic future and seemed satisfied with his progress; at others, he was in love with grandiose plans, as in March and April when he speculated about obtaining world monopolies for, first, a textile-designing machine and, then, a process by which peat moss and wool could be made into cloth.

What made his situation more puzzling was his occasional conviction that the order of reality in which his problems took place—the mundane, sensuous, waking world—was less valuable than another kind of existence, one not easily defined or explained, but hinted at in articles that he read, or in dreams and telepathic experiences that tantalized him.[3]

2. *MTHL*, 2:670.

3. In his introduction to *WWD?*, John Tuckey discusses some of the literature on the relationship between the conscious and unconscious levels of the mind with which Clemens was familiar: William James's *The Principles of Psychology*, Sir John Adams's

Each of these issues—his right to enjoyment, his financial needs, even the essence of the "real" life—impinged upon and affected his literary identity: the subjects that he would treat, the audience that he would write for, the attitude toward life that his work would manifest, the genre (or genres) in which he would express himself. Evidence of his uncertainty may be found in the several, almost bewilderingly abrupt shifts and would-be shifts that he made during this first year.

Clemens began his stay in Vienna by rejecting still another of Major Pond's enticements, asserting in his 17 September letter that he no longer needed to lecture. Yet he mentioned elsewhere that Livy had quashed the scheme; moreover, he obviously enjoyed the response that his appearances in and around Vienna provoked (and a year later, in November 1898, he almost committed himself to a thirty-stop American speaking tour). On 4 November he informed Bliss that reports that he was writing books for publication were fallacious; on the other hand, scattered throughout notes and letters from this period are references to ideas for popular projects. After putting aside a "rattling good subscription book" early in 1898, he plunged headfirst into plays —his own, collaborations, translations—and talked semifacetiously of needing seven rooms in a modern New York building to handle his dramatic business upon his return to America.[4] After his fervor for drama cooled and during his months as a business tycoon, he seemed to be pondering— perhaps unconsciously—the possibility of giving up literature altogether.

Yet, when he was not wallowing in dreams of himself as a John D. Rockefeller, or a potentate of the stage world, or a dismal drifting derelict, he was writing superbly, particularly during the first few exciting months in Vienna. At this time, for example, he wrote both the "Early Days" episode of his autobiography and the initial section of "The Chronicle of Young Satan," two manuscripts whose contrasting tones and purposes provide additional evidence of their

---

Herbartian Psychology, and Georg Lichtenberg's writings on dreams, for example. See *WWD?*, p. 17.

4. SLC to James Pond, 17 September 1897, PS, MTP; SLC to Frank Fuller, 2 July 1897, PS, MTP; see *HHR*, p. 374; SLC to Frank Bliss, 4 November 1897, MTP; *HHR*, p. 316.

creator's vacillating attitudes toward life during these months.[5]

When I think of certain passages from "Early Days," the phrase that I am reminded of most frequently—perhaps surprisingly—is one from the preface to Walt Whitman's 1855 edition of *Leaves of Grass*: "The facts showered over with light." The facts of the writer's past—the physical environment, the sounds of people talking—are there; yet they are sometimes seen in such a way, through memory and imagination, as to create the impression of something almost holy. Consider the following passage in which Mark Twain's ecstatic discovery that he can "call back" the Quarles farm inspires him to write a kind of prose poetry reminiscent of "Song of Myself":

—I can call it all back and make it as real as it ever was, and as blessed. I call back the prairie, and its loneliness and peace, and a vast hawk hanging motionless in the sky, with his wings spread wide and the blue of the vault showing through the fringe of their end feathers. I can see the woods in their autumn dress, the oaks purple, the hickories washed with gold, the maples and the sumachs luminous with crimson fires, and I can hear the rustle made by the fallen leaves as we plowed through them. I can see the blue clusters of wild grapes hanging among the foliage of the saplings, and I remember the taste of them and the smell. I know how the wild blackberries looked, and how they tasted, and the same with the pawpaws, the hazelnuts, and the persimmons; and I can feel the thumping rain, upon my head, of hickory nuts and walnuts when we were out in the frosty dawn to scramble for them with the pigs, and the gusts of wind loosed them and sent them down.[6]

It was not until Florence in 1904 that he hit upon a satisfying method for composing his autobiography: "Start at no particular time of your life; talk only about the thing

5. The manuscript of "Early Days" is written on cross-barred paper that is lighter and greener than the paper used at Weggis. According to Vic Fisher of the Mark Twain Papers, there is evidence that the writer used this paper at least as late as 4 November 1897 (a letter to Frank Bliss is written on it) and perhaps even as late as 26 November (a letter to Bliss is dated then, but only a photocopy of this letter is at MTP; the original is at Yale).

6. *Writings*, 36:110. Henceforth, references to "Early Days" will be made in the text.

which interests you for the moment; drop it the moment its interest threatens to pale, and turn your talk upon the new and more interesting thing that has intruded itself into your mind meantime" (p. 193). Mark Twain used this associational method in composing "Early Days"; but since he also kept to a more or less chronological path, he avoided one of the weaknesses of the worst of the later work: the tendency to focus on topics of such triviality that even his incandescent personality could not vitalize them. Linked to this modified free-association method was his desire and ability to highlight, through the creation of dramatically conceived episodes, whatever he discovered to be most important during his mental peregrinations. The result is that "Early Days" combines in a truly memorable way a sense of freedom with a sense of significant structure.

The sketch begins with a delightful parody of the "my ancestors" section of the typical autobiography. The writer brags of his pirate progenitors whom, he admits, he would love to emulate, as would the reader—"but never mind what he will find there. I'm not writing his autobiography, but mine" (p. 82). He illustrates his mock pride in the ancestor who helped sentence Charles I to death with the following beautifully told anecdote:

> A case of the kind happened in Berlin several years ago. William Walter Phelps was our minister at the Emperor's court then, and one evening he had me to dinner to meet Count S———, a Cabinet Minister. This nobleman was of long and illustrious descent. Of course I wanted to let out the fact that I had some ancestors, too; but I did not want to pull them out of their graves by the ears, and I never could seem to get the chance to work them in in a way that would look sufficiently casual. I suppose Phelps was in the same difficulty. In fact, he looked distraught now and then—just as a person looks who wants to uncover an ancestor purely by accident and cannot think of a way that will seem accidental enough. But at last, after dinner, he made a try. He took us about his drawing-room, showing us the pictures, and finally stopped before a rude and ancient engraving. It was a picture of the court that tried Charles I. There was a pyramid of judges in Puritan slouch hats, and below them three bareheaded secretaries seated at a table. Mr. Phelps put his finger upon one of the three and said, with exulting indifference:
> "An ancestor of mine."

I put my finger on a judge, and retorted with scathing lan-
guidness:

"Ancestor of mine. But it is a small matter. I have others."
(pp. 84-85)

Moving rapidly through other casually selected relatives
and episodes—the "Lamptons," spelled with a *p*, for example; his brother; the Tennessee land; the death of his
father—he arrives finally and with seeming serendipity at
James Lampton, and then climaxes with a portrait of Lampton that I find superior to that of his fictional avatar in *The
American Claimant* and even *The Gilded Age*. The portrait
is worth lingering over; he tells of meeting Lampton acci-
dentally while on a lecture tour with George Washington
Cable, of sneaking away from his uncle to bring Cable to
him, of Lampton orating:

> I went back and asked Lampton what he was doing now. He
> began to tell me of a "small venture" he had begun in New Mexi-
> co through his son; "only a little thing—a mere trifle—partly to
> amuse my leisure, partly to keep my capital from lying idle, but
> mainly to develop the boy—develop the boy. Fortune's wheel
> is ever revolving; he may have to work for his living some day—
> as strange things have happened in this world. But it's only a
> little thing—a mere trifle, as I said."
> And so it was—as he began it. But under his deft hands it grew
> and blossomed and spread—oh, beyond imagination. At the end
> of half an hour he finished; finished with the remark, uttered
> in an adorably languid manner:
> "Yes, it is but a trifle, as things go nowadays—a bagatelle—but
> amusing. It passes the time. The boy thinks great things of it,
> but he is young, you know, and imaginative; lacks the experi-
> ence which comes of handling large affairs, and which tempers
> the fancy and perfects the judgment. I suppose there's a couple
> of millions in it, possibly three, but not more, I think; still, for
> a boy, you know, just starting in life, it is not bad. I should not
> want him to make a fortune—let that come later. It could turn
> his head, at his time of life, and in many ways be a damage to
> him."
> Then he said something about his having left his pocketbook
> lying on the table in the main drawing-room at home, and about
> its being after banking hours, now, and——
> I stopped him there and begged him to honor Cable and me
> by being our guest at the lecture—with as many friends as might
> be willing to do us the like honor. He accepted. And he thanked

me as a prince might who had granted us a grace. The reason I
stopped his speech about the tickets was because I saw that he
was going to ask me to furnish them to him and let him pay next
day; and I knew that if he made the debt he would pay it if he
had to pawn his clothes. (pp. 92–93)

Finally, Lampton leaves and Cable concludes, "That was
Colonel Sellers" (p. 93). Although Mark Twain has apparently been wandering since he began with his talk of his
ancestors, the section concludes so strikingly that the reader
is almost convinced that it is to this point that the narrator
has been leading all along.

The next two sections are organized analogously: the
narrator meanders in a roughly chronological way, occasionally leaping forward or backward in time or alternating
between life and its fictional representation. There is one
structural difference, however: in retrospect, a reader can
discern that the narrator has been moving inexorably toward
a bittersweet center—the Quarles farm—even while his memories, his humorous remarks about Hannibal doctors, for
example, have lingered on the circumference. When he arrives almost magically at this subject, he enshrines his childhood in a language as emotionally charged as anything he
ever wrote. The following is only one example, and practically any passage taken from this section would be appropriate:

I remember the 'coon and 'possum hunts, nights, with the
negroes, and the long marches through the black gloom of the
woods, and the excitement which fired everybody when the distant bay of an experienced dog announced that the game was
treed; then the wild scramblings and stumblings through briers
and bushes and over roots to get to the spot; then the lighting
of a fire and the felling of the tree, the joyful frenzy of the dogs
and the negroes, and the weird picture it all made in the red
glare—I remember it all well, and the delight that everyone got
out of it, except the 'coon.
I remember the pigeon seasons, when the birds would come
in millions and cover the trees and by their weight break down
the branches. They were clubbed to death with sticks; guns were
not necessary and were not used. I remember the squirrel hunts,
and prairie-chicken hunts, and wild-turkey hunts, and all that;
and how we turned out, mornings, while it was still dark, to go
on these expeditions, and how chilly and dismal it was, and how

often I regretted that I was well enough to go. A toot on a tin horn brought twice as many dogs as were needed, and in their happiness they raced and scampered about, and knocked small people down, and made no end of unnecessary noise. At the word, they vanished away toward the woods, and we drifted silently after them in the melancholy gloom. But presently the gray dawn stole over the world, the birds piped up, then the sun rose and poured light and comfort all around, everything was fresh and dewy and fragrant, and Life was a boon again. After three hours of tramping we arrived back wholesomely tired, overladen with game, very hungry, and just in time for breakfast. (pp. 114–15)

One of the effects of "Early Days" is to dissolve completely the distinction between the real and the fictional, as Mark Twain turns the dream of his past into the reality of his creative memory. The result is a myth more intense and meaningful than the actual facts could ever have been. Given his achievement of arriving at this still point, it is entirely understandable that, for the moment, he would be compelled to shelve the manuscript and to wait for further inspiration before again "writing autobiographies for a living" (p. 89).

What is remarkable is the facility with which he moved from this kind of writing and this kind of world into the environment of the immediate political present for the creation of "Stirring Times in Austria," his extremely skillful exposition of the uproar in the Austrian parliament that he observed firsthand in October and November 1897. Almost all of his essays written during the Vienna period are more than competent; they are always clear, often incisive, at times witty, and usually display an admirable dramatic and imaginative flair. Many of his topics may strike the modern reader as trivial—the fate of most "occasional" literature —but of course these sketches were written to be sold, not for posterity. Thus, whatever ideas seemed to him to be new and topical became treatable in prose: queer religions like Christian Science, Swedish health resorts, Austrian inventors, and so on.

In "Stirring Times in Austria," the writer and the occasion unite to create a really fine essay by any standard. The best thing about it is the blend it achieves between the subject itself, the writer's perspective on the subject, and his sense of the audience for whom the piece is written. In the opening section—"The Government in the Frying Pan"—the author telegraphs the situation: "an atmosphere . . . brimful of political electricity."[7] Then he rapidly sketches in the reasons Austria has not ignited: factionalism preventing a unified opposition against the government, the government's skill in diverting the people's attention from crucial issues, the censorship of newspapers, the army. Then, he describes the immediate situation: the dominant party has made an unpopular decision in order to gain enough support outside its ranks to try to push through the *Ausgleich*—the "Arrangement, Settlement, which holds Austria and Hungary together. It dates from 1867, and has to be renewed every ten years" (p. 204). The facts are given economically and through differing means—"informal sources," quotes from a Hartford article several years old—and summarized in a language that sounds spoken, at times with a staccato rhythm that conveys directly the tension that exists:

> The ten-year rearrangement was due a year ago, but failed to connect. At least completely. A year's compromise was arranged. A new arrangement must be effected before the last day of this year. Otherwise the two countries become separate entities. The Emperor would still be King of Hungary—that is, King of an independent foreign country. There would be Hungarian custom-houses on the Austrian frontier, and there would be a Hungarian army and a Hungarian foreign office. Both countries would be weakened by this, both would suffer damage. (pp. 204–5)

Throughout this first section, the subject, not the writer, seems to dominate; yet even in this essentially expository portion, Mark Twain's personality thrusts through, as in his lengthy description of the plight of the newspapers. The description is, from a purely functional point of view, too long; yet it conveys the reassuring sense of a writer in complete control, not afraid to include "superfluous" information if this strikes his fancy:

> If the censor did his work before the morning edition was printed, he would be less of an inconvenience than he is; but of course the papers cannot wait many minutes after five o'clock

7. *Writings*, 22:197. Henceforth, references to "Stirring Times in Austria" will be made in the text.

to get his verdict; they might as well go out of business as do that; so they print, and take the chances. Then, if they get caught by a suppression, they must strike out the condemned matter and print the edition over again. That delays the issue several hours, and is expensive besides. The government gets the suppressed edition for nothing. If it bought it, that would be joyful, and would give great satisfaction. Also, the edition would be larger. Some of the papers do not replace the condemned paragraphs with other matter; they merely snatch them out and leave blanks behind—mourning blanks, marked *"Confiscated."* (p. 201)

The second section, "A Memorable Sitting," describes the thirty-three-hour October meeting of the parliament in which the efforts of the government to force a decision were thwarted by the opposition obstructionists, particularly by an amazing twelve-hour speech by Dr. Lecher. Much of the section is written in dialogue because, as the narrator stresses, the episode was exceptionally dramatic. At appropriate moments the actors are introduced; the president is described in a lengthy set piece memorable for the writer's fascination with the president's smile; the obstreperous Wolf is quickly individualized through Mark Twain's account of a duel: "He shot Badeni through the arm, and then walked over in the politest way and inspected his game, shook hands, expressed regret, and all that" (p. 210). At this point, it might have been easy for the author to have allowed theatrics to submerge significance; this does not happen, because he does not permit the reader to get too close to the action. After describing the controversy for several paragraphs in the present tense, for example, he halts the flow in order "to change the tense" (p. 208); then, while being entirely successful in conveying the quality of Lecher's physical and forensic achievement, he also demands that the reader not lose sight of its meaning:

It was the Majority's scheme—as charged by the Opposition—to drown debate upon the bill by pure noise—drown it out and stop it. The debate being thus ended, the vote upon the reference would follow—with victory for the government. But into the government's calculations had not entered the possibility of a single-barreled speech which should occupy the entire time-limit of the sitting, and also get itself delivered in spite of all the noise. Goliah was not expecting David. But David was there; and during twelve hours he tranquilly pulled statistical, historical, and argumentative pebbles out of his scrip and slung them at the giant; and when he was done he was victor, and the day was saved. (p. 217)

In "Curious Parliamentary Etiquette," the essay's third section, there is even more drama. This drama is primarily farce, but a farce complicated by the tone of wonder in which the narrator responds to the spectacle of professional men cursing one another like stevadores:

Meantime Wolf goes whooping along with his newspaper-readings in great contentment.

Dr. Pattai. "Shut up! Shut up! Shut *up!* You haven't the floor!"

Strohbach. "The miserable cub!"

Dr. Lueger (to Wolf, raising his voice strenuously above the storm). "You are a wholly honorless street brat!" [A voice, "Fire the rapscallion out!" But Wolf's soul goes marching noisily on, just the same.]

Schönerer (vast and muscular, and endowed with the most powerful voice in the Reichsrath; comes plowing down through the standing crowds, red, and choking with anger; halts before Deputy Wohlmeyer, grabs a rule and smashes it with a blow upon a desk, threatens Wohlmeyer's face with his fist, and bellows out some personalities, and a promise). "Only you wait—we'll teach you!" [A whirlwind of offensive retorts assails him from the band of meek and humble Christian Socialists compacted around their leader, that distinguished religious expert, Dr. Lueger, Bürgermeister of Vienna. Our breath comes in excited gasps now, and we are full of hope. We imagine that we are back fifty years ago in the Arkansas Legislature, and we think we know what is going to happen, and are glad we came, and glad we are up in the gallery, out of the way, where we can see the whole thing and yet not have to supply any of the material for the inquest. However, as it turns out, our confidence is abused, our hopes are misplaced.] (pp. 228–29, Mark Twain's brackets)

The narrator expresses his puzzlement when he observes such men engaging in offal flinging; he is even more perplexed when he discovers that the language will not provoke violence. At one point he compares the legislators to schoolboys, but:

School-boys blackguard each other fiercely, and by the hour, and one would think that nothing would ever come of it but noise;

but that would be a mistake. Up to a certain limit the result would be noise only, but that limit overstepped, trouble would follow right away. There are certain phrases—phrases of a peculiar character—phrases of the nature of that reference to Schönerer's grandmother, for instance, which not even the most spiritless school-boy in the English-speaking world would allow to pass unavenged. One difference between school-boys and the lawmakers of the Reichsrath seems to be that the lawmakers have no limit, no danger-line. Apparently they may call each other what they please, and go home unmutilated. (pp. 234–35)

Mark Twain's tone—his quizzical sense of the scene's mystery—conveys better than anything he says directly the impression of hilarious actions that border on the insane.

Section 4 is entitled "The Historic Climax" and describes the meeting in which parliament finally exploded: the government pushed through a law—the Lex Falkenhayn—empowering the chair to evict troublemakers; outraged opposition members attacked and took over the chair; police entered the building and dragged out the invaders; it is now December, and the government is in shambles. In this section there is no dialogue, although as the narrator says, the situation is "imposingly dramatic" (p. 241); it is all picture, with the central episode, which is presented almost cinematically, framed by two passages of analysis to which the essay has been leading. The first passage reads as follows:

However, there were doubters; men who were troubled, and believed that a grave mistake had been made. It might be that the Opposition was crushed, and profitably for the country, too; but the *manner* of it—the *manner* of it! That was the serious part. It could have far-reaching results; results whose gravity might transcend all guessing. It might be the initial step toward a return to government by force, a restoration of the irresponsible methods of obsolete times. (p. 239)

The second appears below:

It was an odious spectacle—odious and awful. For one moment it was an unbelievable thing—a thing beyond all credibility; it must be a delusion, a dream, a nightmare. But no, it was real—pitifully real, shamefully real, hideously real. These sixty policemen had been soldiers, and they went at their work with the cold unsentimentality of their trade. They ascended the steps of the tribune, laid their hands upon the inviolable persons of the representatives of a nation, and dragged and tugged and hauled them down the steps and out at the door; then ranged themselves in stately military array in front of the ministerial *estrade*, and so stood.

It was a tremendous episode. The memory of it will outlast all the thrones that exist to-day. In the whole history of free parliaments the like of it had been seen but three times before. It takes its imposing place among the world's unforgettable things. I think that in my lifetime I have not twice seen abiding history made before my eyes, but I know that I have seen it once. (p. 242)

The language of this second passage is conventional; it is almost trite, in fact. But since it appears at a time when Mark Twain's readers expect to be enlightened clearly and moralistically, it is rhetorically appropriate; moreover, contrasting as it does with the comic and ironic understatement that precedes it, it creates a devastating impression of sincerity and conviction. One of the things that is most effective about this essay is its tonal variety and the narrator's control of the variety: he can be flat, objective, anticipatory, wondering and admiring, amused and perplexed. And appalled. Yet the laconic tone of the last sentence is absolutely right as a final response to the entire situation: "Yes, the Lex Falkenhayn was a great invention, and did what was claimed for it—it got the government out of the frying pan" (p. 243).

One additional quality of this essay should be elucidated: its blend of the obvious and the subtle, the presence of this latter ingredient giving the essay a kind of resonance that "occasional" literature seldom possesses. At times, Mark Twain as narrator is so insistent about the significance of these "stirring times" that he verges on the tendentious; this preachy clarity was of course necessary in an article written for a solid, well-educated audience that expected meat-and-potatoes moralizing in the magazines that it bought. But there is an additional dimension, created by the writer's use of language that is suggestive of both the drama and children at play: "By and by he struck the idea of beating out a *tune* with his board. . . . And so he and Dr. Lecher now spoke at the same time, and mingled their speeches with the other noises, and nobody heard either of them" (p. 216). The references to the theater are of course appropriate because the situation is dramatic; further, as one thinks about it, the stage merges with the references to children to form an important metaphorical complex. These men whom Mark Twain has been observing, it seems, have fallen so in love with performing and playing at politics that they have probably forgotten whatever mature purposes they may have begun with. Members of the government congratulate themselves "almost girlishly" (p. 239) for the subterfuge by which the Lex Falkenhayn is validated. And throughout the turmoil of the sessions, the participants are

> attitudinizing; . . . playing to the gallery. However, they are all doing that. It is curious to see. Men who only vote, and can't make speeches, and don't know how to invent witty ejaculations, wander about the vacated parts of the floor, and stop in a good place and strike attitudes—attitudes suggestive of weighty thought, mostly—and glance furtively up at the galleries to see how it works; or a couple will come together and shake hands in an artificial way, and laugh a gay manufactured laugh, and do some constrained and self-conscious attitudinizing; and *they* steal glances at the galleries to see if they are getting notice. It is like a scene on the stage—by-play by minor actors at the back while the stars do the great work at the front. (p. 232)

What the narrator succeeds finally in describing is a group of Davids not really trying to defeat "Goliahs" (p. 217), but throwing stones both for the sake of the activity and the pleasure of being observed in it. Tom Sawyers were everywhere.

Prior to becoming so closely involved with Austrian politics, Mark Twain had made a tentative beginning to the version of "The Mysterious Stranger"—"The Chronicle of Young Satan"—that, along with his autobiography, is the most ambitious manuscript to which he devoted himself during these last thirteen years.[8] Then, probably after he had finished "Stirring Times in Austria," and to a certain extent because of what he had seen in Vienna during this

8. It is possible that a still unpublished twenty-eight-page manuscript entitled "Conversations with Satan" (Paine 255) that Mark Twain seems to have worked on in the fall of 1897 might have preceded "The Chronicle of Young Satan." The "Conversations" center mostly on the merits of a German stove and of tobacco, the best line in the sketch being the following from an urbane Satan: "It's good; very, very, good; it burns freely & smells like a heretic" (p. 13).

period, he returned to the "Mysterious Stranger" story, working on it until the plot had been begun in a promising fashion. In *Mark Twain and Little Satan,* John Tuckey speculates that Clemens's interest and involvement in the Austrian political maelstrom in late October and November is reflected in "Chronicle" in several ways: the names of several characters, a few plot details, and possibly the writer's important decision to shift the original St. Petersburg setting to Austria.[9] There are several other reasons he might have decided to make such an immense temporal and spatial change in the setting for his story, each of which is linked to the probability that, when Mark Twain began his tale, he hoped to publish it. This, I realize, is not a conventional idea about "Chronicle," but I see no reason to assume otherwise. Clemens referred in a letter written at Weggis to books not intended for publication, but he did not name them.[10] Even if his original intention was not to publish "Chronicle," he was constantly changing his mind about what could and could not reach print, particularly during this time, when he wanted to produce something that would make money and signal his literary rebirth (*Following the Equator* never functioned this way for him because of the conditions under which it was written and because he came to see it as a book that disguised his personality, rather than expressed it). Moreover, he refers in a 5–6 February letter to Rogers to a "rattling good subscription book" that he has put aside, and "The Chronicle of Young Satan" seems to have been the only potentially long book that he was working on at that time.[11] Finally, certain aspects of the first version of the story suggest one written for publication.

We should not forget that while Mark Twain was working on "The Chronicle of Young Satan," "Tom Sawyer's Conspiracy" was very much alive; another reason he changed the setting for "Chronicle" could be that it occurred to him

9. See *MTLS,* pp. 17–24. In a later article, Tuckey demonstrates the resemblances between Eseldorf and Weggis, which he sees as "a kind of proximate Hannibal" ("Hannibal, Weggis and Mark Twain's Eseldorf," n. 18, p. 240).

10. See SLC to Mr. Skrine, 22 August 1897, MTP.

11. *HHR,* p. 317.

that to bring two St. Petersburg manuscripts narrated by Huck Finn to a completion at around the same time would be unwise from the standpoint of publication and sales. Another reason could have been his recognition of the value of remoteness, for as he wrote in his notebook in April 1896, "All world-distances have shrunk to nothing. . . . The mysterious and the fabulous can get no fine effects without the help of remoteness; and there are no remotenesses any more."[12] Certainly "The Chronicle of Young Satan" was to be "mysterious and fabulous," and certainly Austria of the early eighteenth century was more remote than St. Petersburg of around 1840. It is also possible that, by changing the setting, he hoped to stimulate his imagination to create the long book that, thus far, he had been unable to produce using such settings as the undisguised Hannibal past ("Villagers," the autobiography), the disguised Hannibal past ("Hellfire Hotchkiss," "Tom Sawyer's Conspiracy"), Washington, the West, the sea ("Which Was the Dream?"), the European past ("Fragment of Prussian History").[13] A work set in the Austrian past but suggestive of both Hannibal and the Austrian present might be the answer.

A final, plausible reason for the change is that if Mark Twain wanted to include significant religious satire in a story written to be read by someone other than himself in lonely isolation—if, in other words, he wished to write a "serious" and publishable work—it was still (as it had been with his first popular book, *The Innocents Abroad*) much more judicious to attack a foreign version of Roman Catholicism than a homegrown brand of Presbyterianism. And, of course—as notebook entries illustrate—while in Austria he was occasionally angered by what he interpreted to be deleterious Roman Catholic influence.[14] A number of remarks made early on by his new narrator, Theodor Fischer, seem designed primarily to satisfy the tastes of a predominantly

12. Notebook 29 (II), TS, p. 37, MTP.
13. Although he was quoted in a 1900 interview as saying that he believed the settings of stories to be unimportant (see *MTLS*, p. 80) it is evident that, in most cases, the setting of his stories *did* matter to Mark Twain.
14. See, for example, Notebook 32b (II) TS, p. 38, MTP.

Protestant audience, rather than to function as devastating religious satire. Consider the following:

> Father Adolf had actually met Satan face to face, more than once, and defied him. This was known to be so. Father Adolf said it himself. He never made any secret of it, but spoke it right out. And that he was speaking true; there was proof, in at least one instance; for on that occasion he quarreled with the Enemy, and intrepidly threw his inkstand at him, and there, upon the wall of his study was the black splotch where it struck and broke. The same was claimed for Luther, but no one believed it, for he was a heretic and liar. This was so, for the Pope himself said that Luther had lied about it.[15]

Further, a few of Theodor's comments seem out of character coming from a pious Roman Catholic, yet they are understandable when viewed as the manipulations of a wily author who wished to be published and read: "It was in conducting funerals that Father Adolf was at his best, if he hadn't too much of a load on, but only about enough to make him properly appreciate the sacredness of his office" (pp. 38–39). It may be unfair to suggest that the ethnic persuasion of the moneylender, Solomon Isaacs, could have been influenced by the author's desire to ingratiate himself with his readers before risking his cogent satire; but it is true that Clemens had recently encountered virulent pageants of Austrian anti-Semitism.

In any event, after the young stranger's identity has been revealed to the boys, after Mark Twain has begun a story with a certain appeal, and after he has had little Satan play fascinating games with fire, fruit, food, and a castle created ex nihilo, the writer suddenly, shockingly darkens the

---

15. *MSM*, p. 41. Henceforth, references to "The Chronicle of Young Satan" will be made in the text. Readers interested in familiarizing themselves with the most significant research about the "Mysterious Stranger" compex of fiction written prior to 1968 should begin with Tuckey's *MTLS* and his collection of criticism entitled *Mark Twain's Mysterious Stranger and the Critics*. Since that date, in my opinion the most useful information may be found in the introduction and notes to *MSM*, in William Gibson's *The Art of Mark Twain*, in Stanley Brodwin's "Mark Twain's Masks of Satan: The Final Phase," and in Sholom J. Kahn's *Mark Twain's Mysterious Stranger: A Study of the Manuscript Texts*.

tone: while observing two tiny workmen quarreling, "Satan reached out his hand and crushed the life out of them with his fingers, threw them away, wiped the red from his fingers on his handkerchief and went on" (p. 49).[16] Satan follows this display of godly petulance with a few comments about the despicable human race and the paradoxically harmful effect of the Moral Sense. None of the ideas regarding human fatuity and pride, however, are pushed to offensiveness; moreover, they are introduced so imaginatively and humorously —the contempt of the divine boy *is* funny in this context— that the writer makes his points while maintaining his friendly relationship with his reader. Almost immediately after this, the plot veers toward an involvement with Father Peter: he is charged with theft by Father Adolf and jailed; then he is exonerated because of Wilhelm Meidling's arguments, which are suggested to the lawyer by little Satan.

At this point, although the idea looked promising, Mark Twain put the manuscript aside.[17] His inspiration had been thwarted, he said in a 5–6 February letter to Rogers, because of disturbing news received from Bliss about the travelbook sales.[18] Yet he knew that if his imagination could be reinvigorated and the story extended, the project could be very worthwhile.

In the middle of January he zestfully began playwriting,

16. Gladys Bellamy suggests the source of episodes such as this when she mentions the influence of an Apocryphal New Testament on Sam Clemens, particularly the portrait of Jesus bringing clay birds to life and being "charged with causing the death of various boys who have displeased him." See *Mark Twain as a Literary Artist,* pp. 352–53.

17. It was only after he returned to the manuscript in 1899 that Clemens decided to have young Satan shock Father Peter into madness by lying about the results of the trial. See William Gibson's introductory comments in *MSM,* p. 6. Gibson's conclusion differs from that of Tuckey in his *MTLS,* pp. 38–39, where he argues that Mark Twain had written this sequence before putting aside the manuscript in 1897. Gibson's conclusion is supported by the following evidence: although the posttrial result is written on the buff paper of the 1897 version (originally, p. 93; later, p. 386) it is written in the ink of the 1899 continuation. The 1897 ink stops near the top of p. 93/386; the ink used to describe Father Peter's madness is that of the 1899 version of the manuscript.

18. *HHR,* p. 317.

vowing to commit himself wholeheartedly to that pursuit until he discovered whether he was talented enough to be as successful as he wished to be. Some of his time was spent translating two German plays—*Bartel Turaser* by Ernst Gottke and Georg Engel and *Im Fegefeuer* by Philipp Langmann—that had been popular in Europe and that he believed could have a similar destiny in the United States. He also planned to collaborate with Sigmund Schlesinger on a play entitled "Women in Politics," a plan that persisted tepidly even after his enthusiasm for the stage had abated.[19]

It is difficult to decide why at this particular moment he threw himself so fervently and with such high hopes into writing for the stage, although he had for many years flirted with the idea. One reason was probably his high admiration for Adolf von Wilbrandt's *The Master of Palmyra,* a very long tragic play that he described in "About Play Acting."[20] A purpose of this essay was to persuade the American public to alter its dramatic tastes and take an interest in something other than the vapid comedies that were then popular. Given this expressed point of view, one may conclude that Mark Twain saw himself as a contributor to the rebirth of American drama (he felt that conditions had deteriorated greatly since earlier in the century), if not through his own original plays, then through his willingness to support atypical kinds of drama and to translate serious European plays as well as comedies. Another possibility is that since his attempts at long fiction had reached hiatuses, this was the psychological moment to attempt a different type of writing. He may also have felt that now was the time—because of the fresh impetus provided by the European example, because his own stock was high and his public amenable—to become successful in a medium that he had often found alluring. Moreover, Clemens's actions during the first few months of 1898 indicate that for a period he felt himself capable of doing almost anything: speaking; writing fiction, nonfiction, and drama; collaborating on plays; investing. He had come a long way since

19. Ibid.
20. See *Writings,* 23:213–25. For a discussion of Mark Twain's personal and critical responses to *The Master of Palmyra,* see Sidney J. Krause, *Mark Twain as Critic,* pp. 284–95.

the death of his daughter, and his buoyant recognition of this fact is reflected strongly in his Viennese activities.

Whatever the reasons, he worked hard and joyously for at least a month, engaging Bram Stoker as his British agent, asking Rogers either to be his American representative or to select some worthy substitute, writing a comedy called "Is He Dead?," and translating plays. By 15 March, however, he was referring to his "so-called play" in a letter to Rogers, was temporarily discouraged by Stoker's response to the play, and was preparing to throw himself into a new activity—investing.[21]

Only one remnant survives from this period: the comedy "Is He Dead?."[22] Based upon the story of the incredible rise in the value of François Millet's paintings very late in his life and after his death, the farce tells how the indigent Millet and his attractive, conniving cohorts decide to fake the painter's death, thus driving up the value of his paintings and saving from bankruptcy the family of Millet's girl friend, which has been victimized by the villain, André. A few of the farcical scenes are unfunny, particularly an early one in which Millet's paintings are snubbed by a variety of noncustomers (much of the humor here depends upon dialectical monstrosities reminiscent of Mark Twain and Bret Harte's *Ah Sin,* such as a Chinese student's "Go to helly"). Also, Mark Twain is uncertain about whether to use a chimney sweep as a skeptical chorus, as someone who could stare at paintings from a "realistic" perspective and snip dully at their idiocy. Further, there are moments near the end of the play when the tone is inappropriate: the audience knows that Millet is really alive but his girl friend thinks him dead, and her grief is so convincing that it destroys the comic mood that the author wants to create. Finally, a scene in which Millet disguises himself as a woman (his sister) and is courted by the villain, André,

21. See *HHR*, pp. 323, 324, 326.

22. "Is He Dead?," TS, MTP. Henceforth, references to "Is He Dead?" will be made in the text. The play is based on a short story published in 1893 by Mark Twain entitled "Is He Living or Is He Dead?" An eight-page manuscript entitled "Shackleford's Ghost," which Tuckey dates 1897–1898, also is linked to this period of dramatic activity. This farce about the shenanigans of an invisible man reads, in fact, like the scenario for a play.

amidst much physical display of affection is one that undoubtedly would have made a nineteenth-century American
audience uncomfortable.

Despite these weaknesses, it is not a bad play, certainly no
worse than the popular drama of the United States (although
in England this is the time of Gilbert and Wilde and of the
beginning of Shaw's career). Moreover, it could have been—
and still could be—made into an entertaining, playable piece
with some judicious cutting.[23] The "unpromising hero" plot
structure, for example, creates many chances for healthy audience identification, and the scheme that will turn the hero
into a success is ingenious. Also, the play contains some excellent scenes, particularly the sequence in act 2 in which Millet,
supposedly dead and dressed as his twin sister, nervously
and at times almost maniacally tries to persuade prospec-
tive customers that "she" is who she says she is; explaining
that "she" is the younger twin ("He was born on a Tuesday
morning and I—I think—. . .Yes, I was born the next Satur-
day night" [p. 36]) and bragging of her "slathers" of children
("Seven in two years. . . .Some in the spring, some in the fall,
others along here and there" [p. 39]).

The state funeral given by France in the last act also has
some fine comic moments (it takes place offstage and is reported by Millet's friends), particularly those deriving from
the method used to prevent royal mourners from inspecting
the remains: Millet's colleague Dutchy shoves his lunch of
Limburger cheese in the coffin—which is already filled with
bricks—and bores holes in it when he hears of the funeral
plans. In this act as well, Mark Twain makes a satiric point
dear to his heart: predicting that there is no real danger of
repercussions even if France discovers that she has been
fooled, Millet says, "When France has committed herself to
the expression of a belief, she will die a hundred thousand
deaths rather than confess she has been in the wrong" (p. 41).
The allusion here is to the Dreyfus affair, which Clemens
had been observing with fascinated horror for a number of
months and which during the early part of 1898 was making
headlines around the world. Clemens's own 1897 plans to

23. The dramatic agents, Marc Klaw and Abraham Erlanger,
made the same point in a letter to Alf Hayman, manager for
Charles Frohman's Travelling Companies. See *HHR*, n. 1, p. 394.

write a book about the situation had been ruined because he had not received the information that he needed. Writing to Andrew Chatto, his English publisher, on 8 February he spoke of the irony of having his travel book live while the Dreyfus book died.[24] Yet he refused to allow the affair to escape untouched. "Is He Dead?" is clearly influenced by it, as is "Concerning the Jews," an essay written during the summer, of which he was very proud. Finally, a peculiar short story entitled "From the London Times of 1904," written when he was considering buying the American patent for a textile-designing machine that employed a photographic process, exploits not only his fascination with the inventions of the Austrian Jan Szczepanik but also his continuing interest in Alfred Dreyfus.

The story is a good example of Mark Twain's ability and willingness to use practically any aspect of his immediate experience as a source for magazine sketches, a lucrative tendency that I have already referred to. Thus, at the same time as he was having difficulty sorting out the multiplicity of his past experiences in order to create good, long fiction, he had few problems focusing on life practically as he was living it and producing competent, salable material. It is entirely possible, of course, that the habits he had developed to enable him to write short things in such a facile fashion inhibited his ability to write longer work; for example, since he could write magazine material so easily, he might often have been tempted to mine this talent when his longer work languished, rather than to persevere with the more difficult tasks.[25]

During February and March he plunged deeply into investment speculations relating to Szczepanik's inventions;[26] immediately he threw off two publishable sketches, "The Austrian Edison Teaching School Again" and the "London Times" story mentioned above. The former sketch is a brief

24. SLC to Chatto and Windus, 8 February 1898, PS, MTP.

25. This is not to say that Mark Twain was always able to finish and publish the short tales and sketches that he worked on during these years. Enough interesting unfinished material remains unpublished, in fact, to form the nucleus of a volume that the Mark Twain Papers hopes eventually to publish under the editorship of John Tuckey.

26. Letters to Rogers and notebook entries written during this period are full of references to Clemens's investments.

account of the Austrian government's method of avoiding
the potentially harmful effects of letting the inventor serve
his required spell of military duty. Since he had once been a
teacher, he would fulfill his obligation by being one again
for the rest of his life—but only for one half-day every two
months—rather than by being in the army three full years
during the prime of his creative life.[27] This, like the more
substantial "From the London Times," not only capitalizes
on the public interest in the Austrian's inventions, but also
encourages it. The latter purpose would have been important to Clemens, because he was hoping eventually to make
millions by obtaining patent rights for one of these inventions (and perhaps for other inventions as well) in America. In the "London Times" tale, the narrator—an American
foreign correspondent—first tells of a quarrel between Szczepanik and an American army officer, Clayton, over the value
of the telectroscope (a precursor of television); next, he reports that there is a murder charge against Clayton deriving
from the mysterious disappearance of the inventor and the
appearance of an unidentified corpse in the American's base-
ment; then, the reader is informed of the last-second post-
ponement of Clayton's execution because of the discovery—
via the telectroscope—that the inventor is alive in China. All
does not end happily, however; even though the corpse is not
the Austrian's, Clayton will be executed for murdering Szczepanik:

> "Several of us have arrived at the conclusion, your Excellency,
> that it would be an error to hang the prisoner for killing Szcze-
> panik, but only for killing the other man, since it is proven that
> he did not kill Szczepanik."
> "On the contrary, it is proven that he *did* kill Szczepanik. By
> the French precedent, it is plain that we must abide by the find-
> ing of the court."
> "But Szczepanik is still alive."
> "So is Dreyfus."
> In the end it was found impossible to ignore or get around the
> French precedent. There could be but one result: Clayton was de-
> livered over to the executioner. It made an immense excitement;
> the state rose as one man and clamored for Clayton's pardon
> and re-trial. The governor issued the pardon, but the Supreme

27. See *Writings*, 23:263–67.

Court was in duty bound to annul it, and did so, and poor Clayton was hanged yesterday. The city is draped in black, and indeed, the like may be said of the state. All America is vocal with scorn of "French justice," and of the malignant little soldiers who invented it and inflicted it upon the other Christian lands.[28]

The story is clever and the ending is shocking, in a sense prefiguring Mark Twain's refusal in "The Man That Corrupted Hadleyburg" to conform to his readers' hopes for a happy ending. A reader who judged from the evidence of Mark Twain's involvement in other circumstances during these months might conclude that he tossed off this tale while having his shoes shined; yet it is still another example of his remarkable ability to produce sketches that possess both commercial value and a mordant sting that lifts them above the ordinary.

28. Ibid., 22:327–28.

4

The "Gospel" and Beyond
May to October 1898

During the late spring and early summer of 1898, most of which time he was at a health resort outside Vienna called Kaltenleutgeben, Mark Twain finally got down in earnest to his "Gospel"—the work that was published anonymously in 1906 as *What Is Man?* and that he had tinkered with for a number of years, most recently in 1897.[1] Several factors evidently combined to persuade him to focus on this project during this period. For one thing, when he began writing in April, the time did not seem ripe for major fiction because he was finishing up other things. The translating he now referred to as "dull and stupid work," but he was dutifully bringing it to a close. He was also still an investor and expected to travel to London in June to gather data concerning his peat-wool project.[2] Once he began working on his "Gospel," he became very interested in it and persevered until he had completed a useful draft by the end of the summer.

Before I discuss this draft, it is important to refer to three topics related to it. It should be emphasized, first of all, that when he began the manuscript, he was just terminating an ecstatic involvement in a financial world where his pride had undergone a spectacular roller-coaster ride. His March notebook entries and letters are filled with self-congratulatory comments like the following: "My extraordinary familiarity with the subject—paralyzed the banker for a while, for he was merely expecting to find a humorist." Yet, almost at the same time he was talking about the relationship between the inventor, the fool (the original investor, who usually loses), and the wise man (the man who enters after the damaging period

1. See *What Is Man?*, p. 12. For abbreviations used in the footnotes, see "Short References," pp. ix–x.
2. *HHR*, pp. 343, 345.

is over and makes a profit), arguing that this inventor is not a James Paige, this fool not a credulous Samuel Clemens.[3] And in a letter of 24 March to Rogers he remarked, "I feel like Colonel Sellers" even while he saw himself blundering along on the road to billions.[4] The point I am leading to is that "What Is the Real Character of Conscience?"—the probable original title of this philosophical dialogue—is filled with references to pride.

The consensus of critical opinion about the later version of the dialogue—published in 1906 under the more grandiose title *What Is Man?*—has always been that the most plausible explanation of the work's deterministic sections involves Clemens's sense of guilt.[5] I am convinced, on the other hand, that although as the manuscript developed it became considerably longer and differently structured, the function of the deterministic ideas remained the same as in the first im-

3. Notebook 32 (I), TS, pp. 13, 16–18, MTP.

4. *HHR*, p. 337.

5. I oversimplify to a certain extent here, because there has been significant scholarly interest in such topics as the scientific sources of the ideas in *What Is Man?*. See, for example, Sherwood Cummings, "*What Is Man?* The Scientific Sources." More recently, information relevant to *What Is Man?* has been published in Howard Baetzhold, *Mark Twain and John Bull: The British Connection*, pp. 218–25 (Baetzhold's discussion of the Lecky influence is particularly useful); Alan Gribben, "Mark Twain, Phrenology and the Temperaments: A Study of the Pseudo-Scientific Influence"; and John Tuckey, "Mark Twain's Later Dialogue: The 'Me' and the Machine." Of course Paul Baender's discussions of the background to *What Is Man?* in the Mark Twain Papers edition of the text is also revealing. Of the material published before 1960, still particularly useful is Hyatt Waggoner's 1937 article, "Science in the Thought of Mark Twain." The best single article on the work was published in 1957 by Alexander Jones: "Mark Twain and the Determinism of *What Is Man?*." Despite the information available regarding the intellectual sources of this work, it is significant that the writer of the last major full-length biography on Mark Twain—Justin Kaplin—quotes Bernard De Voto on *What Is Man?* with approval: "Without choice there can be no responsibility, and—as if Clemens dimly perceived the logical goal of his illogic—without responsibility guilt has no meaning. 'No one,' Bernard De Voto wrote, 'can read this wearisomely repeated argument without feeling the terrible force of an inner cry: Do not blame me, for it is not my fault'" (*Mr. Clemens and Mark Twain*, p. 340).

portant draft: to make human pride look ridiculous. Almost none of the examples in any of the versions of the dialogue seem designed to encourage the reader to feel sympathy for individuals who have done wrong. Instead, almost all the examples serve to deflect admiration from those who have done right, who have performed patriotic acts, given money to the poor, written great plays, shown courage in battle, and so on. Man's pride is unwarranted, the author repeatedly suggests, because human achievements (such as his own) depend to such a large extent on the luck of the draw in the games of heredity (which he calls temperament) and environment (or training).

Two other ideas are worth mentioning as a preliminary to a more detailed analysis. The first is that the dominant tone of the short dialogue is not despairing; if one reads the work freshly, without being prejudiced by the critical consensus, he should discover that it contains many optimistic passages filled with exhileration and wonder, particularly when the author describes the world of insects and animals. In *What Is Man?* such passages occur with relatively less frequency than in "What Is the Real Character of Conscience?," but the passages are there. The final point to be made is much more applicable to the shorter, tighter early dialogue than to the longer, differently structured, more diffuse *What Is Man?*: the ideas do come together—at times shakily to be sure—and form a piece of literature. Perhaps because of Mark Twain's recent interest in playwriting, "What Is the Real Character of Conscience?" is not contemptible as a dialogue; the writer is trying not only to make his philosophy intellectually impressive (which is his primary purpose in *What Is Man?*, as I will argue later), but also to make it dramatically interesting. The resulting dialectic has on occasions a genuine dramatic thrust. Moreover, the two combatants, the Old Man and the Young Man, are not merely mouthpieces for Clemens's ideas, although they are remembered as such by most readers of *What Is Man?* because of the hundreds of lines in the later work in which the two speakers function in this way. In the short early dialogue, on the other hand, they resemble people (although the Old Man certainly has the best lines).

In his introduction to *What Is Man?*, Paul Baender writes

of Mark Twain's use of the dialogue form: "He tended toward this form when his material was controversial, for he liked to envision a masterfulness in speakers who represented his views, and sophistry and humiliation in their antagonists."[6] However true this statement may be about the author's typical use of the form, it is misleading concerning "What is the Real Character of Conscience?" The Old Man, for example, is generous, frequently tentative concerning his conclusions, and quite good natured; moreover, he seemingly possesses a genuine desire to help his young opponent.

The dialogue begins abruptly, in medias res, and establishes the character of the generic young man—smug, arrogantly self-confident, proud of ideas that he has never examined, and singularly deserving of a penetrating defeat.[7] The Old Man, on the other hand, is almost humble, content in this opening scene to criticize only the most patent and obnoxious idiocies of his young adversary. By the end of this sequence, he has succeeded to an extent, because the Young Man is not as confident as he had been earlier.

With the beginning of the second section, "Personal Merit," the Old Man's strategy changes, as does the structure of the dialogue. Now, he begins to attack, forcing the Young Man into a Socratic situation where, through a series of questions, the Old Man reveals the vagueness and weakness of the Young Man's ideas and the clarity and strength of his own. As the Old Man becomes more outrageous and more interesting, his opponent's (and pupil's) attitude toward the situation changes; the Young Man becomes quizzical, ostensibly eager—at least temporarily—to explore the Old Man's ideas, but he does not capitulate totally. When he sees himself losing the debate, he redirects the dialogue, attempting to divert it to an area where he is more likely to be successful, although not admitting that he has been defeated in the

6. *What Is Man?*, p. 12.
7. The essential difference between the first two sections of the early dialogue and those in *What Is Man?* is that they are reversed: section 1 in the former is section 2 in the latter, and vice versa. There are also a few verbal changes. For these reasons, the text I will refer to in the first part of this discussion is the 1898 typescript of "What Is the Real Character of Conscience?" For textual information about the development of the dialogue see *What Is Man?*, pp. 603–5.

original arena. Yet, by the end, the hesitancy of his contributions—"You really think man is a mere machine?" (p. 16), "In earned personal dignity, then, and in personal merit for his achievements, a man is on the same level as a rat?"—suggests that he is being convinced.[8]

Section 3, "Instinct and Thought," appears almost verbatim as the first part of the sixth section in *What Is Man?* Because it appears so late in the published work, the ideas that it embodies may seem overly repetitive to the reader. This is not a problem, however, in the early dialogue; there, one is more easily able to appreciate Mark Twain's skill in vivifying the presentation of his ideas. Another factor contributing to the effect of this section in "What Is the Real Character of Conscience?" is the dramatic context: in terms of it, the conflict between the characters has moved into a recognizably new stage. During this section, the Old Man draws parallels between man and the so-called lower animals, arguing first that animals and insects can think, then showing that, in some situations they can outthink people. Here, as elsewhere, the writer's main purpose is to destroy man's foolish pride in his own superiority, yet a parallel purpose—perhaps an unconscious one—seems to be to reveal some of the miraculous aspects of the physical world. The structure of the section is clear, but not mechanical, since each stage of the argument grows out of the dialectic between the two men. As it begins, the Young Man has evidently been reflecting upon what he has heard and has returned to an attitude that he had held before and that he will hold again: "It is odious. These drunken theories of yours advanced a while ago—concerning the rat and all that—strip Man bare of all his dignities, grandeurs, sublimities." In responding, the Old Man makes a point that Mark Twain insists on throughout—the necessity of honesty: "He hasn't any to strip—they are shams, stolen clothes. He claims credits which belong solely to his maker." When the Young Man replies petulantly that the other has "no right" to compare him with the rat, the reply is, "I don't morally. That would not be fair to the rat" (p. 189). Ex-

8. See TS, p. 17, and *What Is Man?*, p. 184. Chapter 3 of the early dialogue is almost identical with the first section of chapter 6 in *What Is Man?*. In the rest of this discussion, therefore, I will quote from the published text.

amples such as this indicate the writer's continual attempt to surprise and shock—often humorously.

When the Young Man asserts that man possesses reason, animals only instinct, the Old Man is led into a train of thought in which, after defining instinct as *"petrified thought;* . . . thought which was once alive and awake, but is become unconscious" (p. 191), he proceeds through several other examples that show the ability of animals to draw inferences, to a final example of a bird finding its way home. This prompts him to exclaim, "Edison couldn't have done it any better himself" (p. 192). The Young Man is a bit slow to grasp the implications of this information, and his obtuse question, "Do you believe that many of the dumb animals can think?," gives the Old Man a chance to reinforce his conclusions by discussing examples of elephants and birds. Typically, the climax is comic: "Fleas can be taught nearly anything that a congressman can" (p. 193). The Young Man's exasperating response, "It elevates the dumb beasts" (p. 194), provokes from his teacher further explanation, which begins patiently and concludes, "It is just like man's vanity and impertinence to call an animal dumb because it is dumb to *his* dull perceptions" (p. 195). Then, characteristically, the Old Man's sense of wonder for the physical world manifests itself:

> O.M. That is what she surely does. In all his history the aboriginal Australian never thought out a house for himself and built it. The ant is an amazing architect. She is a wee little creature, but she builds a strong and enduring house eight feet high—a house which is as large in proportion to her size as is the largest capital or cathedral in the world compared to man's size. No savage race has produced architects who could approach the ant in genius or culture. No civilized race has produced architects who could plan a house better for the uses proposed than can hers. Her house contains a throne-room; nurseries for her young; graneries; apartments for her soldiers, her workers, etc.; and they and the multifarious halls and corridors which communicate with them are arranged and distributed with an educated and experienced eye for convenience and adaptability. (p. 195)

The Young Man cannot stomach this type of enthusiasm, so he foolishly falls back upon his previous response: "That could be mere instinct" (p. 195). With this inadequate reply, the rhythm of the argument changes, and the Old Man rains such a flurry of examples on his pupil that even he cannot explain them away. Then, the Old Man goes beyond the exigencies of his argument, carried away by the quality of the miraculous in what he has been describing. The Young Man is not unaffected. By now he is able to admit errors. When he does, the Old Man responds kindly because he has been hoping to create this quality all along:

> Y.M. Perhaps I lacked the reasoning faculty myself.
> O.M. Well, don't tell anybody, and don't do it again. (p. 198)

When the Old Man begins to make concessions, however, the Young Man's competitive urge flares again and the session halts, open-endedly, with him probing for a weakness. Mark Twain's knowledge of the rhythm of argumentation is evident throughout this dialogue and helps to make it quite believably dramatic.

Mark Twain apparently wrote during this period several other sections that he hoped to include in "What is the Real Character of Conscience?," but he was uncertain about their relationship to the whole. A section entitled "The Moral Sense" was originally to have followed "Instinct and Thought," and one entitled "The Quality of Man" was to have been the fifth.[9] "The Moral Sense" has an almost stichomythic quality as the Old Man attacks relentlessly and the Young Man gradually crumbles, returning at the end to a point that he cannot relinquish: the effect of the Old Man's conclusions on his own sense of man's dignity. In "The Quality of Man" the Old Man responds to his pupil's question, "What is your general opinion of man, anyway?," by saying, "he is a very poor thing," proving his point by his observation that only in intellect is man superior to animals and that God—according to descriptions of activities in Heaven—does not value intellect. The last argument might have been influenced by Mark Twain's perusal sometime during this period of the almost completed manuscript of *Captain Stormfield's Visit to Heaven*. Not many of the ideas are new in either of these two sections, a fact that helps explain the stale quality of the dialogue.

Perhaps the major reason Mark Twain did not complete

9. See *What Is Man?*, p. 603.

"What Is the Real Character of Conscience?" is that his thoughts about God were confused, and he evidently wanted to include a section on God in the manuscript. The section he wrote, if included, would have been the longest in the dialogue. It also would have been by far the most bitter, in its comments both on God and on man, as passages such as the following illustrate:

> Y.M. Our Father who art—
> O.M. Don't misuse that title. Leave that to the pulpit. Earthly fathers do not torture and harry and burn children—for discipline's sake or any other. Shall there be *no* honorable title among us sacred from the slanders of the pulpit? God is not a father in any kindly sense. The Book attributed to Him shows it, all Nature shouts it. Plainly if he cares for his children it is not in a spirit of love. It seems strange that he should care for them, or even think of them. Strangest of all that He should value men's flatteries. I cannot conceive of myself caring for the compliments of the wiggling cholera-germs concealed in a drop of putrid water. I cannot conceive of myself caring whether they appointed microbe-popes and priests to beslaver me with praises or didn't. I cannot conceive of myself being "jealous" about whether they mouthed and twaddled at me or didn't. I cannot conceive of myself reducing myself to invisibility and going down into the drop of water to beget myself on a microbe, and be re-born as a microbe, reared as a microbe, crucified as a microbe— suffering such small momentary pain as the evanescent microbe is capable of feeling—and all this foolishness to "save" the microbe species for the rest of time from the consequences of some inconsequential offence. (p. 485)

Although there are links between "God" and the earlier sections—references to ants and the Moral Sense, for example— the at times vitriolic, at times despairing tone of the Old Man suggests a character at odds with the one Mark Twain had created earlier. The section is intellectually confused as well because the Old Man cannot decide whether the God he inveighs against is the real one or only the insane conception of the Bible and conventional Christianity.

This shift in direction could have derived from Clemens's depression over family misfortune. The following interchange, for example, seems to have been written around the August anniversary of his daughter's death:

Y.M. He gives us many, many happinesses; and He never gives us pain except by our own fault or for our own good.

O.M. The happinesses seem to be traps, and to have no other intent. He beguiles us into welding our heart to another heart—the heart of a child, perhaps—the years go by, and when at last that companionship has become utterly precious, utterly indispensable, He tears the hearts apart, He kills the child. Sleep comes upon us and in it we forget our disaster. In the morning we wake; we are confused; we seem to have had a bad dream. Then suddenly full consciousness comes, and we know! All the happiness that could be crowded into a lifetime could not compensate the bitterness of that one moment. And thenceforth the rest of our years are merely a burden. This is to discipline us? Is that your idea? (p. 483)

One of the curious aspects of this section is how radically it contrasts not only with most of "What Is the Real Character of Conscience?," but also with a long notebook entry that Clemens wrote around 30 May. Here, the joy evinced in the following description is reminiscent of the Old Man's tone when he exclaims over the activities of certain insects:

The Being who to me is the real God is the One who created this majestic universe and rules it. . . .

He is the perfect artisan, the perfect artist. Everything which he has made is fine, everything which he has made is beautiful; nothing coarse, nothing ugly has ever come from His hand. Even His materials are all delicate, none of them is coarse. The materials of the leaf, the flower, the fruit; of the insect, the elephant, the man; of the earth, the crags and the ocean; of the snow, the hoar-frost and the ice—may be reduced to infinitesimal particles and they are still delicate, still faultless; whether He makes a gnat, a bird, a horse, a plain, a forest, a mountain range, a planet, a constellation, or a diatom whose form the keenest eye in the world cannot perceive, it is all one—He makes it utterly and minutely perfect in form, and construction. The diatom which is invisible to the eye on the point of a needle is graceful and beautiful in form and in the minute exquisite elaboration of its parts it is a wonder. The contemplation of it moves one to something of the same awe and reverence which the march of the comets through their billion mile orbits compels.[10]

10. *MTN*, pp. 360–61.

Here, as well, the writer has solved a problem that remains unsolved in "God": whether the God of the churches is the real One:

> His real character is written in plain words in His real Bible, which is Nature and her history; we read it every day, and we could understand it and trust in it if we would burn the spurious one and dig the remains of our insignificant reasoning faculties out of the grave where that and other man-made Bibles have buried them for 2000 years and more.
>
> The Bible of Nature tells us no word about any future life, but only about this present one. It does not promise a future life; it does not even vaguely indicate one. It is not intended as a message to us, any more than the scientist intends a message to surviving microbes when he boils the life out of a billion of them in a thimble. The microbes discover a message in it; this is certain—if they have a pulpit.
>
> The Book of Nature tells us distinctly that God cares not a rap for us—nor for any living creature. It tells us that His laws inflict pain and suffering and sorrow, but it does not say that this is done in order that He may get pleasure out of this misery. We do not know what the object is, for the Book is not able to tell us. It may be mere indifference. Without a doubt He had an object, but we have no way of discovering what it was. The scientist has an object, but it is not the joy of inflicting pain upon the microbe.[11]

The pressure of events and moods, however, was continually to undermine Clemens's faith in such conclusions. It was this kind of uncertainty that undoubtedly was one of the most important reasons he had not finished "What Is the Real Character of Conscience?" when he put it aside in the summer of 1898.

A conclusion to be drawn from a few of the strange decisions that Clemens made during July, August, and September (and on occasions in October and November—right up to the signing of the Bliss/Harper contracts) is that one of the results of his work on the "Gospel" was that it helped to throw him into a mild panic. A major problem was that during the summer and early fall several factors combined to compel him to realize that he was *not* superhuman. Thus, it

11. Ibid., p. 362.

must have seemed folly to have worked, during his tradition-
ally most productive and remunerative season, on an unpublishable manuscript.[12] It was some time within these months,
for example, that he seems to have recognized the inevitable failure of his investment speculations.[13] Moreover, his
dreams of dramatic entrepreneurship had died: in late July,
Charles Frohman had refused *In Purgatory*; on 28 August,
the author asked Rogers to burn "Is He Dead?"; and in late
September the situation did not look good for *Bartel Turaser*. The *Century* had accepted his "From the London Times
of 1904" in July for $140 a manuscript page (well above his
normal rate); on the other hand, he had written "About Play
Acting," "The Great Republic's Peanut Stand," and "Concerning the Jews," but he did not know until 5 October (when
Harper's accepted the latter article) whether any of this work
was going to be bought. He would have suspected that the
dialogue about copyright, "The Great Republic's Peanut
Stand," would lack a market because of its length and its
subject; he would have worried about "Jews" because of
what he considered to be its iconoclastic point of view; and
he definitely worried about "Play Acting," because he wrote
both Rogers and Pond, asking them concerning the whereabouts of the article.[14]

His response to a sketch entitled "My Platonic Sweetheart," finished in early August, is revealing. At first, he considered it "thundering good" and mailed it off proudly to
Cosmopolitan; after it was rejected there, it was mailed to

12. According to a late August notebook entry, he had decided
at that point not to publish the dialogue because of his fear of
harming his reputation and of his wife's disapproval. He felt that
printing the dialogue would be to do a real service for thousands
of people, but he considered himself "too selfish" to damage his
own comfort. See Notebook 32 (I), TS, p. 29, MTP.
13. When we notice the dearth of references to his peat-wool
scheme both in letters and notebook entries after the end of May,
it seems legitimate to conclude that Clemens's interest had either
waned or died.
14. *HHR*, p. 353; *HHR*, p. 358; see the pessimistic reference
to the play in Notebook 32 (II), TS, p. 46, MTP; see *HHR*, p. 353;
see Henry Alden to SLC, 5 October 1898, MTP; see *HHR*, p. 354
(Clemens, however, was very proud of "Concerning the Jews");
HHR, p. 363, and SLC to James Pond, 7 October 1898, TS, MTP.

Henry Alden at *Harper's Monthly* and finally to Richard Gilder at the *Century*. Significantly, it was only *after* Clemens heard "immense" financial news from Rogers in late October (Rogers had purchased $17,000 of Federal Steel stock, representing $50,000 "par of stock") that he wrote the *Century*, admitting the poor quality of "My Platonic Sweetheart" and asking Gilder to reject the sketch if he had not done so already.[15] Prior to this time, the writer had been very eager to publish the sketch anywhere, although it is uninteresting in itself (the narrator tells of several times throughout his life that a young girl appeared to him in dreams), deriving its meager allure from its revelations about the author's buried life, a topic about which he normally was reticent.[16]

Two decisions made in late August also suggest someone not thoroughly under control. On 30 August, Clemens wrote J. H. Harper, "O dear, dear, I'm in despair! I was hoping for that new arrangement whereby you would handle all my books in the trade and Bliss the uniform sets—and it didn't materialize."[17] This letter worried Clemens a great deal, for he wrote Rogers on 18 October:

> I am undergoing crucifixion (deserved!) on account of my blunder that I made in exposing to the Harpers the fact that I should have been glad if Bliss (had been) could have been crowded into giving the Harpers *all* the books for the trade, leaving Bliss only the sets by subscription. (Apparently the) I only ventured to write that because the contract had already been *settled*—whereas I guess nothing is really settled with the Harpers until they have *signed*.
>
> Reflection has taught me what you had already perceived, no

15. *HHR*, p. 357; *HHR*, p. 371; SLC to Richard Gilder, 6 November, 1898, PS, MTP.

16. Gladys Bellamy disagrees totally with my evaluation of "My Platonic Sweetheart." She writes, "For complete artistry, this small dream story is perhaps the most perfect of Mark Twain's short fictional pieces" (*Mark Twain as a Literary Artist*, p. 367). Readers interested in judging for themselves will find a copy of the story in *Writings*, 27:287–306. For an article that identifies the real-life model for the "dream sweetheart" (Laura M. Wright) and proceeds to a wide-ranging discussion of the significance of this person in the author's life and work, see Howard Baetzhold, "Found: Mark Twain's 'Lost Sweetheart.' "

17. SLC to Mr. Harper, quoted in *HHR*, n. 1, p. 368.

doubt: that if Harper had the trade-use of all the books it would kill Bliss's edition or badly cripple it; and so I wish I had kept my foolish tongue still.[18]

On 30 August he also asked Harper to return to him an article that was essentially the same as one he had published thirty years previously—an account of the harrowing voyage of the *Hornet*, which was bound for Honolulu and shipwrecked over a thousand miles from its destination.[19] Eventually published as "My Début as a Literary Person," it also is related to his off-again, on-again autobiography, dribs and drabs of which he had begun to pull out of his files in order that they might be published. Thus, while he talked confidently in a 1 October letter to Rogers about having enough material to fill two new volumes of sketches and regretted in his 18 October letter sending out "A Memorable Assassination" and "My Platonic Sweetheart" since "I don't want to be in print too frequently—it can hurt my market," it is clear that he worried very much about being published, particularly since he was looking forward to a return to Vienna and its distracting social season.[20]

His actions concerning a long sketch entitled "Wapping Alice" are also noteworthy. The first thing to observe is that the sketch was originally written for the autobiography, probably in the summer of 1897. Sometime in the late summer or early fall of 1898, he took out the manuscript, changed the name of the narrator from Clemens to Jackson, and began to send it around as a short story (and a tedious one at that, despite a funny last scene).[21]

18. *HHR*, p. 369.
19. SLC to Mr. Harper, 30 August 1898, PS, MTP. A copy of "My Début as a Literary Person" may be found in *Writings*, 23:78–105. The material dealing with the *Hornet* disaster also became relevant to Mark Twain's plans for the plot of "The Great Dark," as Daryl E. Jones convincingly demonstrates in "The *Hornet* Disaster: Twain's Adaptation in 'The Great Dark.' "
20. See *HHR*, pp. 367–68, 370.
21. The manuscript of "Wapping Alice" is written on the distinctive cross-barred paper of the Weggis period. For evidence of his attempt to sell the manuscript, see SLC to Mr. Tuohy, 2 November 1898, PS, MTP. According to a 19 November entry (Notebook 32 (II), TS, p. 51, MTP), he mailed out "Wapping Alice" again, although he said in a 12 November letter to Rogers that he

The most accurate way to characterize Clemens's attitude at this time is with the well-worn word *ambivalence*: he wanted to publish—sometimes almost desperately—yet he worried about publishing too much and in the wrong magazines. Thus, he produced many short manuscripts while at his Kaltenleutgeben retreat, of which a few were of poor quality and uncertain genre; and he wavered between wanting everything in print or only his selected best. His relationship with Harper's was similarly confused: at times he castigated the organization for its niggardliness; yet, he subsequently confided to Rogers that, even while he was negotiating with other journals, he had very much wanted Harper's to accept "Concerning the Jews" (which it eventually did).

Given Clemens's frame of mind, which persisted even after his situation had improved, it seems fair to conclude that one of the reasons he significantly changed the proposed narrative shape of his "Which Was the Dream?" idea was that the new comic beginning and the plan to extend the comedy through three-quarters of the story before springing the "tragedy trap" would make the tale potentially more publishable. (The possibility that it might become a universal satire was dropped entirely.)[22] Bernard De Voto's ominous title for this work—"The Great Dark"—and his inclusion of it in his so-called despair group is particularly inappropriate for the incomplete tale that Mark Twain actually wrote; the proposed continuation as it was outlined in late September notebook entries is, in more ways than one, another story.[23]

---

was going to set its price so high that nobody would buy it (*HHR*, p. 376). In his *Mark Twain & the South*, Arthur Pettit shows how, in Mark Twain's portrait of the black servant, George, in "Wapping Alice," his own ambivalence toward George Griffin manifested itself: "Yet in striking contrast to everything Clemens ever said about the nonfictional Griffin, the most conspicuous trait of the fictional George is not his loyalty but his vanity and selfishness" (p. 102).

22. Clemens discusses his story in a 16 August 1898 letter to Howells. See *MTHL*, 2:675–76.

23. I realize that in viewing "The Great Dark" in terms other than those suggestive of the writer's despair or pessimism, I am being definitely atypical. In his "Mark Twain and the Dark Angel," for example, Larry Dennis asserts, "In 'The Great Dark' life is seen as a horror and death as a horror" (p. 196).

As a work intended for publication, his latest version of "Which Was the Dream?" is definitely superior to the manuscript that he had begun a year earlier. In the first version, Mark Twain had left his narrator—Major General X (whose story begins as an autobiography written for his children)—convalescing with his family in a log cabin; here, he recuperates from the "disasters" (which occur, of course, only in his dream) that have caused his fall from a position close to the presidency of the United States. The author had mapped out in notebook entries ideas for continuing the plot—details concerning a voyage toward Australia to be taken by the narrator and his family—but the continuation had not gone beyond the planning stage. This newer version of the story, however, moves quickly into the idea of voyage as dream, after an initial explanation about the diary being a birthday gift for the narrator's elder daughter. In the earlier manuscript, Mark Twain had tried to account realistically for the narrator's sudden change in fortune—the fire, the brother-in-law's betrayal, the bankruptcy, the fall from an imminent presidency to a rustic shack—but he had succeeded only in being awkwardly implausible.

In the newer version, he did not disguise the fact that he was writing a fantastic tale. The resulting almost immediate movement into the marvelous is effective, particularly because the events take place aboard ship, a setting with which Mark Twain was very familiar, rather than in Washington, an environment that he did not know well. For another thing, by deciding to begin humorously he compelled himself to derive his episodes from pleasant situations in his own life—his relationship with his wife and daughters relatively early in his marriage, for example—and he had an easier time controlling this material than the tragic events that he was too close to. Moreover, in the earlier version he wanted to create a sympathetic narrator who would appear far more sinned against than sinning; but the character's business relationship with his brother-in-law is so obtuse as to undermine this sympathy. It is difficult also to believe that a man so naive could be an extremely successful soldier and politician. In the latest version, on the other hand, the reader's relationship with the narrator creates no problem:

he is now someone living a fascinating adventure that he is able to describe with an attractive sense of humor.

A couple of scenes during the voyage may seem crudely farcical to many readers: in one, for example, the ship's mate tells a story while a personage called the "Superintendent of Dreams" makes himself invisible and drinks the mate's coffee.[24] Yet the character of the mate—good natured; earnest; eager to discover the truth about, but perplexed by, his environment; almost too willing to ascribe mysterious happenings to his love of grog—is well drawn. Moreover, the story he tells (one that Mark Twain tried to use often) is very funny. It concerns a captain who takes a temperance pledge before leaving on a voyage, labors heroically against temptation amidst hard-drinking cronies, then discovers on returning home that his membership application to the temperance society has been refused.[25] What increases the humor is a variation on an old technique; the mate who tells the tale does not find it particularly funny.

The plot is entertaining as well: there is always the threat of sea monsters, for example; and in the second book there is a horrible attack by a giant squid. Then there is the possibility and finally the actuality of a mutiny by the crew, which is quelled only through the courage and quick-wittedness of the captain; here, the Ned Wakeman character is not a cynic as he was in the earlier version.[26] As the writer puts the story aside, left hanging is the destination of the ship and the real nature of the existence that the characters have been living. At this point, Mark Twain had made an effective beginning to a fantasy that had definite potential as a popular book.

The manuscript is not simply entertaining, however; like practically everything that the writer wanted to be published, it possesses a dimension that could be labeled "serious": it

24. Bernard De Voto considers that such actions are "wildly out of tune with this story. It introduces burlesque into a sombre, even terrible narrative" (*LE*, p. 237).

25. *WWD?*, pp. 115–17. Henceforth, references to "Which was the Dream?" will be made in the text.

26. Jones, "The *Hornet* disaster," suggests that Mark Twain's portrait of the captain may also have been influenced by Captain Josiah Mitchell of the *Hornet*.

has a quality of metaphysical speculativeness. Mark Twain's fascination with several ideas related to the nature of dreams is communicated to the reader through a narrator who is not so much terrified by his situation as deeply interested in exploring its meaning. He learns, for example, when he dreams of being alive in a drop of water, that the dimensions of this new world are not illusory, but real, and that "nothing but the laws and conditions have undergone a change. You came from a small and very insignificant world" (p. 123). The narrator finds something "overpowering" and "sublime" in his discovery and has no regrets whatsoever about the voyage, although he is ignorant of its destination. He learns also that his previous life—and not this one—was a dream (p. 124), a fact that his wife confirms; yet when he discusses some of his memories of this "dream" with his wife, he discovers that their memories touch at certain points. Then, they devote much of their time to resurrecting the past: "It was fascinating, enchanting, this spying among the elusive mysteries of my bewitched memory" (p. 139). Here, Mark Twain suggests a definition of reality that would make it commensurate with intensity; he suggests further that "realities" that have become "dreams" because of the passage of time or a change of environment can in a sense be made "real" again if the "dreamer" searches for them with someone whose experiences have been similar. The narrator's pleasure in ruminating over these ideas is infectious, and the reader leaves the manuscript disappointed that there is no continuation.

Unfortunately, Clemens's familial responsibilities caused him to interrupt his story: he had promised to take Livy and the girls on a brief "pleasure" trip in late August. He did, and the trip turned into a disaster because Livy had an infected eye, their accommodations were miserable, and the weather was unbearably hot.[27] When he returned to Kaltenleutgeben, he had lost his inspiration, he became involved with more easily salable projects, the empress of Austria was assassinated, and he did not pick up the story until the end of September. At this point, the notebook entries indicate a wild shift in direction. A few excerpts will convey what I mean:

27. See *HHR*, pp. 357–58.

The whole (crew) list go crazy. The stewardess becomes Mad^me
V.D., & imagines herself the Herrscherin der Welt— . . . finally
even suspects the cats of immoralities. . . .
The bloody footprint appears. . . . Some are religious
mad, & their greeting is—
"Life is a boon." Reply—
"Let us be thankful for it."
At which the idiot always laughs.
"He is to us a tender Father, & His loving mercies have
no limit."
The idiot laughs.
The blind squid appears at intervals.
Often the footprint appear [sic] & go about terrifying
everybody, then fade out harmless. It is only when the
invisible hand *touches* a person that he shrivels &
shudders & goes mad.[28]

What seems to have happened is that when he returned
to the story, the environment of the ship no longer stimulated his imagination; since he was unwilling, however, to
retire gracefully to some more congenial setting and topic—
probably because he was still very much worried about publication—he decided to shove his creation forward even when
he had no real energy for it, when instead he had only
dismal, unintentionally comic, cosmic pessimism and memories of bad melodrama. On the other hand, later in the notebook entry, he strikes something that, in terms of his fantastic premise, his memories of the *Hornet* disaster, and—
perhaps—his own worst fears, sounds chillingly plausible:

The sea begins to dry up. The beasts get worse. . . .
The great animals begin to get stranded, & struggle &
fight & die & stink.
Ship aground at last—the other ship ditto, faraway.
Capt. & Edwards & others take several days' provisions &
walk overland. Arrive too late. All hands dead. They
carried the mummied bodies (aged 16 and 25) back to their
ship. Too late again. All dead—& he was going to
ask forgiveness of her and Jessie. Looks up—is at
home—his wife & the children coming to say goodnight.
His hair is white.[29]

28. Notebook 32 (II), TS, pp. 43–44, MTP.
29. Ibid., pp. 45–46.

Gone are the repetitions of "the idiot laughs" and the melo-dramatic underlinings, and remaining is a plot line that could have worked. At this point, however, Mark Twain apparently did not want to make the revisions that would have been necessary to link the story in manuscript with the notebook plot; he may also have felt that the shift from com-edy to "tragedy" had come too early and have decided to wait for more comic inspiration. The simplest explanation may also be the best: the move to the Hotel Krantz may have been enough to cool his enthusiasm.

Almost as a necessity after his remuneratively unsuccessful summer and after his involvement with a long fictional proj-ect that was not close to completion, Mark Twain began to apply his considerable technical skill and his tough-minded attitude toward human nature to the writing of a single piece of short fiction. He finished it and published it as "The Man That Corrupted Hadleyburg." Since so much has al-ready been written about this superb fable, I will not devote a great deal of space to my analysis of it.[30] There are, how-ever, a few aspects of the tale that I would like to comment on.

Most noteworthy about this unequivocally "serious" com-edy is Mark Twain's success in employing fictional means to embody those ideas from his "Gospel" (which he may now have been calling "Selfishness") that had made it too con-troversial to publish. Because he was writing popular fiction for an audience that expected to be entertained as well as instructed, the writer had to avoid the sermonizing tone present in some sections of the dialogue. He had to treat his characters, therefore, so that the reader would feel that they were participants in a story; the first impression could not be that they were mouthpieces in what was really a disguised essay designed to promote Mark Twain's ideas.

And the characters do seem to be participants in a story— a very interesting, mysterious, and suspenseful one, in fact.

30. It seems to me that the most thoughtful analysis of the story is contained in Pascal Covici, Jr., *Mark Twain's Humor: The Im-age of a World* (Dallas: Southern Methodist University Press, 1962), pp. 189–205. An interesting recent essay about the tension between free will and determinism in the story is Mary E. Rucker, "Moralism and Determinism in 'The Man That Corrupted Hadleyburg.'"

Thus, when the ideas that they enunciate in response to the pressure of events clearly coincide with the ideas of the author, this fact does not seem presumptuous to the reader; he does not feel that his confidence has been betrayed. Because of the narrator's focus on the old Richards couple, for example, and because of his occasional willingness to help us share their thoughts and feelings, we become interested in their lives. We even care about them, although we see that their greed is leading them toward behavior that is clearly wrong. When, therefore, in frustration and anger Mary Richards lashes out at her husband, we accept her speech as a perfectly natural response to the dynamics of the situation. That she may also be speaking for Mark Twain is of secondary importance:

> "Oh, I know it, I know it—it's been one everlasting training and training and training in honesty—honesty shielded, from the very cradle, against every possible temptation, and so it's *artificial* honesty, and weak as water when temptation comes, as we have seen this night. God knows I never had shade nor shadow of a doubt of my petrified and indestructible honesty until now—and now, under the very first big and real temptation, I—Edward, it is my belief that this town's honesty is as rotten as mine is; as rotten as yours is. It is a mean town, a hard, stingy town, and hasn't a virtue in the world but this honesty it is so celebrated for and so conceited about; and so help me, I do believe that if ever the day comes that its honesty falls under great temptation, its grand reputation will go to ruin like a house of cards. There, now, I've made confession, and I feel better; I am a humbug, and I've been one all my life, without knowing it. Let no man call me honest again—I will not have it."[31]

Later in the story, when Howard K. Stephenson also speaks for Mark Twain, the reader first feels that Stephenson's letter is integral to the plot, since the letter finally reveals the motives and strategy of the mysterious and threatening man who has succeeded in "corrupting" Hadleyburg. The letter is lengthy, so I will quote only a few lines from it:

> You were easy game. You had an old and lofty reputation for honesty, and naturally you were proud of it—it was your

31. *Writings*, 23:15–16. Henceforth, references to "The Man That Corrupted Hadleyburg" will be made in the text.

> treasure of treasures, the very apple of your eye. As soon as I
> found out that you carefully and vigilantly kept yourselves and
> your children *out of temptation*, I knew how to proceed. Why,
> you simple creatures, the weakest of all weak things is a virtue
> which has not been tested in the fire. . . . I am hoping to eter-
> nally and everlastingly squelch your vanity and give Hadleyburg
> a new renown—one that will *stick*—and spread far. (pp. 52–53)

It is of course not only by means of judiciously placed big
speeches like the two I have just cited that Mark Twain
embeds his ideas in the story. The actions of almost all the
characters, for example, reinforce the author's point about
the power of selfishness and greed. The structure of the
plot, leading as it does with seeming inevitability to the
change in the town motto—from Lead Us Not Into Temptation to Lead Us Into Temptation—reinforces Mark Twain's
ideas about training. Moreover, when at the very end of the
story the narrator reveals the motto, he also sheds a final,
penetrating light upon the ironic relationship between the
essence of real virtue—the humility embodied in "The Lord's
Prayer"—and the pride of Hadleyburg.

Another noteworthy aspect of the story is Mark Twain's
success, during the portions when he functions as a third-
person-limited narrator, in conveying the *feel* of the process
of rationalization: the process by which an individual can
convince himself that what he knows to be false is actually
true. His dramatization of the Richards' musings is particularly well done:

> The couple lay awake the most of the night, Mary happy and
> busy, Edward busy but not so happy. Mary was planning what
> she would do with the money. Edward was trying to recall that
> service. At first his conscience was sore on account of the lie he
> had told Mary—if it was a lie. After much reflection—suppose
> it *was* a lie? What then? Was it such a great matter? Aren't we
> always *acting* lies? Then why not *tell* them? Look at Mary—
> look what she had done. While he was hurrying off on his honest
> errand, what was she doing? Lamenting because the papers
> hadn't been destroyed and the money kept! Is theft better than
> lying?
>
> *That* point lost its sting—the lie dropped into the background
> and left comfort behind it. The next point came to the front:
> *Had* he rendered that service? Well, here was Goodson's own
> evidence as reported in Stephenson's letter; there could be no

better evidence than that—it was even *proof* that he had rendered it. Of course. So that point was settled. . . . No, not quite. He recalled with a wince that this unknown Mr. Stephenson was just a trifle unsure as to whether the performer of it was Richards or some other—and, oh dear, he had put Richards on his honor! He must himself decide whither that money must go—and Mr. Stephenson was not doubting that if he was the wrong man he would go honorably and find the right one. Oh, it was odious to put a man in such a situation—ah, why couldn't Stephenson have left out that doubt! What did he want to intrude that for? (p. 24)

Often, in handling the analysis of thought as a third-person narrator, Mark Twain expresses the cerebration of his characters in asides and soliloquies. And, typically, readers familiar with the fiction of practically any good writer in English after Henry James will find this use of direct discourse to be stagy and amateurish. To his credit, Mark Twain considered the dramatization of thinking to be a forte of his friend William Dean Howells and recognized that he himself was not very good at this type of thing.[32] But he frequently is good in "The Man That Corrupted Hadleyburg."

32. Writing to Howells on 19 October 1899, Clemens complains, "Ah, if I could look into the insides of people as you do and say, and tell *how* they said it" (*MTHL*, 2:710).

5

Still Another Beginning
November 1898 to March 1899

Although the previous several months had contained episodes not conducive to Clemens's peace of mind and healthy outlook on life, November 1898 offered a great deal of compensation. Two events early in the month were crucial: Rogers's purchase of Federal Steel stock and—finally—the signing of the Bliss/Harper contract. The writer's response to news of the steel-stock purchase was predictably flamboyant: he planned to ask Rogers to buy $25,000 more of the stock and to pay for it by mortgaging the Hartford home; then, he would pay off the mortgage by completing and publishing his autobiography and embarking on a lecture tour managed by Pond. It was only after deliberation that he reluctantly rejected his inspiration, accounting for his change of heart by explaining that he did not want to risk bankruptcy again, but at the same time querying his financial godfather, Was I a coward? Should I have bought the extra stock? Despite his decision not to purchase the extra steel stock, it is evident that by this time he was becoming confident of his ability not merely to pay his debts, but to become wealthy. A clue to this state of mind was his only half-ironic reference to a prediction by a palmist (Cheiro) that he would be rich when he reached sixty-eight. Perhaps he had been foolish, therefore, in giving up playwriting so hastily: possibly someone could tinker with "Is He Dead?" and vivify it; perhaps the Austrian playwright who wanted to translate *Pudd'nhead Wilson* would create a European hit; perhaps the London man who wished to dramatize "The Million Dollar Bank Note" would do so successfully.[1] More

1. For information about this period, see *HHR*, pp. 374–78. For abbreviations used in the footnotes, see "Short References," pp. ix–x.

realistically, however, he knew that his best chances lay with his books. In this connection, he recognized that if he could publish a new work during the next year, it would boost the sales of Bliss's Uniform Edition of the "old books," the introduction to which Brander Matthews would furnish in early December.[2] And his desire to publish a new book was undoubtedly one of the reasons that, in November, he began sporadic work on his autobiography.[3] It is probably also a major reason that, in the same month, he began another "Mysterious Stranger" manuscript—this one more obviously amiable than "The Chronicle of Young Satan."

Mark Twain worked on "Schoolhouse Hill" for only a few weeks, but by the time he set it aside near the end of November or beginning of December, he had made a splendid beginning to a story combining elements of "The Chronicle of Young Satan," "Tom Sawyer's Conspiracy," and "Hellfire Hotchkiss" with new ones that complemented the old.[4] The writer apparently hoped that by combining ingredients from his earlier projects he would inspire himself to write the long book that a number of promising beginnings had still not stimulated.[5] The plot revolves around the adventures of another young Satan figure (this time a son of the devil) with the odd name of "44" (Quarante-Quatre") who materializes in the wintry St. Petersburg schoolyard; dazzles the teacher and pupils (including Tom and Huck) with his abilities; reluctantly defeats the bully Henry Bascom and, in self-defense, snaps the wrist of Henry's slave-trader father; is housed with the compassionate Oliver

2. See SLC to Frank Bliss, 17 November 1898, PS, MTP. In November, after many exasperating and unsuccessful hours, Mark Twain tore up a number of pages, submitted a short discussion to Bliss, and left the long introduction to Brander Matthews.

3. It is difficult to decide exactly what was written for the autobiography during these months. It is possible, in fact, that Mark Twain wrote nothing new, contenting himself instead with reading over what he had already written, tinkering with this material, and then dropping the project when inspiration failed to come.

4. For information regarding the dating of "Schoolhouse Hill," see William Gibson's comments on p. 8 in *MSM*. Henceforth, references to "Schoolhouse Hill" will be made in the text.

5. It is evident that by this point he was occasionally worrying about his inability to exceed short narrative limits. See *MTHL*, 2:685.

and Hannah Hotchkiss; rescues townspeople from the ravages of the Great Blizzard; reveals his identity to Oliver; and prepares to enlist Oliver's aid in learning about humanity, so that 44 can alleviate the problems created by his own father. At this point, the writer halts to refuel.

Technically, the unfinished story is superb, particularly Mark Twain's handling of the various functions of the third-person-omniscient point of view: he etches the winter environment in the reader's imagination; creates character through humorous summary statements; builds suspense for scenes through his control of the rhythm of withholding and disseminating information; then lets the action advance primarily through dialogue once the scenes have been prepared for; and, instead of always reporting speech directly, he summarizes for the sake of variety and economy, as in the following example:

> Hotchkiss sank into his chair weak and limp, and began to pour out broken words and disjointed sentences whose meanings were not always clear but whose general idea was comprehensible. To this effect: from custom bred of his upbringing and his associations he had often talked about Satan with a freedom which was regrettable, but it was really only talk, mere idle talk, he didn't mean anything by it; in fact there were many points about Satan's character which he greatly admired, and although he hadn't said so, publicly, it was an oversight and not intentional—but from this out he meant to open his mouth boldly, let people say what they might and think what they chose— (p. 212)

In the following passage, the narrator's skill is exemplified by the unobtrusive manner by which he modulates between reporting the thoughts and emotions of the two slaves and Oliver Hotchkiss and ironically commenting on them:

> The gratitude of the two negroes was deep and honest; this speech promised relief for them; their situation had been a cruelly embarrassing one; they had sat down with these white men because they had been ordered to do it, and it was habit and heredity to obey, but their seats had not been more comfortable than a hot stove would have been. They hoped and expected that their master would be reasonable and rational, now, and send them away, but it didn't happen. He could manage his *seance* without Meadows, and would do it. He didn't mind

holding hands with negroes, for he was a sincere and enthusiastic abolitionist; in fact had been an abolitionist for five weeks, now, and if nothing happened would be one for a fortnight longer. He had confirmed the sincerity of his new convictions in the very beginning by setting the two slaves free—a generosity which had failed only because they didn't belong to him but to his wife. As she had never been an abolitionist it was impossible that she could ever become one. (pp. 205–6)

Throughout the story, in fact, Mark Twain is almost entirely successful in an old-fashioned, pre-Jamesian way, choosing not to focus the action in the mind of a central consciousness and not worrying about the respective merits of showing and telling.

The most noteworthy aspect of the story is the narrator's attitude toward its events and people: his genially tolerant tone, which is filled with nostalgic affection, yet is seldom sentimental. The description of Hannah Hotchkiss's admiration of her husband, for example, escapes sentimentality because of the narrator's humor:

She was fond and proud of her husband, and believed he would have been great if he had had a proper chance—if he had lived in a metropolis, instead of a village; if his merits had been exposed to the world instead of being hidden under a bushel. She was patient with his excursions after the truth. She expected him to be saved—thought she knew that that would happen, in fact. It could only be as a Presbyterian, of course, but that would come—come of a certainty. All the signs indicated it. He had often been a Presbyterian; he was periodically a Presbyterian, and she had noticed with comfort that his period was almost astronomically regular. She could take the almanac and calculate its return with nearly as much confidence as other astronomers calculated an eclipse. His Mohammedan period, his Methodist period, his Buddhist period, his Baptist period, his Parsi period, his Roman Catholic period, his Atheistic period—these were all similarly regular, but she cared nothing for that. She knew there was a patient and compassionate Providence watching over him that would see to it that he died in his Presbyterian period. (pp. 140–41)

Her generosity in sheltering the homeless 44 is made to seem less saintly, more human, by the narrator's following recognition:

Hannah Hotchkiss exulted in the wonders brought by the visitors, and the more they brought the happier she was in the possession of that boy; but she was very human in her make-up, and she felt a little aggravated over the fact that the news had to come from the outside; that these people should know these things about her lodger before she knew them herself; that she must sit and do the wondering and exclaiming when in all fairness she ought to be doing the telling and they the applauding; that they should be able to contribute all the marvels and she none. (p. 191)

The writer's treatment of the black cook, Aunt Rachel, does threaten to become sentimental:

"How does it come you didn't tell us these things sooner, Rachel?"

"*Me* tell you! Hm! You reckon you'd a b'lieved me? You reckon you'd a b'lieved Jeff? *We* b'lieves in bewitchments, caze we knows day's so; but you-all only jist laughs at 'em. Does you reckon you'd a b'lieved me, Miss Hannah?—does you?"

"Well—no."

"Den you'd a laughed at me. Does a po' nigger want to git laughed at any mo' d'n white folks? No, Miss Hannah, dey don't. We's got our feelin's, same as *you*-all, alldough we's ign'ant en black." (p. 196)

But the threat disappears when the narrator remarks, "Her tongue was hung in the middle and was easier to start than to stop. It would have gone on wagging, now, but that the wax candle had long ago been waiting for exhibition" (p. 196). Even the villain, Henry Bascom, is not totally one-dimensional; the narrator evokes admiration for his "pluck" (p. 188) even while dramatizing his cruel pride.

"Schoolhouse Hill" is pervaded with a sense of life's dualities, but the negative aspects are accepted, rather than lamented or made the subject of strident tirades. The snow, for example, that creates for the children such joyous opportunities in the tale's opening scene, takes twenty-eight lives during the Great Blizzard. The children empathize with 44 when he is threatened by the bully, marvel at his schoolroom ability, and also envy him when his talents are fully revealed. The adults' interest in 44 derives both from compassion and from their awareness of his skills, particularly his ability to create real gold. The slaves are discriminated against by the whites, but, through their compliance, they also discriminate against themselves. They are in one sense "inferiors" in the families that they serve; but in another, they are equal members whose opinions on some topics are respected. Even the biblical Satan's dualities are observed: on the one hand, he is the conventional betrayer of the human race; on the other, the angel who is cruel while attempting to be kind—hoping to bring to the inhabitants of the new world a gift that he himself had benefitted from. In "What Is the Real of Conscience?" Mark Twain developed ideas to demonstrate that man should be more tolerant of human frailty, even while he clearly recognizes it. The same ideas dominate "Schoolhouse Hill."

Probably the most surprising beneficiary of the story's mood is the Orion figure, Oliver Hotchkiss. As I have mentioned before, several of Clemens's earlier attempts to use his brother as fictional fodder had resulted primarily in revealing the writer's own somewhat mean intolerance toward his exasperating sibling. Here (as the following example reveals), although Orion is a "weather-vane," he is also a kind, likable man whose weaknesses are viewed as peccadilloes, not as the failings of a stupid clod:

> Mr. Hotchkiss's pride and joy were frank and simple; every new marvel that any comer added to the list of his lodger's great deeds made him a prouder and happier man than he was before, he being a person substantially without jealousies and by nature addicted to admirations. Indeed he was a broad man in many ways; hospitable to new facts and always seeking them; to new ideas, and always examining them; to new opinions and always adopting them; a man ready to meet any novelty half way and give it a friendly trial. He changed his principles with the moon, his politics with the weather, and his religion with his shirt. He was recognized as being limitlessly good-hearted, quite fairly above the village average intellectually, a diligent and enthusiastic seeker after truth, and a sincere believer in his newest belief, but a man who had missed his vocation—he should have been a weather-vane. He was tall and handsome and courteous, with winning ways, and expressive eyes, and had a white head which looked twenty years older than the rest of him. (p. 190)

During the year between Orion's death and the beginning of "Schoolhouse Hill," Clemens's attitude toward his brother seems to have mellowed because of comments from other people, such as the following from Twichell: "Our memory of him is of a gentle and amiable spirit—remarkably disposed to the things of good will."[6] In this story, Oliver is even viewed by 44 as the proper man to aid him in his quest for knowledge about the world. If he had continued the narrative, Mark Twain might have used this relationship—the blind leading the omniscient—as a source of comedy; yet, at this point, 44's choice apparently is intended to reflect on Oscar's good qualities.

An interesting aspect of the thoroughly tolerant tone of "Schoolhouse Hill" is that many of the notes that relate to it suggest a different kind of book. The writer, for example, considered having the little Satan figure possess "an immortal's contempt for evanescent mortals" and wonder "at their interest in life—not worth the trouble; and their childish ambitions" (p. 433). According to a lengthy November notebook entry, little Satan would, for part of the story, become a victim of human contempt and indifference (p. 428). Another plot possibility had him establishing an "Anti-Moral Sense Church," which would have preachments such as "Everything is insane—upside down. The idle sit on thrones, the workers in the gutter. . . . You punish attempted suicides —whereas if a man owns anything at all (according to your own scheme of life) it is his life—a foolish possession" (p. 446).

Further notes suggest a farcical Satan fooling with magic tricks, or Satan as a kind of Captain Stormfield who will lecture mortals on the silliness of their attitudes toward Heaven (pp. 434, 439–46). If Mark Twain had decided to finish the story, he might have pushed it in one or other of the directions seemingly dictated by his differing conceptions of the little Satan character. But the wonderful boy who dominates the pages of "Schoolhouse Hill" is neither contemptuous of mortals nor a magical buffoon. He is a being—unlike the figure in "The Chronicle of Young Satan" —who wants to help human life, who is able to learn humanity's standards as easily as he learns its languages, who intuits that its difficulties may be related to its vanity and a diseased

6. Joseph Twichell to SLC, 27 December 1897, MTP.

Moral Sense, and who deeply wishes to right the wrongs initiated by his misguided and notorious father. The little Satan Mark Twain creates in "Schoolhouse Hill" is really a potential Christ figure, but one who has no desire to sacrifice himself for the sake of anyone's afterlife; he proposes to live and experiment in this world for the sake of this kind of reality. Moreover, a possibility that the writer considered as a plot continuation was to have 44 fall in love with one of the village beauties and thus discover that the actual experience of this emotion was superior to the cool, intellectual pleasures of his former fiery home (pp. 438–39).

Unfortunately, the narrative proceeds no further, and a book beautifully begun remains unfinished. There were probably two immediate reasons Mark Twain set aside the manuscript. Judging from the notes, he wanted somehow to extend the story to a point where he could include some of the more radical material from "What Is the Real Character of Conscience?" and *Captain Stormfield's Visit to Heaven*; yet he could not determine how to do this in the benign environment that he had created, particularly in a book that contained references to Tom and Huck. Another important reason was more mundane: writing to Rogers on 8 December, he mentioned being sick for eleven days—because of fatigue, he guessed.[7] If, as seems quite likely, he had written the six and one-half chapters of "Schoolhouse Hill" in two weeks, his exhaustion was understandable. When he returned to work after his illness (and after he had asked Bliss in a 10 December letter if he would consider publishing a book of sketches by subscription[8]), he moved on to something else in his quest for a new, long, publishable, and potentially popular book.

It is possible that the "something else" was a continuation of "Tom Sawyer's Conspiracy," a manuscript that he may well have worked on in December and January.[9] His memory

7. *HHR*, p. 380.
8. SLC to Frank Bliss, 10 December 1898, PS, MTP.
9. In his remarks about the dating of this section of the manuscript of "Tom Sawyer's Conspiracy," Walter Blair says only that "he worked on it in 1898, 1899 or 1900—perhaps in all three years" (*HH and T*, p. 154). Henceforth, references to "Tom Sawyer's Conspiracy" will be made in the text.

and imagination were of course full of the Hannibal environment during these weeks. Also, he may have decided that the best possible salesman for the old Mark Twain volumes would be not a story that only tantalized his readers with references to Tom and Huck, but rather one that centered on their adventures. Moreover, he had a year previously made an excellent start on such a book, abandoning it at the point where the town had been deliciously frightened by the prospect of a "conspiracy" to steal its slaves; and Tom, Huck, and Jim had prepared to launch the conspiracy by stealing one of Bat Bradish's slaves (Tom in blackface), before someone else did the same thing, because Tom had discovered that one of Bradish's Negroes was really a white man in disguise.

When Mark Twain returned to his story, the somewhat leisurely pace of the earlier version accelerated considerably, the result being that before setting the manuscript aside again, he had created a tale that is at times humorous, almost always exciting, and also significant in its treatment of the freed slave's predicament.

When the narrative begins again, Jim is sent to inform Tom's aunt that the boys are engaged in detective work; then, Tom and Huck discover Bradish's body, Tom tracks down the murderers—one of whom seems to be wounded—and overhears their conversation in the haunted house. At the same time, Jim is jailed on suspicion of the murder. Tom is overjoyed at this development; and—having provided Jim with a motive (Bradish had been the man who persuaded Miss Watson to sell Jim down the river in *Huckleberry Finn*)—he abets the town's fears of an attack by "Burrell's Gang," planning to drag in the true villains at the last minute, thus rescue Jim, and then bask in a torchlight celebration. Unfortunately, the murderers disappear and Jim's situation looks dismal until Huck meets the Duke and the King on a steamboat. When they hear of Jim's incarceration, they propose to print fake Wanted notices about him, tell the authorities that he is charged with a previous murder in the South, and sell him for a large profit after he is released. The entry of the Duke and the King gives Tom some breathing space: if the real murderers cannot be found, he will allow the two frauds to carry out their plan; then (with

Huck's help) he will either steal Jim from his new Southern owners or buy him from the Duke and the King; and finally he will escape the St. Petersburg law officers by heading for Canada and/or England for further adventures.

The pages of "Tom Sawyer's Conspiracy" that were written during this period contain several elements that would have guaranteed popular success. The author uses the element of surprise skillfully, for example, to manipulate reader response to Jim's imprisonment: first, when it seems as if Jim will be freed easily, Mark Twain has the real murderers escape; then, when Jim's situation looks hopeless, the plan of the Duke and the King is introduced. The blend of humor and suspense is also well done. The story is constantly suspenseful because of the seriousness of the charges against Jim; yet, Mark Twain does not make the same mistake as he did in *Tom Sawyer, Detective*, where his interest in the ratiocinative plot led him almost to forget humor. In this section of "Tom Sawyer's Conspiracy" there are episodes that would appeal to readers who admired clever detective work: Tom's use of "clews," for example, to deduce the temporary whereabouts of the murderers and the fact that one of them has been injured (p. 209). But there are also a number of crude but amusing one-liners: Huck's reference to the "lawyer for the prostitution" (p. 216); the Duke's "stick your feet in your mouth and stop some of your gas from escapin', Majesty" (p. 224); Huck's summary of Jim's conversation—"still, he knowed me and Tom wouldn't let him be a slave long if industriousness and enterprise and c'ruption was worth anything" (p. 229). There is also one very funny scene in which Flacker the detective astounds an audience of St. Petersburg worthies with his inane deductions that "Burrell" is the head conspirator and that Jim is the murderer with "two 'complices' to the murder and he seen their footprints—dwarfes they was, one cross-eyed and t'other left-handed; didn't say how he knowed it, but he was shaddering them, and although they had escaped out of town for now, he warn't worrying, he allowed he would take them into camp when they was least expecting of it" (p. 230).

As well, Mark Twain's handling of this brief scene helps create that mixture of the entertaining and the serious that is a quality of his best published work. Most notable here is the "shuddering, enough to shake the house and sour the milk" (p. 230), with which practically every one of Flacker's revelations is greeted by his audience. The towns-people are almost wallowing in the fear that the situation provokes—they are using this fear, in fact, as a source of entertainment—and because they do indulge their emotions at every opportunity, Jim's danger is augmented consider-ably. In the earlier version of "Tom Sawyer's Conspiracy," the author had also illustrated this tendency, but he had not clarified its implications. In this section, however—particu-larly at the point when the murder is discovered—the sinister aspect of emotional self-indulgence is displayed clearly:

> It was only just the beginning, the place was going to swim in blood, you'll see. That is what they said. . . . And the way they was taking on about Bat Bradish you would a thought they had lost a angel; they couldn't seem to get over grieving about him and telling one another no end of sweet little beautiful things he had done, one time or another, which they had forgot till now; and it warn't no trouble, nuther, becuz they hadn't ever happened. Yesterday there wouldn't anybody say a good word for the nigger-trader nor care a dern about him, becuz every-body despised nigger-traders, of course; but today, why, they couldn't seem to get over the loss of him, nohow. Well, it's people's way; they're mostly puddnheads—looks so to me.
>
> Of course they was going to lynch Jim, everybody said it; and they just packed all the streets around the jail, and talked excited, and couldn't hardly wait to commence. (pp. 216–17)

What makes Jim's situation even more frightening is that —as Huck casually asserts on several occasions—"he was a free nigger this last year and more, and that made every-body down on him, of course, and made them forget all about his good character" (p. 217). Throughout this sec-tion, the writer's interest in suggesting the implications of freedom for blacks in this friendly community is continually manifest, as the following make clear: "He was going to explain, but they shut him up and wouldn't let him say a word—said a nigger's word warn't any account anyway" (p. 215); "It's easy to show that you *probably* killed him, and of course that is pretty good, but it can't hang a man—a white one anyway" (p. 215); "I didn't like it; I was scared of it; it was

too risky; something might happen; any little hitch, and
Jim's a goner! A nigger don't stand any show" (p. 218); "It's
white man's talk and Jim's only a nigger" (p. 223); "Everybody says he'll be hung, and of course he hain't got any
friends, becuz he's free" (p. 223). Particularly disturbing—and
real—about so many of these statements from Huck the adult
narrator is his total acceptance of the situation: "of course"
Jim will be treated this way; "naturally" people will want to
lynch him. Jim is Huck's best friend, but even looking back
from the vantage point of his maturity at this pre–Civil War
experience, Huck is unable to feel anything approximating
moral outrage or to question at all a social system that "naturally" could turn a black man into the depersonalized outlet
for ugly emotions.

The plot of "Tom Sawyer's Conspiracy" is exciting and
entertaining; and both the excitement and entertainment
are inextricably linked with the serious social theme of
how white men treat blacks. One further example should be
usefully illustrative:

> "My goodness, Marse Tom, I never *killed* him."
>
> "I know. That's the weak place. It's easy to show that you
> *probably* killed him, and of course that is pretty good, but it
> can't hang a man—a white one, anyway. It would be ever so
> much stronger if you had a *motive* to kill him, you see."
>
> "Marse Tom, is I in my right mine, or is it you? Blame my
> cats if I kin understan'."
>
> "Why, plague take it, it's plain enough. Look at it. I'm going
> to save you—that's all right, and perfectly easy. But where's the
> glory of saving a person merely just from jail. To save him from
> the gallows is the thing. It's got to be murder in the first degree
> —you get the idea? You've got to have a *motive* for killing the
> man—*then* we're all right! Jim, if you can think up a rattling
> good motive, I can get you put up for murder in the first degree
> just as easy as turning your hand over." (p. 215)

Tom's mangled priorities—glory at the apex, a black man's
sensibilities somewhere at the nadir—are mordantly comic;
they are also the major cause of the excitement of this section's plot. In *Huckleberry Finn*, Mark Twain strung out
his book—in chapters that many critics consider an excres-
cence—by enlarging on similar values introduced by Tom

Sawyer. Here, on the other hand, these motivations are central to the book and help to create a narrative that, as far as it goes, is quite successful.

Yet the narrative stops far short of the length at which it could have been sold as a major new Mark Twain creation. Several plot possibilities seem to have been considered: making the murderers members of "Burrell's Gang" and having Huck and Tom follow them to their hideout; having the Duke and the King sell Jim in the South, and then having the boys steal him out of slavery. The possibility foreshadowed most frequently was for Jim and the boys to escape to England:

> Then we would take him over to England and hand him over to the Queen ourselves to help in the kitchen and wait on table and be a body-guard and celebrated; and we would have the trip, and see the Tower and Shackspur's grave and find out what kind of a country we all come from before we struck for taxation and misrepresentation and raised Cain becuz we couldn't get it. (p. 227) [10]

If the writer had decided to explore this latter possibility he might have turned the second half of "Tom Sawyer's Conspiracy" into a kind of travel book in order to produce the desired length; the detective plot had taken him about as far as he could go. Each of these possibilities, however, would have involved him in a setting very different from the one in which he had been immersed and in a book of a very different type. Since at this point he was not ready to force his imagination in this direction, he halted "Tom Sawyer's Conspiracy" again—teetering, as with so many of the tales that he worked on during these years, on the edge either of an ending or of an essentially new beginning: he had to decide whether to be satisfied with a good, long short story—instead of the subscription book that he hoped to publish—or to make the shift in direction that might lead toward a novel.

By the beginning of 1899 he had completely left his Hannibal world: "Schoolhouse Hill" had been postponed before Christmas, "Tom Sawyer's Conspiracy" possibly some time

10. This plot possibility is also mentioned in *HH and T*, pp. 229, 232.

in January. His autobiography had also sputtered to a stop.[11] During January and February, however, he finished three articles—"The New War Scare," "Diplomatic Pay and Clothes," and "Government by Article 14";[12] and he hoped that these could be used to complete a volume of sketches that could then serve, as he had hoped that his unfinished projects would, to provide useful, immediate remuneration and to keep his name in the public eye, thus aiding the sales of the Uniform Edition of his works.[13] By the end of March he suggested to Frank Bliss that the articles that he had been writing about Mary Baker Eddy and Christian Science might also contribute to the new volume.[14] These articles, particularly the four sections that were published in *Cosmopolitan* magazine, contain some gloriously funny writing. Mark Twain's first paragraph, for example, with its monumental "Germanic" first sentence (reminiscent of the sections on the German language in *A Tramp Abroad*), its deadpan tone, its lovely irrelevancies concerning asses and manure piles, is an extremely humorous set piece:

> This last summer, when I was on my way back to Vienna from the Appetite-Cure in the mountains, I fell over a cliff in the twilight and broke some arms and legs and one thing or another, and by good luck was found by some peasants who had lost an ass and they carried me to the nearest habitation, which was one of those large, low, thatch-roofed farm-houses, with apartments in the garret for the family, and a cunning little porch under the deep gable decorated with boxes of bright-

11. See SLC to Richard Gilder, 25 February 1899, PS, MTP.

12. In a 3 January 1899 letter to Joe Twichell (PS, MTP) he mentioned having difficulty in writing "Diplomatic Pay and Clothes," a sketch about America's failure to dress or pay its diplomats commensurately with their high office. In a 19 February letter to Rogers (*HHR*, pp. 389–90) he exulted in the rates paid by a new London journal, *Lords and Commons*, which was to publish his "Government by Article 14," a forgettable article about the Austrian government. In another letter to Rogers (*HHR*, p. 385) he referred to a sketch about gambling at Monte Carlo called "The New War Scare" (Paine 46, MTP), an innocuous piece that he considered to be more daring than "The Man That Corrupted Hadleyburg."

13. See SLC to Frank Bliss, 2 February 1899, PS, MTP.

14. See SLC to Frank Bliss, 31 March 1899, PS, MTP.

colored flowers and cats; and on the ground floor a large and light sitting-room, separated from the milch-cattle apartment by a partition; and in the front yard rose stately and fine the wealth and pride of the house, the manure-pile. That sentence is Germanic, and shows that I am acquiring that sort of mastery of the art and spirit of the language which enables a man to travel all day in one sentence without changing cars.[15]

Before quoting at greater length from this Christian Science material, I must stress one thing: for Mark Twain's audience the subject was important and controversial, much more so than for modern readers. When the first installment appeared in the October 1899 issue of *Cosmopolitan*, it was so popular that the editor sent Clemens two hundred dollars more than the piece had been sold for. Edward Hale, the author of *The Man Without a Country*, wrote, "You have tackled a problem which all the rest of us have shirked." And Joe Twichell remarked, "Some judge it the best you ever did." It was even rumored in the *Christian Observer* that the Christian Science church had been so badly wounded by the *Cosmopolitan* article that it had bribed the journal's editor not to publish any more of Mark Twain's commentary on the subject.[16]

As Paul Baender points out in his introduction to *What Is Man? and Other Philosophical Writings* (pp. 24–26), many readers were puzzled by the seemingly ambiguous stance that the writer took toward Christian Science. The ambiguity is more obvious in the book that he eventually published, but even in the first eight sections it is present: his respect for the religion's basic concept, for example—that mind can dominate matter (even though this concept seems to be at odds with ideas in his "Gospel")—along with his contempt for its totalitarian tendencies and skepticism concerning the ultimate destination of the vast amounts of money gathered in by the movement. The reason the eight sections written at this time are still eminently readable, however, is that they are frequently hilarious—even for someone who knows little,

15. *What Is Man?*, p. 216. Henceforth, references to these articles will be made in the text.

16. See *MTHL*, 2:709; Edward Hale to SLC, 11 October 1899, MTP; Joseph Twichell to SLC, 8 November 1899, MTP; see John Walker to SLC, 23 April 1900, MTP.

and cares less, about Christian Science. Consider, for example, the description of the method of a Christian Scientist (Mrs. Fuller—a "widow in the third degree"):

> She unpinned and unhooked and uncoupled her upholsteries one by one, abolished the wrinkles with a flirt of her hand and hung the articles up; peeled off her gloves and disposed of them, got a book out of her handbag, then drew a chair to the bedside, descended into it without hurry, and I hung out my tongue. She said, with pity but without passion:
> "Return it to its receptacle. We deal with the mind only, not with its dumb servants." (pp. 218–19)

The juxtaposition of the woman's controlled, stately pomposity (she "descended into" her chair and spoke "with pity but without passion") and the narrator's eager indecorum is memorably comic. So also in the following passage is the placid narrator's willing subservience to still another would-be healer:

> The horse-doctor came, a pleasant man and full of hope and professional interest in the case. In the matter of smell he was pretty aromatic, in fact quite horsy, and I tried to arrange with him for absent treatment, but it was not in his line, so out of delicacy I did not press it. He looked at my teeth and examined my hock, and said my age and general condition were favorable to energetic measures; therefore he would give me something to turn the stomach ache into the botts and the cold in the head into the blind staggers; then he should be on his own beat and would know what to do. He made up a bucket of bran mash, and said a dipperful of it every two hours, alternated with a drench with turpentine and axle-grease in it would either knock my ailments out of me in twenty-four hours or so interest me in other ways as to make me forget they were on the premises. He administered my first dose himself, then took his leave, saying I was free to eat and drink anything I pleased and in any quantity I liked. But I was not hungry any more, and did not care for food. (p. 228)

The narrator's problems remain, however; so he attempts a synthesis of the two scientific worlds, Christian and veterinary:

> I took up the Christian Science book and read half of it, then took a dipperful of drench and read the other half. The resulting experiences were full of interest and adventure. All

through the rumblings and grindings and quakings and effer-
vescings accompanying the evolution of the ache into the botts
and the cold into the blind staggers I could note the generous
struggle for mastery going on between the mash and the drench
and the literature; and often I could tell which was ahead, and
could easily distinguish the literature from the others when the
others were separate, though not when they were mixed; for
when a bran mash and an eclectic drench are mixed together
they look just like the Apodictical Principle out on a lark, and
no one can tell it from that. The finish was reached at last, the
evolutions were complete and a fine success; but I think that
this result could have been achieved with fewer materials. I
believe the mash was necessary to the conversion of the stomach
ache into the botts, but I think one could develop the blind
staggers out of the literature by itself; also, that blind staggers
produced in this way would be of a better quality and more
lasting than any produced by the artificial processes of a horse-
doctor. (p. 229)

Then, in the final section of the *Cosmopolitan* article, the
narrator's naivety triumphs, rescuing him from Mrs. Fuller's
attempt to gouge him for $234:

"Nothing exists but Mind?"
"Nothing," she answered. "All else is substanceless, all else is
imaginary."
I gave her an imaginary check, and she is suing me for substantial dollars. It looks inconsistent. (p. 234)

In the next four, primarily analytical sections, Mark
Twain to a large extent drops the persona whose inspired
idiocy may remind the reader of early sections of *The Innocents Abroad*; he then discusses the various claims of the
church, its possibilities for expansion, and so on. Some of his
statements seem obtuse—for example, his idea that on matters of religion and politics "*all* opinions . . . are brass-far-
thing opinions" (p. 237). And on occasion he seems to be pad-
ding. Yet this part still contains enough comic passages to
make it worthwhile, particularly the now-sardonic narrator's
incredulous inventory of Mrs. Eddy's profitable literary activities:

Also we have Mrs. Eddy's and the Angel's little Bible-Annex
in eight styles of binding at eight kinds of war-prices; among
these a sweet thing in "levant, divinity circuit, leather lined

to edge, round corners, gold edge, silk sewed, each *prepaid*, $6,"
and if you take a million you get them a shilling cheaper—that
is to say, "prepaid, $5.75." Also we have Mrs. Eddy's *Miscel-
laneous Writings*, at 'andsome big prices, the divinity-circuit
style heading the extortions, shilling discount where you take
an edition. Next comes *Christ and Christmas*, by the fertile
Mrs. Eddy, . . . Then follow five more books by Mrs. Eddy, at
highwayman's rates, some of them in "leatherette covers," some
of them in "pebbled cloth" with divinity circuit, compensation
balance, twin screw, and the other modern improvements; and
at the same bargain-counter can be had the *Christian Science
Journal*. (p. 250)

Although it is sometimes difficult to decide what Mark Twain
is attacking in this Christian Science material—whether, in
fact, he is attempting to make any satiric point at all—many
of the sections remain extremely funny. Primarily for this
reason his early Christian Science articles are still worth
reading.

6

Longings for Home
April 1899 to September 1900

In contrast with the comic high spirits of so much of the
Mary Baker Eddy material (which, according to a letter to
Frank Bliss, the writer had not quite completed by the end
of March[1]), Clemens wrote to Howells on 2 April,

> I suspect that to you there is still dignity in human life, & that
> Man is not a joke—a poor joke—the poorest that was ever con-
> trived—an April-fool joke, played by a malicious (urchin) Crea-
> tor with nothing better to waste his time upon. Since I wrote
> my Bible, (last year) which Mrs. Clemens loathes, & shudders
> over, & will not listen to the last half nor allow me to print any
> part of it, Man is not to me the respect-worthy person he was
> before; & so I have lost my pride in him & can't write gaily nor
> praisefully about him any more. And I don't intend to try. I
> mean to go on writing, for that is my best amusement, but I
> shan't print much. (For I don't wish to be scalped, any more
> than another.)[2]

What makes these words particularly anomalous is that, since
Mark Twain had written his "Gospel," he had also worked
on his autobiography, the "Great Dark," "Schoolhouse Hill,"
"Tom Sawyer's Conspiracy," and the Christian Science articles; and much of this had been full of gaiety. The tone of
the letter may be explained in part as being the writer's attempt to rationalize his inability to complete any of these
works, which contained so much good material. And this
rationalization may be seen as a stage in the process by which
he tried to propel himself—once and for all—to decide about
the publishability of some of this material.

By 13 May he seems to have made up his mind:

1. SLC to Frank Bliss, 31 March 1899, PS, MTP. For abbreviations used in the footnotes, see "Short References," pp. ix–x.
2. *MTHL*, 2:689.

6 p.m. For several years I have been intending to stop writing for print as soon as I could afford it. At last I can afford it, & have put the pot-boiler pen away. What I have been wanting was a chance to write a book without reserves—a book which should take account of no one's feelings, no one's prejudices, opinions, beliefs, hopes, illusions, delusions; a book which should say my say, right out of my heart, in the plainest language & without a limitation of any sort. I judged that that would be an unimaginable luxury, heaven on earth. There was no condition but one under which the writing of such a book could be possible; only one—the consciousness that it would not see print.

It is under way, now, & it *is* a luxury! an intellectual drunk. Twice I didn't start it right; & got pretty far in, both times, before I found it out. But I am sure it is started right this time. It is in (story) tale-form. I believe I can make it tell what I think of Man, & how he is constructed, & what a shabby poor ridiculous thing he is, & how mistaken he is in his estimate of his character & powers & qualities & his place among the animals. . . .

I hope it will take me a year or two to write it, & that it will turn out to be the right vessel to contain all the ordure I am planning to dump into it.[3]

And in an article in the *London Daily Chronicle* on 3 June he is quoted as saying,

No, I'm not expecting to write any more for publication. . . . The man is entitled to a holiday for the rest of his life who has written for twenty-five years, or been a soldier that long, or made himself useful or ornamental in any capacity for such a period. My holiday will consist in writing two books, simply for the private pleasure of writing. One of them will not be published at all; the other written for the remote posterity of a hundred years hence.[4]

It is important to note, however, that despite his talk of "not expecting to write any more for publication," he obviously was still thinking about it, because he had already written the notes for "Indiantown," which apparently was intended to be the introduction to another attempt at long fiction. Yet such a statement should not be surprising coming from a writer who had left unfinished so many would-be publishable projects; perhaps he felt that if he *said* he was

3. Ibid., pp. 698–99.
4. 1899 Clippings file, MTP.

not going to worry about publication, he actually would not. And perhaps he hoped that his readers would no longer waste their time awaiting his new publications and would begin to reread the old favorites. Then, if a new book did appear, they would be pleasantly surprised.

Certainly the two manuscripts to which he devoted most of his literary time in the late spring and summer seem to have been written for two different purposes and for two different audiences.[5] That the new section of "The Chronicle of Young Satan" was composed for an audience of one is clear almost from the point where Mark Twain began again. When he had set aside the manuscript almost two years before, Father Peter had just been exonerated of Father Adolf's charges that he had stolen money actually provided by young Satan. Upon resuming the story, the writer held his dramatization of the trial in abeyance, backtracked to the point where Father Peter had been imprisoned, and invented new plot material. Almost all the new episodes seem designed to reveal openly, as Mark Twain had written to Howells, "What I think of Man, and how he is constructed, and what a shabby poor ridiculous thing he is."[6] Marget's servant, Ursula, finds a kitten and smugly prophesies, "It's only the poor that have a feeling for the poor, and help them. The poor and God. God will provide for this kitten. . . . Not a sparrow falls to the ground without His seeing it." Then young Satan snaps, "But it falls, just the same. What good is seeing it fall?"[7] The cat, of course, is a "Lucky Cat"; it provides the household with money every morning, and with other goods upon request. According to the narrator, Theodor, Ursula probably guesses it is an agent of the devil, "but no matter . . . for in matters of finance even the piousest of our peasants would have more confidence in an arrangement with the devil than with an Archangel" (p. 67). Next, young Satan is introduced to the family. After he has spoken warily of his own family in the "tropics"—and after Mark Twain has taken some gra-

5. During this period he was at Sanna, Sweden, where he, Livy, and Jean were taking the "Swedish Movement Cure." Numerous letters that he wrote during this time attest to his enthusiasm for the Kellgren treatment, after some initial skepticism.

6. *MTHL*, 2:698.

7. *MSM*, p. 68. Henceforth, references to "The Chronicle of Young Satan" will be made in the text.

tuitous but personally satisfying shots at the French[8]—he advises Marget about how to visit her uncle; then he provides supper magically, through an act that sounds a bit like a blasphemous parody of Christ's miracle with the loaves and fish. After the meal, by flattering Ursula he has her "mincing and simpering around in a ridiculous girly way," causing the narrator to conclude, "I was ashamed, for it showed us to be what Satan considered us, a silly race and trivial" (p. 71).

Later, after young Satan and Theodor have visited the jail and have witnessed tortures, they journey—by floating through space—to France and see more of the same. All this leads young Satan—who in the earlier "Chronicle" had been rarely bitter, merely indifferent—into a long, acrimonious tirade against man's moral sense. The passage is familiar but deserves to be quoted again:

> It is some more Moral Sense. The proprietors are rich, and very holy; but the wage they pay to these poor brothers and sisters of theirs is only enough to keep them from dropping dead with hunger. The work-hours are fifteen per day, winter and summer—from 5 in the morning till 8 at night—little children and all. And they walk to and from the pig-sties which they inhabit—four miles each way, through mud and slush, rain, snow, sleet and storm, daily, year in and year out. They get four hours of sleep. They kennel together, three families in a room, in unimaginable filth and stench; and disease comes, and they die off like flies. Have they committed a crime, these poor mangy things? No. Have they offended the priest? No; they are his pets—they fatten him with their farthings, or he would have to work for his living. What have they done, that they are punished so? Nothing at all, except getting themselves born into your foolish race. You have seen how they treat a misdoer there in the jail, now you see how they treat the innocent and the worthy. Is your race logical? Are these ill-smelling innocents better off than that heretic? Indeed, no, his punishment is trivial compared with theirs. They broke him on the wheel and mashed him to rags and pulp after we left, and he is dead, now, and free of your precious race; but these poor slaves here —why, they have been dying for years, and some of them will not escape from life for years to come. It is the Moral Sense

8. Apparently hell is composed primarily of Frenchmen, *MSM*, p. 69.

which teaches the factory-proprietors the difference between right and wrong—you perceive the result. They think themselves better than dogs. Ah, you are such an illogical, unreasoning race! And paltry—oh, unspeakably! (pp. 73–74)

When they return home, the narrator's friend Seppi talks of the disappearance of Hans Oppert, whom previously the boys had tried to prevent from cruelly mistreating his dog. Young Satan learns of Hans's accident through a conversation with Hans's dog, who, in his kindness and concern for his master, helps emphasize man's real "place among the animals." After a search party has discovered the man, he dies without the benefit of the last rites, which causes the narrator to assert, "if we had been an hour earlier the priest would have been in time to send that poor creature to heaven, but now he was gone down into the awful fires, to burn forever. . . .It gave me an appalling idea of the value of an hour, and I thought I could never waste one again without remorse and terror" (p. 76). The Hans Oppert episode thus allows Mark Twain not only to underline the cruelty of man, man's worthlessness as compared with animals, and the inhumane dimension of certain religious dogmas, but also to introduce the theme of the inestimable value of time—a theme that becomes crucial in the "Chronicle" section written in the summer of 1900.

Several additional episodes give him opportunities to pour his "ordure" upon the human race: for example, the beautifully written, poignant, tragic section in which the grandmother of the family's new servant, Gottfried Narr, is cruelly burned as a witch. Just prior to putting aside the manuscript again, Mark Twain creates a situation—the rivalry of the narrator's sister, Lily, and Marget for young Satan's favors—in which the satire is more subtle, but is nonetheless there. The two girls "love" Satan primarily out of pride, since they hope to be envied for capturing this remarkable being; in their pursuits, moreover, they trample on the feelings of the two men who have been faithful to them. The attitude toward love exemplified in this narrative contrasts radically with the attitude suggested in the notes for the continuation of "Schoolhouse Hill": there, 44 was to have discovered the preeminent worth of sexual love.

Mark Twain's choice and handling of his narrator create

a paradoxical effect. On the one hand, Theodor contributes to the author's ostensibly cynical attack on the human race because of his eagerness to quote young Satan's words (he tells us many times that he is proud to have his friendship) and his inability to counteract their import. Further, since he is telling the story as an adult looking back on his youth—and as one who has been deeply influenced by his experiences—he is able to draw the proper, cynical conclusions about human motivation even when young Satan is not present, conclusions that he would be unlikely to draw if he were a youthful narrator. On the other hand, there is the contrasting effect that I suggested when referring to the writer's "ostensibly" cynical attitude. Despite the occasional bitterness, the overall tone of this section transcends cynicism not only because young Satan's comments seem designed in a sense to help the human race by calling attention repeatedly to the deleterious effects of pride, but also because the narrator is deeply interested in the past that he remembers. He has not been numbed by his experiences and still—like his creator—retains his remarkable capacity for wonder.

In the following episode, for example, although the narrator begins by remarking, "I was in raptures to see him show off so" (because such displays reflect well on himself), it becomes clear as his description continues that his motives for appreciating young Satan's music go beyond the merely selfish:

It was not one instrument talking, it was a whole vague, dreamy, far-off orchestra—flutes, and violins, and silver horns, and drums, and cymbals, and all manner of other instruments, blending their soft tones in one rich stream of harmony. And it was mournful and touching; for this was the lover realising his loss. Then Satan began to chant the words of that poor fellow's lament—gentle and low; and the water rose in those two people's eyes, for they had heard no voice like that before, nor had any one heard the like of it except in heaven, where it came from. Little by little the music and the singing rose louder out of the distance—the lover was coming, he was on his way. And ever the singing and the music grew; and the storm began to gather and move toward us, with the wind sighing, the thunder muttering and the lightning playing; and on it came, just as if you could see it, and see the lover's horse racing and straining down in the pursuing front of it; and so, with a boom and a roar and a crash it burst upon us in one final grand explosion of noble sounds, and then the battle began, the victory was won, the storm passed, the morning came, and the lover lay dying in the maiden's arms, with her tears falling upon his face and the precious music of her endearments fading upon his ear.

It was finished, and we sat drowned in that ecstasy, and numb and dumb and only half conscious. (p. 93)[9]

One of the intended effects of the narrator's admiration for, and descriptions of, young Satan's miracles is to reveal by contrast man's limitations. Another effect—perhaps only unconsciously intended by Mark Twain—is to reveal man's admirable capacity for large, impersonal awe when viewing phenomena of genuine worth. Livy's response to the manuscript—"It is perfectly horrible—and perfectly beautiful"—is perfectly appropriate.[10]

The same thing, unfortunately, can not be said about the other piece of major fiction (entitled at this point "Which Was Which?") that Mark Twain worked on during approximately the same period. In his introduction to *Which Was the Dream?*, John Tuckey conjectures that "Indiantown"—the delightfully rambling sketch that serves as a type of preamble to the longer work—was probably begun during Clemens's trip to London in June and early July, when he was negotiating with Chatto and Windus concerning the English rights to the Uniform and Deluxe editions and also publicizing these books.[11] More precisely, "Indiantown" was probably written during the ten-day period at the beginning of June when, because of Clara's illness, Clemens was relaxing at the Grand Hotel at Broadstairs on the Dover beach, before being swirled into a hectic London social schedule.[12] Just prior to leaving for this retreat, he spoke in an interview

9. Generalizing from the importance of music in specific works such as "The Man That Corrupted Hadleyburg" and "The Chronicle of Young Satan," William Gibson writes of Mark Twain's work as a whole: "Humor and music as catharsis, and satire as corrective and perspective, are omnipresent in Mark Twain's theory and writings" (*The Art of Mark Twain*, p. 199).

10. *MTHL*, 2:699.

11. *WWD?*, p. 20. Henceforth, references to "Indiantown" will be made in the text.

12. For evidence supporting this dating, see *HHR*, pp. 398–400, and *Writings*, 22:1085–87.

of his autobiography;[13] and "Indiantown" is filled with auto-biographical references, particularly in the narrator's des-cription of David and Susan Gridley, who are only very skimpily disguised versions of Clemens and Livy. In "Indian-town," Mark Twain seems to be trying to write the introduc-tion for a long novel, because he spends an inordinate num-ber of pages establishing his Mississippi setting and then sketching a multitude of the town's characters. It is possible that another reason he devotes so much space to this prelim-inary material without using it to lead toward a plot is that he is using it to familiarize himself again with an en-vironment that he may have lost touch with. The Hannibal that he had been describing in the previous two years was primarily a children's world; in "Indiantown," on the other hand, the adult focus, although not the tone, resembles "Vil-lagers" and *Pudd'nhead Wilson*.

One notable aspect of this sketch is that the narrator's perspective on the people in the town is opposed almost total-ly to the misanthropy that Clemens had exemplified in his March and April letters to Howells and that was on display in "The Chronicle of Young Satan." Consider the following, for example: "With his intimates the Squire was *like the average man* [my italics]—easy, companionable, interested in what was going on and not reserved in the matter of exhib-iting the natural play of his feelings" (p. 158); "But in spite of their detestable faults they were dear good generous peo-ple, always ready for good works, and people were obliged to like and respect them—and did" (p. 162); "Her special friend was the widow Pilgrim. Mrs. Pilgrim was a kind-hearted creature who didn't know anything, but didn't know she didn't know anything, and this protected her from em-barrassment. . . . She had good instincts and was an ass, and this made her welcome everywhere" (p. 162). In "Indian-town" Mark Twain as narrator functions as an extremely chatty, amiable God who sees all and accepts what he sees, as he had done in "Hellfire Hotchkiss."

Given the disparity in tone that exists between a poten-tially "public" manuscript like "Indiantown" and an ostensi-bly "private" one like "The Chronicle of Young Satan," it is

13. See the 3 June interview in the *London Daily Chronicle* in the 1899 Clippings file, MTP.

tempting to generalize and draw a simplistic conclusion: the tonal differences in Mark Twain's works are caused by his sense of his audience—when speaking to a mass audience he affects an insincere mask; when speaking to a small audience, of as few as one, he is the "real" Mark Twain. I suspect, however, that the causal situation in some instances is considerably more complex: these effects may not derive from these causes and in some cases they may be reversed. It is possible, for example, that having written or while writing something *like* "Indiantown" in a benign mood—although not this particular manuscript because Mark Twain probably had publication in mind *before* he began to write—he would decide to use it as the basis for a publishable manuscript; or, that having written or while writing something like a section of "Chronicle" in a bitter mood, he would decide not to publish it. Probably the sometimes extreme tonal disparity that separates certain manuscripts and even portions of manuscripts from each other can best be explained (as has been done by other critics), by pointing to relatively "innocent" and "experienced" sides of the writer's personality. The innocent side is tolerant, forgiving, and responsive to the world's positive dimensions; the experienced side is condemnatory, cynical, and bitter about the world's negative aspects. Each side is an essential part of the writer's identity, and each *tends to be* inspired by the possibility of a certain kind of rhetorical situation. What is most interesting to observe are the strategies that the conscious professional writer begins to employ when he realizes that an idea—perhaps one deriving from "unconscious cerebration"—may be led toward a publishable manuscript; or, conversely, how he reacts when an idea he has been developing with publication in mind leads toward something quite different.

In the case of "Indiantown," it would appear that when Mark Twain began writing, he hoped to create a popular novel. The friendly narrator sounds like a person eager to interest an audience ("at the time of which we write"); he establishes his setting using a technique solidly within the conventions of popular narrative: he gives a picturesque overview of the region, then of the particular time (June). He draws the town in terms of its people (Andrew Harrison's mansion is a mile north of Burt Higgins's blacksmith shop), makes a few conventional sociological observations ("of course the most of the people were of the commonplace sort"); then begins to focus on the characters, introducing his individuals in relation to their class. This process is familiar, as is the town (so the narrator implies). These people are "our" people.

In this way he begins a chronicle quite different from that of young Satan. What happens to "Indiantown," however, is also what happened to "Hellfire Hotchkiss": the writer's interest in creating fictional characters wanes; he neglects the strategies necessary to make character serve plot; and the fictional world dissolves into autobiography as his memories of the past intrude. Finally, a would-be novel meanders to a stop.

Later in the summer, while he and his family were in Sanna, Sweden, experiencing the "Swedish Cure" administered by Jonas Kellgren, Mark Twain returned imaginatively to Indiantown.[14] At this point, he seems to have taken careful steps to insure that his ideas would lead toward fiction. Perhaps recognizing that one cause of his earlier problems was his lack of distance from the material, he changed the body of water bordering the town from the resonant Mississippi into a stream. Also, he made the protagonist, George Harrison, into a primarily fictional creation, even though he retained the name of the "Indiantown" character who resembled Orion Clemens and gave to him one distinctive quality of David Gridley, the character who resembled Sam Clemens—the deceptiveness of his supposedly high principles.

To eliminate another problem with "Indiantown" as fiction—the lengthy exposition that never moved into a plot—the writer here goes to the opposite extreme: "Which Was Which?" is crammed almost immediately with incidents. Due to his worry over a debt to Squire Charles Fairfax, George Harrison's father becomes unbalanced, trying to pay off the squire with counterfeit cash, then imagining that Fairfax is planning to prosecute him, although the squire is so sympathetic to the old man that he tears up the voucher for the debt. Harrison, frightened by his father's fabrications, first considers burning down the family's mill for the insurance,

14. See John Tuckey's comments on dating in *WWD?*, p. 177.

then decides upon stealing money from Fairfax—telling himself it is only a loan—in order to pay back the debt. Upon entering the squire's house at night, he meets and by accident kills another intruder—Jake Bleeker. When Bleeker's body is discovered, Fairfax is charged with the crime because, just previously, he had humiliated the victim in a public street. Harrison considers confessing, decides not to, and then—in a cloyingly ironic sequence—befriends Fairfax in jail, becomes a second father to his daughter (who is the fiancée of Harrison's son, Tom), and promises to help discover the real murderer. During the period when he was writing this material, Mark Twain also wrote a type of ending for the story—in one chapter the trial leads to a hung jury and Fairfax's freedom; in another, Harrison's father's "dying deposition" asserts that he had seen Fairfax kill the intruder (it is not clear whether this is a true account of the event—and therefore Harrison did not actually kill Jake Bleeker—or simply another example of the elder Harrison's delusions). The pages written during these months, however, do not come close to constituting a novel, so it is not surprising that Mark Twain again resumed the story when he returned to the United States.

As a narrative, "Which Was Which?" is very weak, a major problem being that, as opposed to "Indiantown," it relies too indiscriminately upon the strategies—the most obvious and ineffective ones—of popular fiction. For example, a minor character—Dug Hapgood—seems primarily intended to provide comic relief; instead, he is largely unfunny, serves to dissipate whatever suspense may have been created, and helps to remind the reader of bad melodrama. The language of "big speeches" like the following should stir similar echoes:

"O, my God, why cannot I die!"
He got up and walked the floor, wringing his hands and uttering despairing ejaculations. Presently he noticed those papers on the mantelpiece, where Martha had left them. He took them absently up, not conscious of what he was doing. . . . He glanced at them and sank, like one smitten mortally, into his chair. "*Canceled*—God pity me! O! O! O! how can a man bear this! . . . I am a thief—stealer of my father's false money—thief to no purpose—thief to save the house's honor, and it was *al-*

ready saved—through what mystery and by whose heaven-sent compassion there is no divining! Oh, if—". (p. 230)

In general, the most crucial difficulty with "Which Was Which?" is that Mark Twain tried to create a quasi-naturalistic novel by employing a rhythm and techniques that are devastatingly ineffective. In order to stress his point about the power of circumstance to mold men's lives, for example, he turned Harrison from a high-principled man into a criminal in an absurdly brief time, depending to an almost ludicrous extent upon coincidences such as the following to bring this about: Harrison's son has a Tom Sawyerish desire to reveal only at the proper moment that the debt has been cancelled—thus permitting Harrison's father to proceed with his criminal plans; the maid decides to remove the note that would have explained all from Harrison's place at the table; Bleeker appears at the Fairfax house at the moment when Harrison is there. Mark Twain's reliance on fast action and coincidence created no problems in his successful subscription books; nor did his relative unconcern about transitions, an attitude perhaps developed in the writing of travel books, where a move to a new area was sufficient justification for the discussion of a new topic.

In naturalistic novels, however, there is usually a slow preliminary movement and a careful accumulation of details; these qualities help to make chance events seem simply part of a long sequence and to make unusual episodes seem plausible and even inevitable. Without this type of crescendo, the ideas of the novel may seem imposed, certain events may seem gratuitous. Consider the effect, for example, if Theodore Dreiser in *Sister Carrie* had pushed Carrie into bed with Hurstwood after fifteen pages, or if Frank Norris in *McTeague* had made Trina sleep with her gold two pages after she marries the dentist. Something similarly disastrous happens in "Which Was Which?" as Mark Twain, eager to hammer home his philosophical points and to create an exciting plot—even borrowing the murderer-discovered-over-the-body gimmick from Tom Sawyer books in order to create the necessary complications—instead begins a story that is as bad as anything he wrote during this last period. Another, one would presume unintended, effect of his technique is that the force of his philosophy is almost destroyed. Harrison changes so quickly from an honest man to a deceiver, and spends so much time rationalizing this change, that it seems to derive not so much from circumstances as from Harrison's own contemptible foolishness and weakness.

After, or perhaps even before, laying aside the manuscript temporarily, probably in late August, Mark Twain finished what was intended to be the introduction to an English translation of the trials of Joan of Arc, and he asked Bliss on 3 September whether the work could be sold by subscription. Bliss wondered about the decorum of selling such a book by such a method, and the writer's enthusiasm subsided. Much later, after he had withdrawn his introduction because he was angered by the stylistic emendations made by the editor, T. Douglas Murray—an English barrister and amateur historian—he included it in *Literary Essays*, one of the two volumes of sketches that were published in 1900. In September, as well, Mark Twain wrote "My Boyhood Dreams," a sketch creating humor by parodying the nostalgic impulse: "Has *any* boyhood dream ever been fulfilled? I must doubt it. Look at Brander Matthews. He wanted to be a cowboy. What is he today? Nothing but a professor in a university. Will he ever be a cowboy? It is hardly conceivable."[15] It was soon published and was subsequently included in *The Man That Corrupted Hadleyburg and Other Essays and Stories*. Thus, although he still had not written his big subscription novel, he had written material that eventually became profitable.

When Clemens returned to London in October, he was—for a while—extremely busy; he was working on a novel (probably "Which Was Which?"), deciding upon the contents of two volumes of sketches that would be published in America and Europe the following year, writing a short (thirty-two-hundred words) article entitled "My First Lie and How I Got Out of It," maintaining his interest in the translation of the Joan of Arc trials, and even considering joining with Canon Basil Wilberforce for several talks to be delivered

15. *MTHL*, 2:708; SLC to Frank Bliss, 3 September 1899, PS, MTP; SLC to Frank Bliss (incomplete), 26 September 1899, PS, MTP; see *Writings*, 23:258.

to "worthy" audiences about his long-cherished heroine.[16] During the remainder of this year and the first half of 1900, however, he seems to have written very little: two forgettable short stories in December 1899 ("How the Chimney Sweep Got the News to the Emperor" and "The Death Disc"); the bare beginnings of a Huck and Tom story with a nautical setting in March 1900; and, apparently in the same month, a fifty-six-hundred-word article describing a postal-check scheme.[17]

It is possible of course that he did write material that he destroyed eventually. In declining, on 29 January, an offer from Felix Volhovsky, who had requested an article for *Free Russia*, he complained about the danger of allowing a new project to interrupt an older one, thus implying that he already was working on something.[18] Perhaps the piece of work that he did not want to intrude on was his introduction to, and continuing involvement with, the Joan of Arc project; in his letter to Murray on 31 January, he enclosed his shortened and emended introduction, acknowledged the absolute need for intelligent running commentary on the text, and predicted that if a master like Henry James could translate it, it would live forever.[19] He also talked on occasion of having written, and of planning to write, material for a humorous magazine that S. S. McClure wanted him to lend his name to as editor upon his return to America.[20] It is doubtful, however, whether Mark Twain actually did much preliminary work for the magazine. Most of the evidence from this period points to a man whose creative reservoir is almost bone dry, who is—as he had written to Rogers in early January—sick of his "everlasting exile," and who is impatient to return home (although it was not until August 1900 that he had decided where home would actually be).[21]

16. See *HHR*, pp. 409–10; SLC to Mr. Harper, 1 October 1899, PS, MTP; and SLC to Mr. Tuohy, 30 October 1899, PS, MTP.

17. See SLC to Miss Harrison, 21 December 1899, "Proposition for a Postal Check" may be found in Paine 211, MTP.

18. SLC to Felix Volhovsky, 29 January 1900, TS, MTP.

19. SLC to Mr. Murray, 31 January 1900, TS, MTP.

20. For information concerning the McClure offer see *Writings*, 32:1099–1102.

21. *HHR*, p. 424.

Upon returning to London in October 1899, he had signed a lease for his accommodations, thinking that Jean needed to be near the English home of Kellgren—the founder of the Swedish Movement Cure—to continue her recovery. Then, soon afterward, he decided that the Kellgren system closely resembled osteopathy; if he had known this before, he remarked, they could have returned to America early in 1900. By February, he was planning to leave England in June; but by the middle of May he had resigned himself to an October departure: Jean had "turned the corner" and needed to remain with Kellgren until she was all the way around. This kind of uncertainty undoubtedly had a harmful effect upon whatever literary ideas he might have hoped to develop. He was also involved in other things during the winter and spring: for example, investing in, and helping to get off the ground, an organization devoted to promoting Plasmon, a new milk product and health food. This, along with the Kellgren system, was his current panacea; Plasmon, moreover, would make him a very rich man, he was certain. In late 1899 and early 1900, as well, he must have devoted a great deal of thought to the McClure offer—not only to the editorship of the magazine, but also to McClure's desire to publish his books.

Part of Mark Twain's dissatisfaction with Harper's—particularly in December—derived from his worry over the very shaky financial situation of the company and from his feeling that it was not advertising his books sufficiently. The financial carrot dangled by the ingenious and aggressive McClure undoubtedly also contributed to his dissatisfaction. His enthusiasm for McClure began to cool in February when the publisher revealed that the editorship would not be the sinecure that he had originally implied (Mark Twain had said that he actually expected to work on the magazine, but not to the extent that McClure's February letter suggested). Yet he still had not rejected the offer on 20 April, when in a letter to Rogers he remarked, "The putting off of the magazine is a good deal of relief to me. It will give me time in which to write some things for the first year's issue without feeling crowded for time."[22] There were other en-

22. Ibid., p. 442. For information concerning this period see *HHR*, pp. 409–49.

tanglements as well: the usual social obligations, his appearance in front of a committee of the House of Lords in early April to discuss copyright problems, negotiations over the dramatic rights to *Tom Sawyer* and "The Man That Corrupted Hadleyburg," more offers of surefire financial bonanzas. All these contributed to a situation in which it was difficult for the writer to do real, creative work.

On the other hand, Dollis Hill House, an estate just outside London where he moved in early July, was an environment in which his literary imagination was revitalized; while here he wrote a magnificent section of "The Chronicle of Young Satan."[23] In his *Mark Twain and Little Satan*, John Tuckey comments at some length about the effect of world events in 1900—the Boxer Rebellion in China, the Boer War, the assassination of King Humbert of Italy—upon this section.[24] Certainly Clemens's fascination and disgust with the slaughters in South Africa and China had been exemplified in numerous letters written before his move to Dollis Hill House in early July,[25] and certainly his interest in these affairs seems to have been the main impetus for many of the "Chronicle" pages. This was fortunate, because when he had set the manuscript aside in the previous summer after having devoted a large number of pages to Satan's romantic entanglements, Mark Twain obviously had been floundering.

That there is a great deal of the writer in the young Satan of the Dollis period is patent, particularly in the contradictions of the character and in his relationship with the human race. On the one hand, there is his professed indifference to humanity—that of the elephant for the ant, he tells the narrator (p. 113)—and on the other, there is the overwhelming

23. Although, upon taking possession of the house on 2 July, Clemens had called it the dirtiest dwelling in Europe, perhaps in the universe (Notebook 33, TS, p. 20, MTP), he wrote on 26 September, "Better 60 days of Dollis than a cycle of Cathay" (Notebook 33, TS, p. 26, MTP). He also wrote in "Travel Scraps" (DV 82, p. 3) that Dollis House came nearer to being a paradise than any other house he had ever owned. The estate was situated close enough to London for Clemens to visit the city easily; yet, it also possessed many of the advantages of a rural environment.

24. *MTLS*, pp 47–50.

25. See, for example, SLC to Joseph Twichell on 27 January (*MTL*, 2:694–95) and on 12 August 1900, (*MTL*, 2:699).

evidence of his concern: his willingness to help the boys and the people they worry about, and in particular the tone of anger and outrage that pervades practically every one of his lengthy comments about civilization. Most significantly, in the several suggestions made by young Satan about ameliorating the human condition, Mark Twain seems to be contemplating possible means of escaping from the morass caused by human weakness, particularly by the weakness of pride. Contrasting with the desolating deterministic implications of ideas such as "every man is a suffering-machine and a happiness-machine combined. . . . For every happiness turned out in the one department the other one stands ready to modify it with a sorrow or a pain—maybe a dozen" (p. 112) is the meliorism of young Satan's often-quoted speech on the iconoclastic power of satiric laughter.

In the following statement also there is an almost Nietzschean belief in the potency of the hero (or heroine, like Joan of Arc): "Some day a handful will rise up on the other side and make the most noise—perhaps even a single daring man with a big voice and a determined front will do it—and in a week all the sheep will wheel and follow him, and witchhunting will come to a sudden end. In fact this happened within these ten years, in a little country called New England" (pp. 154–55). Other episodes in the narrative also have positive implications, although young Satan does not emphasize them and the narrator is not quite able to perceive them himself. A corollary of young Satan's determinism, for example—"His first act determines the second and all that follow after" (p. 115)—is that every act is important, not simply the grandiose ones: "You people do not suspect that all of your acts are of one size and importance, but it is true: to snatch at an appointed fly is as big with fate for you as is any other appointed act" (p. 116). And one of the related implications of the superb episode culminating with Nikolaus's death by drowning is the idea that, viewed from the proper perspective, every second can be ripe with magnificent possibilities:

It was an awful eleven days; and yet, with a lifetime stretching back between to-day and then, they are still a grateful memory to me, and beautiful. In effect they were days of companionship with one's sacred dead, and I have known no comrade ship that

was so close or so precious. We clung to the hours and the min-
utes, counting them as they wasted away, and parting with them
with that pain and bereavement which a miser feels who sees
his hoard filched from him coin by coin by robbers and is help-
less to prevent it. (p. 124)

A difficulty in making this almost existentialistic attitude
really affect one's life, however, is the evanescence of one's
belief in, and concern for, the mortality of others: it is only
during the period prior to his friend's death that the narrator is able to transcend his pride and self-absorption. This
fact, and others related to it, point to a quality of skeptical
awareness that informs the book and seems to prevent Mark
Twain from going beyond a kind of wistful once-over-lightly
dramatization of positive possibilities. Climaxing young Satan's lengthy discussion of the potential power of laughter,
for example, is the narrator's response, "I said I was too much
hurt to laugh. I said our religion was our stay and our hope;
it was the most precious thing we had, and I could not bear
to hear its sacred servants derided" (p. 167). The author is
not criticizing his narrator here, he is simply recognizing the
influence—and I think the value, despite the related weaknesses—of anything believed to be sacred.

Here Mark Twain the radical is being undercut by Mark
Twain the conservative. It is episodes such as these that help
explain why he was unable to commit himself totally to the
kind of satiric stance that his critics would have had him
assume. He recognized that there was often value in the
men and institutions that he might have wished to tear down.
Moreover, he recognized the impossibility of predicting all
the results of even the most well-meaning social action. Surely this is one of the primary implications of the several
occasions upon which the narrator's entreaties for young Satan's help lead to a burning or a drowning or madness.

The writer was much aware, also, of the seemingly infinite
human capacity for turning acts that were intended as in-
structional into a means of self-gratification. Among other
things, young Satan is the artist as potential reformer, in a
certain sense the hero that he himself calls for. Yet—in the
section where "Chronicle" has become a temporal travel
book—instead of learning from young Satan's didactic pageant of civilization, the narrator goes into ecstasies over the

"marvelous night show," especially the Bartholomew's Day massacre (p. 135), or regrets that he is unable to "convert" Satan to his own point of view (p. 137). When young Satan punishes an enemy by turning him into stone, women thrill at the miracle (p. 144), and the bereaved survivors eventually become rich by employing their petrified relative as a relic. After young Satan discovers that the boys have responded to his nightmare vision of history as if it had been presented to them primarily for their delectation, he capitulates momentarily:

> Then he saw by our faces how much we were hurt, and he cut his sentence short and stopped chuckling, and his manner changed. He said gently—
>
> "No, we will drink each other's health, and let civilization go. The wine which has flown to our hands out of space by my desire, is earthly, and good enough for that other toast, but throw away the glasses—we will drink this one in wine which has not visited this world before."
>
> We obeyed, and reached up and received the new cups as they descended. They were shapely and beautiful goblets, but they were not made of any material that we were acquainted with. They seemed to be in motion, they seemed to be alive; and certainly the colors in them were in motion. They were very brilliant and sparkling, and of every tint, and they were never still, but flowed to and fro in rich tides which met and broke and flashed out dainty explosions of enchanting color. I think it was most like opals washing about in waves and flashing out their splendid fires. But there is nothing to compare the wine with, just as there was never anything to compare Satan's music with. We drank it, and felt a strange and witching ecstacy go stealing through us. (pp. 138–39)

There are sections of "The Chronicle of Young Satan" that suggest a writer who has been drinking this wine and who has decided to pour out his vituperation, to allow his imagination to soar, and to indulge himself. When Mark Twain returned to America he would try to suppress his doubts about the damned human race and confront his responsibilities.

7

Mark Twain, Reformer
October 1900 to May 1901

When Samuel Clemens returned to the United States so triumphantly in October 1900, he began almost immediately to involve himself in the politics of his country. This was fortunate, first of all, for the anti-imperialist and municipal reform groups and sympathizers who gained not only an articulate spokesman, but, most significantly, a famous one, one who was perhaps the most famous man in the world at this time. As William Gibson has pointed out, when Mark Twain began to speak out repeatedly against the aggressiveness of the great powers, there was already a large minority—at least in the United States—that had been voicing its disapproval of the English conduct in the Transvaal; of the German, Russian, and French machinations in China; and of the American entanglement in the Philippines. Although this group included such able, intelligent, and respected spokesmen as William Dean Howells, none of these spokesmen had the public following, nor the public influence, of Mark Twain.[1]

It is of course impossible to evaluate the precise influence of the statements Mark Twain made on a variety of issues during this period; yet it is almost certainly true that—at least with respect to the American involvement in the Philippines—many people too timid to express their opinions before the publication of "To The Person Sitting In Dark-

---

1. In addition to William Gibson's excellent article entitled "Mark Twain and Howells: Anti-Imperialists," useful information about this topic may be found in Frederick Anderson, ed., *A Pen Warmed-Up in Hell*; Louis Budd, *Mark Twain: Social Philosopher*; Philip Foner, *Mark Twain: Social Critic*; Maxwell Geismar, *Mark Twain: An American Prophet*; Arthur Scott, "Oracle," chapter 6 in *Mark Twain at Large*, pp. 254–300; and *damned human race*. For abbreviations used in the footnotes, see "Short References," pp. ix–x.

ness" gained courage after the essay appeared in the *North American Review* in the winter of 1901. As one of the essay's admirers wrote, "That paper did immense good. It gave many a 'silent assertion liar' courage to come out and assert his convictions in what his conscience told him was right."[2] Mark Twain did not cause the McKinley government to withdraw from the Philippines; nor is it even likely that he convinced many people of their foolishness in admiring famous men whose actions he himself deplored and whose courage he considered specious, such as Gen. Frederick Funston. It is possible, however, that the kind of public awareness that his writing, speaking, and interviewing helped to create did help to make American policy in the Philippines more just than it might have been. It is possible as well that his criticisms of missionary policy helped to make individual missionaries more sensitive to the values and needs of their benighted would-be converts. It is, finally, probable that his agitations against Tammany Hall corruptions prior to the New York municipal elections in the fall of 1901 helped considerably to defeat an insidious political machine.[3]

All of this is conjecture, but it is conjecture that indicates the social value of Mark Twain during the period from 1900 to 1905. Certainly many of the numerous letters that were provoked by, in particular, "To The Person Sitting In Darkness" speak of readers who had been *moved* by the writer's words. Nobody was more skeptical than Clemens about whether his words would have a lasting effect upon the human natures that he had touched. Yet, if any man of letters in the United States had any positive influence on the governments and citizens of the country, it was this "jolly jokester."[4]

It was fortunate, second of all, for the writer, not only that the causes existed, but also that he was begged to champion them. As Hamlin Hill states in his iconoclastic biography of Clemens's last years, Clemens loved the notoriety and the energy that surrounded him and that he was compelled to exert; he loved his role on center stage that was concomi-

2. A. W. Carson to SLC, 15 October 1901, MTP.
3. See Notebook 34, TS, p. 12, MTP: "It—is—a victory!—& we are here to rejoice. Who won it? Modesty almost forbids."
4. Quoted in Foner, *Mark Twain: Social Critic*, p. 100.

tant of his reforming zeal.[5] As he was the first to admit, his vanity was large, and this plethora of useful activities was hugely stimulating to a man who, during a few of the previous years, had become occasionally too comfortable with thoughts of death. But it does not follow that a vanity-inspired search for excitement was the preeminent reason Clemens drove himself to exhaustion during certain months. Nor does it follow that his political activity was largely frivolous.[6] Samuel Clemens remained sincerely patriotic during this period that so many observers felt would be a watershed in American history.[7] Therefore, he wrote, he spoke, he allowed himself to be interviewed, both because he enjoyed these activities and also because he hoped—at times passionately—to ameliorate American conditions. And he hoped to do so at every level, from the most exalted (by changing American foreign policy, for example) to the most ostensibly mundane (by agitating for the official recognition of osteopaths in the state of New York[8]).

Given the propitious circumstances in which Clemens was able to embrace political issues when he returned to his powerful but troubled country, two speculations seem reasonable: first, some time before the return he had probably decided to make his general reputation as a humorist with a serious side more specific by becoming a moralist and a reformer; second, in view of his skepticism regarding the possibilities of reform—a skepticism most recently on display in "The Chronicle of Young Satan"—it is likely that he had decided to orchestrate his efforts so that they would have maximum impact. The publication of *The Man That Corrupted Hadleyburg and Other Stories* just prior to his de-

5. In particular, see Hamlin Hill's comments in chapter 1, "Indian Summer," of *God's Fool*.

6. This is the impression that Hill seems to be attempting to convey in his biography.

7. Numerous articles written in major American journals such as *Century Magazine, Harper's New Monthly Magazine,* and *Atlantic Monthly* during the last five years of the nineteenth century (and particularly during and after the Spanish-American War) focused on the significance of the period and on America's responsibilities as a world power.

8. See, for example, his speech on "Osteopathy" in *Writings,* 28:232–34.

parture for America undoubtedly was related only acci-
dentally to his incipient reformism, but it was a fortuitous
accident, because many of the reviews of the volume in September and October focused on the title story and on Mark
Twain as a moralist. William Archer's review is one example:

> Perhaps you wonder to find Mark Twain among the moralists
> at all? If so, you have read his previous books to little purpose.
> They are full of ethical suggestion. Sometimes, it is true, his
> moral decisions are a little summary. Often, nay, generally, his
> serious meaning is lightly veiled in paradox, exaggeration, irony.
> But his humor is seldom entirely irresponsible for many pages
> together, and it often goes very deep into human nature. Let me
> merely remind you of that exquisite page—one of how many!—in
> "Huckleberry Finn," where Huck goes through his final wrestle
> with his conscience as to the crime of helping to steal Jim out of
> slavery.[9]

Interviews that Mark Twain gave to the *New York World*
correspondent in London and to reporters greeting him in
New York suggest that he already was considering his role,
as well as ways to use the newspaper medium to make himself
influential. His responses in both interviews give the impression of being delightfully extemporaneous; yet when queried
about the issue of imperialism, he gave answers that are so
pungently clear as to suggest that he wanted to be asked the
questions and was absolutely ready when he was. A few of
his statements made in the New York interview follow:

> I left these shores, at Vancouver, a red-hot imperialist. I wanted
> the American eagle to go screaming into the Pacific. It seemed
> tiresome and tame for it to content itself with the Rockies. Why
> not spread its wings over the Philippines, I asked myself? And I
> thought it would be a real good thing to do. . . .
>
> But I have thought some more, since then, and I have read
> carefully the treaty of Paris, and I have seen that we do not
> intend to free, but to subjugate the people of the Philippines.
> We have gone there to conquer, not to redeem.

9. William Archer, *London Morning Leader*, 22 September 1900,
in 1900 Clippings file, MTP. See also *Academy*, 29 September 1900,
p. 258: "Mark Twain, censor and critic, is rapidly taking the place
of Mark Twain, fun-maker." It should be pointed out, however,
that not all the reviewers were happy with this change, particularly
not the British ones.

We have also pledged the power of this country to maintain and protect the abominable system established in the Philippines by the Friars.

It should, it seems to me, be our pleasure and duty to make those people free, and let them deal with their own domestic questions in their own way. And so I am an anti-imperialist. I am opposed to having the eagle put its talons on any other land.[10]

What makes the denunciations particularly effective in the context of these interviews is the way in which they contrast with the friendly, relaxed, tentative tone of the rest of the material: Mark Twain seems to be saying that, while he may be uncertain (although comfortably so) of many things at this time, he is energetically convinced that imperialism is wrong.

Upon his return, he was briefly subdued while he began to settle in and—perhaps—to await the right moment to begin speaking stridently. He did not write anything for publication for several weeks, and his first few speeches only hovered over reformist causes. His short speech on 18 October on behalf of relief for children orphaned by a catastrophe in Galveston, Texas, contained one cute anecdote, expressed sincere sympathy for the victims, and said nothing about his impressions of America, although he did joke about his dedicated observations, "the object of this diligence being to regulate the moral and political situation on this planet."[11] At the Lotus Club dinner on 10 November, however, in a speech abundantly quoted by the press, several of his remarks pertained to American foreign policy. The tone of these remarks to many old literary friends was decorously casual, but he said enough even in this celebratory context to inform his wider audience that political issues were bothering him.[12]

After he had spoken nonpolitically to the Nineteenth Century Club on 20 November, he was ready to plunge spectacularly into the American scene as a social critic and reform-

10. *New York Herald*, 16 October 1900. In 1900 Clippings file, MTP. Most of the 6 October interview given to the *New York World* correspondent is quoted in Gibson, "Mark Twain and Howells," pp. 444–45.

11. See *Writings*, 28:204.

12. See ibid., pp. 199–200.

er.[13] At the Berkeley Lyceum on 23 November, for example, in a speech to the Public Education Association, he seized upon his audience's special interest and the newspaper headlines that announced Russia's redirection of educational funds toward military purposes, to attack Russian, German, and French greed and power mongering in China and to declare,

> China never wanted foreigners any more than foreigners wanted Chinamen, and on this question I am with the Boxers every time. The Boxer is a patriot. He loves his country better than he does the countries of other people. I wish him success. The Boxer believes in driving us out of his country. I am a Boxer, too, for I believe in driving him out of our country.[14]

Then, on 29 November, he mailed to the Red Cross Society his savage "A salutation-speech from the Nineteenth Century to the Twentieth," intended as one of many toasts to be written by famous people and read at watch-meetings across America on New Year's Eve. When Clemens's request for the names of other contributors was not granted, his "salutation-speech" was withdrawn, subsequently to be published in the *New York Herald* on 31 December.

An action performed by him around this time in response to an ostensibly trivial incident is also indicative of how far he was prepared to go by late November. Katy Leary, the family maid, had been overcharged by a grasping cab driver. Clemens not only took the man to court but also arranged for both the incident and his severe comments about it to be publicized fully.[15] Although he was made the butt of a few

13. "Disappearance of Literature," in ibid., pp. 209–10.
14. See ibid., p. 212.
15. Mark Twain asserted, "If I am clubbed and robbed in the street and I say that maybe the man needed the money and make no complaint, is that acting the part of a good citizen? Here this man comes without a club and tries to rob me. I would be a bad citizen if I did not complain as I would if I kept quiet about being clubbed and robbed. Now I have no feelings against this man. I have no quarrel with him. My quarrel is with the condition of society that makes him possible. The New York public are responsible for such men as he. They submit to the extortions and encourage them by their assistance. Every good citizen is a private policeman. It is his duty to assist and co-operate with the authorities in sustaining the law and in bringing violators to justice. I am here in no other capacity than that. I am not seeking any revenge. I

jokes for his supposed quixotism, the consensus was favorable: here, most people realized, was a famous man who wanted to change conditions by beginning with individual responsibility; such an action should be applauded and emulated.[16]

By the beginning of 1901, Mark Twain's identity as a reformer had taken an even more definite shape as a result of two speeches made during December and of the publication of his "salutation-speech" in the *Herald*. In 6 December remarks to the St. Nicholas Society, he delivered a mock eulogy to New York City in such a bland tone that at first many members of the audience did not know how to interpret his words.[17] He ran no risk of misinterpretation, however, when he made a speech on 12 December introducing the famous youthful Boer War correspondent, Winston Churchill:

> Yes, as a missionary I've sung my songs of praise; and yet I think that England sinned when she got herself into a war in South Africa which she could have avoided, just as we have sinned in getting into a similar war in the Philippines. Mr. Churchill by his father is an Englishman; by his mother he is an American; no doubt a blend that makes the perfect man. England and America; yes, we are kin. And now that we are also kin in sin, there is nothing more to be desired. The harmony is complete, the blend is perfect—like Mr. Churchill himself, whom I now have the honor to present to you.[18]

Noteworthy about these words is that they constituted a definite violation of propriety, since Churchill was being honored at the banquet.

Finally, on 31 December, his "salutation-speech" was pub-

---

simply am here as a good citizen trying to do my duty to society as such." Reprinted in the *Troy* (New York) *Daily Times*, 24 November 1900. See 1900 Clippings file, MTP.

16. The *Troy Daily Times* editorialized, for example: "If every good citizen would make a public example of the offender against the people's rights, as Mark Twain has done, there would be less of the over-reaching that presumes upon the leniency or the laziness that refuses to prosecute such offenders" (1900 Clippings file, MTP).

17. The speech may be found in *Writings*, 28:217. The responses of the audience are referred to in a "Topics of the Time" column from *Century Magazine*. See 1900 Clippings file, MTP.

18. Quoted in Gibson, "Mark Twain and Howells," n. 1, p. 449.

lished in the *New York Herald* and reprinted seemingly everywhere:

> I bring you the stately matron named Christendom, returning bedraggled, besmirched, and dishonored from pirate-raids in Kiao-Chou, Manchuria, South Africa, and the Philippines, with her soul full of meanness, her pocket full of boodle and her mouth full of pious hypocrisies. Give her soap and a towel, but hide the looking-glass.[19]

His blending of grandiloquent and colloquial diction, his repetitive and balanced phrasing, and his careful choice of sentence structure—the long, assertive sentence with its crescendo of denunciatory phrases, then the short imperative sentence with its really memorable personification and image—all combine to create an extremely effective polemical statement. The "salutation-speech" was also a brilliant, controlled beginning of the series of impressive political writings that is the best evidence of Mark Twain's skill during the first few years of the twentieth century.

It may seem to some readers that a conflict exists between this kind of activism and the gist of the author's "Gospel," sections of which he was writing and revising during 1901 and 1902. Yet, portions that he had already written help to explain the seeming disparity between the doctrine of selfishness and his own "altruistic" activities: all acts ultimately derive from selfish motives, but there are higher forms of selfishness involving actions that satisfy not only personal needs but those of others; his actions in late 1900 are examples of this higher form. Earlier sections of the dialogue may also help to reconcile the "Gospel's" deterministic thrust and Mark Twain's own attempts to change American conditions: environment—which he defined as anything, outside of inherited characteristics, that affects individual action—molds lives; Mark Twain was trying to change the environment. Although several earlier portions of the dialogue suggest this kind of reconciliation, it is possible that the writer was not totally satisfied with the explanation. In any event, some of the material written during 1901 and 1902 speaks directly and quite cogently to these questions, a fact that suggests that he was pondering the relationship between his

19. Ibid., p. 451.

almost fully developed philosophy and his actions. Consider, for example, the several times repeated "Admonition": *"Diligently train your ideals upward and still upward toward a summit where you will find your chiefest pleasure in conduct which, while contenting you, will be sure to confer benefits upon your neighbour and the community."*[20]

In the early months of 1901, his words continued to prod upon practically any occasion when they might have some influence. Speaking to the City Club on 4 January, for example, he suggested the formation of an "Anti-Doughnut Party" (a name derived from a childhood experience in political corruption busting), the members of which would compel the dominant parties to select their best men, then would elect the best of the best through their organized, wholehearted, minority support.[21] On 20 January, in a short speech entitled "Votes for Women," he asserted, "If women had the ballot today, the state of things in this town would not exist."[22] This flow of words may strike a contemporary reader as sub-literary or, more significantly, as a waste, even a desecration, of Mark Twain's talent. At the time, however, his actions were immensely important, given the causes that he attacked or defended and given his unique position, which derived from his reputation and his polemical skill: his sense of timing, his understanding of his audience, his ability to use language for maximum argumentative effect. Moreover, although Mark Twain did not create an American *Gulliver's Travels*, he did compose his own version of "A Modest Proposal"—"To The Person Sitting In Darkness."

Much has been written about the circumstances leading to the publication of the essay in the February 1901 issue of the *North American Review*: about the immediate cause (a newspaper report concerning inordinately large reparations demanded by American missionary William Ament for atrocities committed against Christians during the Boxer Rebellion in China); about the general cause (the imperialistic actions of a few powerful countries); and about Clemens's troubled decision to publish (his letter asking the advice of Joe Twichell and the writer's almost incredulous response

20. *What Is Man?*, p. 173.
21. See *Writings*, 28:218–21.
22. Ibid., p. 224.

to his friend's caution, his discussions with Livy and Howells[23]). And much also has been said by critics about the
amount of courage that it may or may not have taken to
publish this and other political statements. With respect to
this latter issue, however, there should be room for another
opinion.

It seems to me that it took considerable courage for the
writer to publish this essay, especially since, unlike many
creative people, Clemens was very concerned about finances,
his family, and his public. For one thing, the issues were
contentious and, although he had every reason to expect
much support for his ideas, he also had reason to anticipate
many attacks. If there was strong opposition, his reputation
could be damaged (and he was very conscious of the vicissitudes of literary stock), the sales of his old books could be
harmed, as could the sales of whatever new books he might
be able to write—although at this point he was not confident
that there would be any. He was an aging man who cared
about his family and who did not want to hurt them badly
again, either monetarily or in other ways. Although Livy
supported his decision to publish, it surely is indicative of
his concern that he bothered to keep track of the responses
to the essay and to report the good ones to his wife.[24]

There is another factor: as much evidence suggests, he
often was extremely concerned about how his books were
received by his readers, not only because he worried about
sales, but also because he wanted to bring people pleasure.[25]
When he was somehow able to convince himself that individual adversaries were villains, he was able to compete against
them gleefully, with practically no compunctions. But he
would not be able to metamorphose everyone who disagreed
with his arguments in "To the Person Sitting in Darkness"
into a reprobate or a fool through the magic of his venom.
The essay, he must have known, was going to disappoint, to
hurt, to enrage many of his faithful sympathizers—his fans,
if you will. And this possibility would have bothered him,

23. For background information, see *damned human race*, p. 5.
24. See *God's Fool*, p. 24.
25. See, for example, his well-known letter about *Connecticut
Yankee* to Andrew Lang. The draft of the letter is quoted in full in
Critical Heritage, pp. 334–36.

despite the support of close friends like William Dean How-ells.

There is one final point: his ideas were going to be pub-lished in the prestigious *North American Review*. He was not speaking, he was not being interviewed, he was not writ-ing an ephemeral statement for a medium like the news-paper, in which his words would be read and discarded, the ideas either forgotten or dimly remembered. A journal arti-cle would be read and copies probably kept, with the ideas in it constantly available for perusal. What I am suggesting is that a substantive article in the *North American Review* would have seemed like more of a political commitment than anything he had done previously, although not the commit-ment that would have been demanded by a book on the subject. It must have been to a certain extent reassuring, therefore, that in the same issue as his own article was an anti-imperialist statement made by former President of the United States Benjamin Harrison and an appreciation of Mark Twain written by William Dean Howells, in which the author argued pointedly that readers should not lose sight of the old humorist because of the shadow cast by the new moralist.[26] To sum up: it took real courage for the writer to publish this essay; readers who fail to recognize this fact also fail to recognize a superior example of a quality that Samuel Clemens did not always possess.

In the essay itself, great propaganda becomes great art; the writer's consideration of the most crucial issue of the time—European and American exploitation of less power-ful countries, American principles in the twentieth century —becomes a timeless discussion about the relationship be-tween self-defined "superior" civilizations and "inferior" ones. After being published, it was referred to and editor-ialized upon by numerous newspapers in the United States and abroad, and it created a cacophony of grateful applause and wounded or derisive jeers. The essay was—to use an anachronistic but appropriate phrase—a happening.

Although "To the Person Sitting in Darkness" has been

26. See Benjamin Harrison, "Musings Upon Current Topics"; and William Dean Howells, "Mark Twain: An Inquiry." "To the Person Sitting in Darkness" appears in *North American Review* 172 (1901): 161–76.

reprinted often, a summary of its contents will be useful. The narrator first juxtaposes two Christmas statements made by New York newspapers (one praising American munificence, the other delineating ugly conditions on the sordid New York East Side), then he moves to another Christmas report describing William Ament's successful attempt to collect indemnities from the Chinese, discusses the report's anomalies, focuses on big power mistreatment of the Chinese and others who "sit in darkness," points to the growing tendency of those in darkness to distrust the "Civilization Trust," demonstrates links between the European "game" and American actions in the Philippines, offers a new plan of deception for the United States, and concludes by suggesting a few future actions: the flag should be painted black "and stars replaced by a skull and crossbones";[27] Richard Croker, the corrupt mayor of New York, should become a one-man replacement for the Civil Commission studying the Philippines.

Most noteworthy about the essay is the writer's skillful and effective use of simple ideas and techniques. The irony, for example, originates from a simple core—showing how supposedly Christian societies act in a sublimely un-Christian fashion—then extends outward to pervade practically every aspect of the essay and to suggest, finally, that nothing is as it seems, or should be. The title, as has been pointed out by Janet Smith, probably derives from Matthew 4–5.[28] What she and other commentators on the essay have failed to mention is the significance of this biblical context, which would have been chillingly clear to readers familiar with their Bible: these chapters describe Christ's temptations in the wilderness, his gathering of worthy disciples, their healing activities, the Sermon on the Mount, Christ's injunctions to love not only one's friends but also one's supposed enemies, and his message that to be a true follower a person must act humanely to those different from himself. In contrast with this context, the essay, from its beginning to its

27. See *damned human race*, p. 21. Henceforth, references to "To the Person Sitting in Darkness" will be made in the text.

28. Ibid., p. 5. Janet Smith actually refers only to Matt. 4:16: "The people which sat in the darkness saw a great light." Allison Ensor's book, *Mark Twain and the Bible* (Lexington: University of Kentucky Press, 1969), does not even refer to this essay.

end, dramatizes how un-Christ-like are the representatives of the "Blessings of Civilization Trust." The narrator's frequent references to the "Person" and to images of light and darkness help to keep the biblical context in mind so that the reader may feel the enormity of the Christian actions. The ubiquitous biblical references also create a standard against which the actions of the great powers may clearly be judged. As do the references to the American and European past: here, simplistically—but with the propagandistic power that derives from this technique—French, German, and Russian avariciousness and mendacity are opposed to British and, particularly, American generosity and honesty. The ironic fact here is that America has come to play the game the European way. The image of the deceitful game is introduced with the narrator's magnificent use of another simple technique—the pun: "heads I win, taels you lose"—and the image of the game unfairly played is repeated throughout the essay.

The scope of Mark Twain's essay is tremendous, touching as it does upon the biblical, European, and national past; speaking directly about imperialistic enormities in South Africa, China, and the Philippines; then drawing these grand and far-flung examples of the abuse of power and trust (another pun) together with an example that is more mundane, more immediate, but equally virulent: Tammany Hall. Yet, despite the seemingly casual manner in which these examples are drawn together, the links seem welded together, a fact indicative of the structural skill that the author displays throughout.

A section that may seem weak to the modern reader is the one in which the narrator suggests means of allaying the suspicions of the "Person": admit all the facts frankly, but, "for the sake of the business we must persuade him to look at the Philippine matter in another and healthier way. We must arrange his opinions for him" (p. 15). The narrator mentions the resemblance between his strategy and that of Mr. Chamberlain in South Africa, then gives a calmly stated history of the American involvement in the Philippines, proposing to rationalize it as follows:

> "They look doubtful, but in reality they are not. There have been lies; yes, but they were told in a good cause. We have been treacherous; but that was only in order that real good might

come out of apparent evil. True, we have crushed a deceived and confiding people; we have turned against the weak and the friendless who trusted us; we have stamped out a just and intelligent and well-ordered republic; we have stabbed an ally in the back and slapped the face of a guest; we have bought a shadow from an enemy that hadn't it to sell; we have robbed a trusting friend of his land and his liberty; we have invited our clean young men to shoulder a discredited musket and do bandits' work under a flag which bandits have been accustomed to fear, not to follow; we have debauched America's honor and blackened her face before the world; but each detail was for the best. We know this. The head of every state and sovereignty in Christendom and 90 per cent of every legislative body in Christendom, including our Congress and our fifty state legislatures, are members not only of the church, but also of the blessings-of-civilization trust. This world-girdling accumulation of trained morals, high principles, and justice cannot do an unright thing, an unfair thing, an ungenerous thing, an unclean thing. It knows what it is about. Give yourself no uneasiness; it is all right."

Now then, that will convince the person. You will see. It will restore the business. Also, it will elect the master of the game to the vacant place in the trinity of our national gods; and there on their high thrones the three will sit, age after age, in the people's sight, each bearing the emblem of his service: Washington, the sword of the liberator; Lincoln, the slave's broken chains; the master, the chains repaired. (pp. 19–20)

The irony is too obvious, too contrived, one might argue. Moreover, the language is too trite and melodramatic, the contrast between the narrator's cool urbanity ("There have been lies; yes, but . . . True, . . . We know this? . . . Give yourself no uneasiness; it is all right") and his often torrid diction, too jarring and unbelievable. But such passages may be defended if the reader is willing to grant that their irony—at least on one level—is intended to be patent; that the passages are supposed to jar. Mark Twain could not afford, given his primary intention of energizing American consciousness and of somehow changing American foreign policy, to be misunderstood, as he sometimes was when he permitted his hoaxes to be too subtle. The diction—which may seem from one point of view to be hackneyed—may from another point of view be called familiar and may be explained and justified as the author's attempt to signal clearly to his reader, "This is what I mean, this is what I believe, now I am being sincere." The contrast, moreover, between this type of language and the narrator's urbanity may seem comic and may be viewed as an example of Mark Twain's attempt to entertain even while he excoriates. There is an almost palpable tension throughout this essay that suggests a writer who fulfills his responsibility to amuse his vast public only through exercising a heroic self-control. That the essay remains funny even while being clearly and simply serious is one of Mark Twain's remarkable accomplishments.

There is still more to be said, however, about the contrasts that I have been discussing. For one thing, when the narrator's guise becomes that of the reasonable man attempting to explain seemingly unreasonable acts by viewing them in a sympathetic light rather than failing to admit their existence, he is doing what many statesmen did (and continue to do); but when he uses the technique of hyperbole and exaggerates the disparity between the facts and their "explanation," he clarifies the horrible absurdity that is the essence of political endeavor. One further point. It is possible that in making his modest proposal for perpetuating the misuse of power, Mark Twain is drawing a final parallel between the contemporary and the biblical: as mocking narrator he becomes Mephistopheles, tempting his Christian readers in a manner analogous to the devil's temptation of Christ in the passages from Matthew suggested by the essay's title.

The writer's achievement here can be measured more easily when its blend of message and control is compared with the powerful, but relatively undisciplined "A Stupendous Procession," which Clemens was working on during the same period but which has been only recently published in *Fables of Man*.[29] This piece, which is not written in any precise genre, begins with the narrator describing a series of grotesque floats, which depict aspects of early-twentieth-century civilization. It then moves through a quasi-dramatic interlude replete with newspaper quotes and dialogue between characters such as Washington's ghost, the Adjutant General, and a Mark Twain mouthpiece named the "Frivolous Stranger." Finally, more heterogeneous floats pass by, climaxing with "The Shade of Lincoln, towering vast and dim

29. See *F of M*, pp. 403–19. Henceforth, references to "A Stupendous Procession" will be made in the text.

toward the sky, brooding with pained aspect over the far-reaching pageant" (p. 49). "The Stupendous Procession" is an interesting experiment, combining as it does a kind of wild symbolic short play with material suggestive of political cartoons—the captions in capital letters, the alternation of horrible and comic images, the totally simplistic message:

CHRISTENDOM,

a majestic matron, in flowing robes drenched with blood. On her head, a golden crown of thorns; impaled on its spines, the bleeding heads of patriots who died for their countries—Boers, Boxers, Filipinos; in one hand a slung-shot, in the other a Bible, open at the text, "Do unto others," etc. Protruding from pocket, bottle labeled "We bring you the Blessings of Civilization." Necklace—handcuffs and a burglar's jimmy. (p. 405)

The elements do not coalesce, however; the humor does not contribute to the satire as it does in "To the Person Sitting in Darkness," but rather provides a relief from it, not so much for the reader as for the writer, who is bursting with savage indignation. The sense that the writer has pondered carefully the most effective way of presenting his material is lacking here. The images and ideas are thrown onto the page, the author seemingly persuaded by his procession principle of structure that the material really does not have to be organized, that it may be chaotically joined, in fact, like a parade. The relationships, therefore, that are so clearly drawn in "To the Person Sitting in Darkness"—between past and present, values supported and values violated, Europe and America—are sketched only murkily in "The Stupendous Procession." What one remembers most are a few pictures and the author's anger.

A common assumption concerning this essay is that it was suppressed because its contents were too incendiary.[30] A more

30. See Hill in *God's Fool*, for example: "Mark Twain's attempt to duplicate his New Year's greeting to the twentieth century was a manuscript called 'The Stupendous Procession'—consigned to the 'unpublished' file as too acetic for publication. Indeed, the pattern developing was for him to write bitterly sarcastic pieces on current topics, consign them to his growing collection of unusable manuscripts (perhaps because his 'corn-pone' instinct told him they would not meet with approval), and attend another banquet or speechmaking event" (p. 40). Of "The Stupendous Procession," Arthur Scott comments "Although Mark Twain got as far as mak-

reasonable conclusion is that it was not submitted for publication because Mark Twain knew that "To the Person Sitting in Darkness" was a much more effective satire. He was
also very sensitive about being in print too often and about
overusing a particular subject or approach; when he decided
to publish an anti-imperialistic statement, therefore, he
would have wanted it to be his best work, something that by
any standard the *North American Review* essay undoubtedly
is. Throughout this period, Mark Twain's strategies as a
social critic and reformer were usually shrewd, and his decision to publish "To the Person Sitting in Darkness" rather
than "The Stupendous Procession" is indicative of this fact.

Almost concurrently with his composition of these two
short pieces, he worked on "The Secret History of Eddypus,
the World-Empire," a fantasy supposedly narrated by a man
living in a future when a Christian Science monarchy holds
religious and political power.[31] Judging from the first few
chapters and from a section entitled "History 1000 Years
from Now," dated January 1901 and excluded from the
manuscript, it seems likely that when Mark Twain began
work on it, he considered having it serve the function that
"To the Person Sitting in Darkness" came to fulfill so effectively. The "1000 Years" fragment, for example, contains
several references to the Philippines, and "Eddypus" includes early passages such as the following:

> Civilization is an elusive and baffling term. It is not easy to
> get at the precise meaning attached to it in those far distant
> times. In America and Europe it seems to have meant benevo-
> lence, gentleness, godliness, justice, magnanimity, purity, love,
> and we gather that men considered it a duty to confer it as a
> blessing upon all lowly and harmless peoples of remote regions;
> but as soon as it was transplanted it became a blight, a pesti-
> lence, an awful terror, and they whom it was sent to benefit
> fled from its presence imploring their pagan gods with tears and
> lamentations to save them from it. The strength of such evi-
> dence as has come down to us seems to indicate that it was a
> sham at home and only laid off its disguise when abroad. (p. 327)

---

ing corrections on a typescript, the paper seems to have been too
outspoken for Livy to allow publication" (*Mark Twain at Large*,
p. 269).

31. See *F of M*, pp. 315–82. Henceforth, references to "The
Secret History of Eddypus" will be made in the text.

Even some of these references are so innocuous when compared to the published essay, however, that they prefigure the private role—as a kind of free-form, relaxing diversion—that the composing of the fantasy came to play for Clemens during the months when the grimacing public man was "stirring up the pharisees until they stop and think."[32] Later, he would ponder finishing and publishing the manuscript, but during this period it must have provided him with many necessary hours of self-indulgence away from his exhilarating, exhausting, disciplined public responsibilities—the jazz riff amidst the antimartial marches. The results of this alternatively speculative, satirical, and playful enterprise are predictable; nuggets and junk bump together, and the work must be dipped into rather than read continuously for any length of time.

Much of the writer's playfulness is directed at the solemn narrator-historian's frequently ludicrous reconstructions of the past. His attempt to determine the significance of the Statue of Liberty, which he calls "Charley's Aunt," is a case in point:

> We search the old writers in vain to find out who she was, or by what noble service she won this splendid homage, we only know that she was Charley's Aunt, and that Mark Twain paid for the statue and presented it to "the city," for he says so. There is evidence elsewhere that she had a nephew named Charles Frohman, or Fromton, and that he wrote a book, presumably upon architecture, called "The House of the Seven Gables," and another one called "The House that Jack Built," but this is all we know of him with certainty. It is the irony of history that it so often tells us much about an illustrious person's inconsequential relatives, and gives us not a word about the illustrious person himself. That stately copper colossus can have but one meaning: Charley's Aunt once filled the ancient world with her fame; and where is it now? Thus perishable are the mightiest deeds of our fleeting race! It is a pathetic thought. We struggle, we rise, we tower in the zenith a brief and gorgeous moment, with the adoring eyes of the nations upon us, then the lights go out, oblivion closes around us, our glory fades and vanishes, a few generations drift by, and naught remains but a mystery and a name—Charley's Aunt! Ah, was it worth the hard fight, the

32. See Abner Goodell to SLC, 30 December 1900, MTP.

weary days, the broken sleep, the discouragements of friends, the insults of enemies, the brief triumph at last, so bitterly won, at such desolating cost—was it worth it, poor lass? But you shall not have served in vain. There is one who loves you, one who mourns you, one who pities you and praises you; one who, ignorant of what you did, yet knows it was noble and beautiful; and banishing time and ignoring space, drops a worshiping tear upon that lost grave of yours made for you by friendly hands a thousand years ago, dear idol of the perished Great Republic, Charley's Aunt. (p. 335)

There is, I think, beneath the burlesque, a point struggling to emerge about the way in which American ideals are being disguised and lost. Unfortunately, this passage is typical of "Eddypus" as a whole in that the meaning evaporates as the writer indulges himself to the limits of his own tolerance and probably beyond that of his readers. Mark Twain's imagination is flying free—to crash almost as often as it soars.

One of the manuscript's most interesting sections appears in the first two chapters of book 2 when the narrator discusses his major clandestine historical source: Mark Twain's "Father of History." Speaking of Twain, the narrator refers both to his "Gospel of Self," whose publication has incensed the Christian Science church, and to his "Old Comrades," which had been published five hundred years after Twain's death, because only then could the book's language be read without its honesty threatening individuals or their descendants. Neither the "Gospel" nor the autobiography had been published by 1901, of course, but references to these philosophical and "historical" works suggest how often Clemens was thinking about them and their possible effect upon his present and posthumous reputation, even while he publicly focused on politics. Later, the narrator analyzes the character of this legendary father—in passing he refers to his numerous bastard children, particularly Tom Sawyer and Huckleberry Finn—concluding on the basis of a phrenological report that Mark Twain lacked a sense of humor and firmness. The phrenologist asserts, "This is the low-downest poltroon I've ever struck" (p. 351). Included among this mixture of biographical fatuousness, falsity, and half-truths is a suggestion of the writer's probable primary aim during this section: to savor the thought that, despite the hardening of his image for his public during these months, his real self was still inaccessible.

After this section of myopic biography, the narrator begins, as a preparation for his analysis of the twentieth century, a zany, sometimes almost awestruck description of the wondrous nineteenth. This description halts in the middle of anecdotes about science and scientists. At this point it seems as if the writer put the manuscript aside because it had done, physically and psychologically, all that he really had wanted it to do during this period, and because he had become tired of it, as has the reader. Moreover, he still may have been unprepared to venture his detailed predictions concerning the twentieth century because he was uncertain as to what tone they would assume, despite his early talk of democracy's demise and the rise of Christian Science. Mark Twain as Jeremiah never could be wholly comfortable, particularly when he was having a good time.

Prior to leaving with his family for a summer in the Adirondacks, Clemens completed this particular period as a reformer with his publication in the *North American Review* of "To My Missionary Critics," a defense of his attacks on William Ament. The essay, which resembles a lawyer's brief, is notable for its reasonable tone, the variety of its arguments, its attempt to blame the Missionary Board rather than individual missionaries, and the manner in which it turns into a strength what had been an ostensible weakness in his earlier criticisms of missionaries: the missionaries did not, as he had charged, demand indemnities thirteen times in excess of damages, only one-and-one-third times:

What was the "one third extra?" Money due? No. Was it a theft, then? Putting aside the "one third extra," what was the *remainder* of the exacted indemnity, if collected from persons not *known* to owe it, and without Christian and civilized forms of procedure? Was *it* theft, was it robbery? In America it would be that; in Christian Europe it would be that. I have great confidence in Dr. Smith's judgment concerning this detail, and he calls it "theft and extortion"—even in China; for he was talking about the "thirteen times" at the time that he gave it that strong name. It is his idea that, when you make guilty and innocent villages pay the appraised damages, and then make them pay thirteen times that, besides, the *thirteen* stand for "theft and extortion."

Then what does *one third* extra stand for? Will he give that one third a name? Is it Modified Theft and Extortion? Is that it? The girl who was rebuked for having borne an illegitimate child excused herself by saying, "But it is such a *little* one."[33]

"To My Missionary Critics" is in many ways an extremely clever, effective performance; yet what is most interesting about it is that it was brought into being because many readers seized upon an issue of relatively peripheral importance in "To the Person Sitting in Darkness" and twisted it into the essay's most crucial dimension. As the writer had hoped, the initial reviews of "Darkness" had focused upon its anti-imperialistic content and its criticism of American policy in the Philippines.[34] But then the missionaries and their sympathizers had grasped their cudgels; the writer had been attacked in print; he had replied briefly, implying that he had little desire to speak further; the press had bounced the issue about; and Mark Twain had felt compelled to reply at some length.[35] As a result, the major purpose for which a brilliant essay clearly had been written began to be forgotten. The focus blurred, and Mark Twain became for many readers the man who was mean to missionaries.[36] "To My Missionary Critics" is an effective defense, and he seems to have enjoyed writing it; yet, the essay is not particularly relevant to the issues with which, only a short time before, he had identified himself. Perhaps by this time he was tired of carrying American foreign policy on his verbal back and welcomed this other issue; perhaps he was mentally preparing to retreat to the wilds of New York state after an incredibly active fall

33. *Writings*, 29:284–85.

34. Almost all of the many reviews contained in the 1901 Clippings file of the Mark Twain Papers stress this aspect of the essay.

35. For a brief history of this controversy, see Foner, *Mark Twain: Social Critic*, pp. 280–81.

36. Judging from some of the references that I have seen made to "To the Person Sitting in Darkness," I conclude that many modern critics also think of the essay as being about missionaries. For example, Lewis Gaston Leary writes, "He hardly ever attacked anyone except patsies, like Boss Tweed and Jay Gould and missionaries, whom it was fashionable to attack" ("The Bankruptcy of Mark Twain," p. 85).

and winter, and he could see in this issue an opportunity to drop his anti-imperialist crusading lance as a preliminary to again becoming a writer of fiction. It is significant that a May notebook entry referred to a potential story in which a natural coward was doomed to a lifetime of heroism in order to live up to the example set by one brave act.[37]

37. See Notebook 34, TS, p. 10, MTP. It is possible that, prior to leaving for the Adirondacks, he wrote even more anti-imperialistic material, because, as Arthur Scott points out in *Mark Twain at Large* (p. 268), there still exists significant unpublished work about imperialism and missionaries. I assume that at least some of this will be published in the volume of Mark Twain's social and political writings that Louis Budd is editing for the Mark Twain Papers.

8

An Indifference to Fiction
June 1901 to May 1902

Although Clemens's lovely, secluded setting during the late spring and summer of 1901 was conducive to writing, and although in the fall he mentioned having written a great deal while at Saranac Lake, it is difficult to say exactly what literary projects he devoted himself to. We do know that he worked on "A Double-Barreled Detective Story," which he finished in early September, and on a short essay entitled "The United States of Lyncherdom," originally planned as the introduction to a subscription book on the history of lynching in the United States.[1] It is quite possible, also, that during the late spring he wrote the first two chapters of "No. 44, The Mysterious Stranger," introducing the Austrian fifteenth-century setting and the environment of the print shop, but not yet bringing young Satan onto the scene.[2] New in the second chapter are the characters and the print-shop setting. The first chapter, on the other hand, is taken from "The Chronicle of Young Satan," only slightly revised. Several names are changed and the time of the story is now 1490, rather than 1702. Mark Twain probably made the temporal change in order to render plausible the isolation and secrecy of the print shop—qualities necessitated by the Church's opposition to "the cheapening of books and the indiscriminate

1. See SLC to Joseph Twichell, 8 September 1901, TS, MTP. For abbreviations used in the footnotes, see "Short References," pp. ix–x.

2. A notebook entry made on 13 May, while he was still in New York, suggests that he was at least considering another Satan manuscript: "Put into *this* Satan's mouth all that was to have been put into the other Satan's." Notebook 34, TS, p. 10, MTP. In *MTLS*, John Tuckey explains why it is impossible to date these two chapters accurately, other than to say that "the story probably could not have gone beyond these chapters until after November 1902" (see pp. 56–57).

dissemination of knowledge," as the narrator explains. Significant about the situation is that working with a small group of characters and an isolated environment should have helped the author to write a fairly tight, unified story whose episodes could be observed easily by a first-person narrator.

Mark Twain probably began the fantasy anticipating that its setting, so suggestive of his own youth, would provide a pleasant contrast to the hectic, adult world he had inhabited during the previous months. Soon after the manuscript was begun, however, it seems to have been shelved because he was unable to devise a plot that would allow him to use material from "The Chronicle of Young Satan," something that, according to a notebook entry, he was hoping to do.[3] Perhaps one reason he was unable to extend "No. 44" by relying upon this material and was unwilling to continue the original young Satan manuscript was related to his involvement in reform activities. As a reformer, Mark Twain had been able to openly express his ideas about, and vent his spleen upon, politics and society in general; even his attacks upon Christian institutions and the behavior of individual Christians had been legitimized by his reform purposes and—to a certain extent—by the genre and medium in which these attacks took place. It is therefore possible that, since his interest in these topics had been at least temporarily sated, he no longer felt a need to write a manuscript like the last section of "The Chronicle of Young Satan." Moreover, at the point where he had stopped working on "Chronicle," the plot had disappeared, a fact suggesting that the writer had lost control of, and interest in, his narrative. It is therefore not surprising that in trying to resuscitate his young Satan idea he grasped for a new plot; neither is it remarkable that, upon recognizing his need to fill out the plot by adapting to it episodes and ideas from "Chronicle," he lost his inspiration.

Some time during the summer he evidently returned to his George Harrison narrative, which he had put aside in late 1899 after the protagonist had inadvertently killed Jake Bleeker, Squire Fairfax had been jailed for the crime, and Harrison's father had moved into madness and toward death. Upon coming back to the story, Mark Twain worked at it sporadically both at Saranac Lake in the summer and at

3. Notebook 34, TS, p. 10, MTP.

Riverside in the fall and winter, by which time he had created enough new characters and subplots to push "Which Was It?" well beyond novella length;[4] yet it was still too short and too untidy for publication as a novel.

The new manuscript begins with the elder Mr. Harrison's death and George's inheritance of $40,000 in cash and a valuable estate from an uncle in Memphis. With the introduction of this latter complication, the story explodes. Sol (Hamfat) Bailey, a new character modeled on Orion Clemens, guesses that the uncle's legitimate heir is a still-to-be-discovered wife and asks feckless Allan Osgood for help in locating the woman. When they reach Memphis, they learn of a likely prospect—a Mrs. Milliken—and invite two more men to help them, both of whom are dishonest and yearn to gain the estate themselves. Another Indiantown resident, Templeton Gunning, is also involved in the search, his mother actually being the object of it (although she is not the heir; there is none). Templeton's mother suffers from the harassment of a revengeful black man, Jasper (or Pomp, as he is variously named), because of his knowledge of her criminal past and her former cruelty to him. When the writer pauses again, Templeton and Allan are planning to search for "Mrs. Milliken," Templeton knowing that the woman is his mother; while the Memphis men are seeking another suspect. By this point, Hamfat Bailey is in the employ of George Harrison, is hoping to prevent the "widow" from securing the wealth, and is oblivious to his partner's treachery.

As the resumé should suggest, the plot of this latest manuscript is tedious, convoluted, and murky, as Mark Twain invents new characters, settings, and subplots in order to shove his story toward completion. The summary also should suggest that as the manuscript pages proliferate, George Harrison and his ironic situation—he is the "defender" of Squire Fairfax, the man accused of murdering Jake Bleeker, while being the real murderer himself—tend to be hidden among the debris. And although the new material is relevant to the main theme—each new subplot underlines the point about the capacity of all people for criminal behavior—it is never really *felt* to be relevant. The reader is reminded of George

4. See the information on the composition of the manuscript in *WWD?*, p. 22.

Harrison because Hamfat Bailey occasionally visits him, but George is no longer the center of the book, which really has no center. As a result the plot seems contrived and almost incoherent.

There are other problems as well, one of which is linked to Mark Twain's decision (probably of this time) to tack the much-used ("Which Was the Dream?" and "The Great Dark") dream frame onto the story:[5] Mrs. Harrison refers to her daughter's birthday party and to her husband nodding over the autobiography he is writing for the girls; a fire breaks out killing all the Harrison family except George and his son Tom; the twin brother of Allan Osgood is also incinerated. Then, Harrison speaks again fifteen years later and the actual plot begins. When the events in the frame are combined with subsequent happenings, the plot seems almost ludicrously bloody. Still another difficulty emerges when the writer decides to have his narrator distance himself from his terrible history by telling it in the third person. This technique (analogous to that of Henry Adams in his *Education*) makes good psychological sense and is also practical; if Mark Twain had made Harrison into a first-person narrator he would have had to revise many pages from the 1899 manuscript written in the third person. Unfortunately, having made this decision, he seems to have forgotten or been indifferent to the fact that the story was Harrison's, not that of a ubiquitous God. Thus, when Harrison begins to describe events that he could not possibly have observed, something he does often, the reader should condemn the author for sloppy technique, not indulge him the way one does Herman Melville when he treats Ishmael with similar recklessness in *Moby Dick*. Mark Twain's disregard of this rudimentary narrative principle is interesting because he was usually careful about such things.

Mark Twain also decided to have Hamfat Bailey, the "Idiot Philosopher," voice material from the writer's "Gospel."[6] This is peculiar because, emanating from someone consistently portrayed as a frivolous, unstable, ideological dilet-

5. For information about the addition of the frame, see ibid., p. 22.

6. Material on pp. 307, 308 of *Which Was the Dream?* is lifted almost verbatim from the "Gospel."

tante, the ideas lack the force that they would have possessed
had they been voiced by a more reliable character. In this
way, the writer undercuts himself even as he presents ideas
important to him. Of course, there is no one else in the story
who could introduce such ideas any more compellingly; yet,
it is significant that Mark Twain did not invent a spokesman, although he invented several other characters in order
to grind out more pages. As a result of these several problems,
this section of "Which was Which?" is lamentably weak,
despite several good scenes (one in an ice-cream parlor, for
example).[7]

There is an important conclusion to be drawn, however,
from a consideration of this fictional hodgepodge: one of the
reasons Mark Twain at this point could not write good,
long fiction was that—perhaps only subconsciously—he did
not want to write it, at least not for any length of time. For
one thing, he no longer appeared to be interested in telling
a lengthy story for its own sake. For another, he seemed impatient with the devices a novelist has to use to justify the introduction of his ideas. Perhaps still remembering the joy
of his polemical involvement and by now no longer plagued
by the fatigue, he wished to speak with relative directness
about his other pet notions. As an aging man who knew that
few years remained in which he would be taken seriously, he
wanted to be heard. He felt more comfortable writing short
fiction than he did writing novels because forms such as the
fable and the moral exemplum allowed him to express his
ideas more freely.

There was another problem with writing novels. Mark
Twain could no longer sustain enough interest in character
per se to carry a novel to conclusion; neither could he
sustain an interest in characters who were only mouthpieces
for his ideas or only relevant to his themes beyond the time
it took him to compose a short story. For these reasons, it
probably would have been impossible for Mark Twain to
have written a novel of ideas—a utopian novel, for example.
One final point. Since we know that both before and after
his return to America he was priming himself to write his

7. Actually, we cannot be certain what title—"Which Was
Which?" or "Which Was It?"—Mark Twain was using at this time.
Nor, I think, does it matter.

autobiography, perhaps the anticipation of this work and also the occasional involvement with it helped to block the flow of long fiction, since he believed that in the autobiography he would be able to tell the whole truth about characters without having to wear the novel's by now irritating disguises. Like practically anything relating to the man, the impatience with long fiction was not consistent, but it seems to have been a pervasive problem in the summer of 1901, after the preaching of the previous months and before the impending New York election in the fall. The impatience, moreover, was a force which in these last years always had to be confronted.

Related to this general problem is the novella "A Double-Barreled Detective Story," which he was able to finish in September and publish.[8] The narrative starts as if to become a somber, even morbid tale about human evil: a young Southern aristocratic belle marries beneath her station; her proud husband takes revenge upon her family's contumely by mistreating her, his cruelty climaxing when he ties her to a tree at midnight, lets his bloodhounds strip her, and leaves her for the eyes of passing strangers to find and humiliate. Since Mark Twain wrote this beginning after researching a book about lynching in the United States, he may have debated having his story move toward a lynch scene. Instead, bizarre convolutions take place in the plot: time passes, the setting changes, a son (Archy) with a bloodhound's sense of smell is born to the woman, he is trained to hate his father and is deployed to search for him. He begins, seems to find his father, the man escapes, then Archy discovers he has been after the wrong man. The search—now with the purpose of telling the man he has been accused wrongly—circles the globe as more time passes; the boy writes to his mother from a California mining community. Then the letters cease, and an omniscient narrator tells of a cruel man living with a boy, Fetlock Jones, who secretly hates the man and plans revenge. The boy's uncle, Sherlock Holmes, visits the town amidst much adulation, the boy murders his tormentor, Holmes accuses the wrong person, Archy deduces the right one, Fet-

8. The source I am using is *Writings*, 23:285–358. Henceforth, references to "A Double-Barreled Detective Story" will be made in the text.

lock is jailed, a brave sheriff prevents a lynching. At this point, Archy finishes the story with a letter to his mother: the man whom Archy had persecuted has wandered into town, half-mad; Archy has prepared to rehabilitate him; and Fetlock has escaped jail, to the relief of all. End of story.

From one point of view, "A Double-Barreled Detective Story" is execrable fiction, certainly one of the worst tales that the writer ever foisted upon his public. But from another it can be seen as a conscious burlesque, not just of Sherlock Holmes fiction, which is the obvious target of the California section, but also of other types of formula fiction, of reader response to such fiction, even of Mark Twain's own temptation to depend too heavily upon this kind of writing in order to stretch short ideas into long books.[9]

Although it is difficult to decide totally about the writer's intentions, there is enough evidence scattered throughout the story to render these conclusions plausible. One of the techniques often employed in literary burlesque is to use elements typical of the target, but to exaggerate them so that the quality of the ludicrous latent in them becomes clear. Another technique is to use these elements in an unusual context and thereby to provoke laughter. Mark Twain throughout his career employed both these techniques frequently and usually in such a way as to make his intentions obvious. But here is an important point: if a writer decides to burlesque through exaggeration, the amount of exaggeration is crucial; if the disparity between the original and the burlesque itself is not great, then it is sometimes almost impossible to decide whether the writer wishes to be taken seriously or to be laughed at.[10] The satiric intention of the

9. In his *Mark Twain and John Bull: The British Connection*, Howard Baetzhold argues that almost all of "A Double-Barreled Detective Story" is a more or less consistent burlesque of Arthur Conan Doyle's *A Study in Scarlet*. Baetzhold concludes, however, that early melodramatic elements "detract from its otherwise superb burlesque" (pp. 299–304). Of this beginning section, DeLancey Ferguson writes, "The story commenced as a grim revenger's tragedy, in which the parody has no lawful place; even the tragedy contained, in the bloodhound scent which was Archy's birthmark, an element peculiarly close to unintentional burlesque" (*Mark Twain: Man and Legend*, p. 286).

10. Mark Twain's burlesque review of English responses to *The*

Sherlock Holmes section of this story is obvious: it ridicules the hero's supposed expertise and the mob's adulation of him. What is more complex, however, is the manner in which the reader's response to the burlesque is manipulated; we are invited to laugh at certain elements of detective fiction, but simultaneously to derive pleasure from observing clever ratiocination, particularly since the deducing is being done by the underdog, Archy. Yet the detective catches Fetlock Jones, a boy whom we do not want to be caught, although we may not realize this until after the capture has been made. Ironically, at this point we want him to avoid punishment.

Our response to this treatment of the deduction and capture suggests something that Edgar Allan Poe stories ("The Cask of Amontillado," for example) sometimes convey: the pleasure we derive from certain types of activities is amoral, a fact that the hero/villain dichotomy of much detective fiction tends to disguise. Mark Twain underlines this point about the reader's potential for amorality in the story's casual ending: a murderer escapes, and his escape is approved by both the townspeople and the readers. Conventional melodramatic fiction tends to reinforce simplistic moral codes; the writer's burlesque of this type of fiction, on the other hand, subtly supports the conclusions of his "Gospel."

Thus far only the mining-camp section of the story has been discussed; what of the first barrel of "The Double-Barreled Detective Story"? Here, also, abundant evidence suggests that the writer was not writing melodrama, but burlesquing it and its readers' willingness to accept its conventions uncritically. The opening is shocking not only because of the husband's gross mistreatment of his wife, but also because the actions are surprising. The writer's attempt to render plausible this relationship is perfunctory, perhaps merely because of carelessness, more probably because he wants to suggest that only cursory treatment is required: to the devourers of this type of popular fiction, shock and surprise are paramount, not plausibility. Critical readers might also wonder whether the narrator's reference to the young

---

Innocents Abroad is only one example of several instances throughout his career when his ironic tone was overlooked. See *Critical Heritage*, p. 39.

girl's pride is sufficient explanation for her ability to endure silently, "all the miseries that the diligent and inventive mind of the husband could contrive" (p. 286).

In the following passage, some phrases could have been copied almost directly from romantic serials: "At the end of the three months he said, with a dark significance in his manner, 'I have tried all things but one'—and waited for her reply. 'Try that,' she said, and curled her lip in mockery" (p. 287). So many aspects of this passage—the formula phrases, the picturesque stances assumed by the protagonists, the titillatingly vague suggestiveness of the promised act—are almost so archetypically melodramatic that it is hard not to conclude that Mark Twain is writing burlesque. More evidence leads to the same conclusion: the incident with the bloodhounds is outré even by the standards of melodrama; the girl decides to have the man's child although there is no previous reference to any sexual relations between her and her husband. It is almost as if she wills it; the news that the child is born with the sense of smell of a bloodhound suggests for a thrilling moment that the girl has been raped by bloodhounds. The expository scene in which the mother concludes that her boy has the scent of a bloodhound is so implausible that it must be burlesque: the boy tells his mother of smelling the postman's scent on the sidewalk; she exclaims, "God has appointed the way!" (p. 290), her eyes burn with a "fierce light," her breath comes "short," her face is lit "with a fell light . . . with vague fires of hell" (p. 291), she informs Archy of his birthright and prepares to take her revenge. In view of his peculiar gift, Archy's naive query, "Mamma, am I different from other children?" (p. 289), is one of the funniest lines that Mark Twain ever wrote.

There follows the revenge motif, plot surprises such as the revelation that the wrong man has been followed and tortured, clues obtained through handwriting, a whirlwind world trip reported on and dispensed with in a paragraph. The writer seems to be piling on his incidents so quickly and with such a minimum of explanation as to almost demand that the reader either condemn the cavalier substitution of variety for plausibility—a substitution that Mark Twain was himself tempted to make in his nonburlesque fiction—or laugh at it. Moreover, the reader is being asked to question stereotypes such as the following:

> Then she told him her bitter story, in all its naked atrocious-
> ness. For a while the boy was paralyzed; then he said:
> "I understand. We are Southerners; and by our custom and
> nature there is but one atonement. I will search him out and
> kill him."
> "Kill him? No! Death is release, emancipation; death is a
> favor. Do I owe him favors? You must not hurt a hair of his
> head."
> The boy was lost in thought awhile; then he said:
> "You are all the world to me, and your desire is my law and
> my pleasure. Tell me what to do and I will do it."
> The mother's eyes beamed with satisfaction, and she said:
> "You will go and find him. I have known his hiding-place for
> eleven years; it cost me five years and more of inquiry, and much
> money, to locate it. He is a quartz-miner in Colorado, and well-
> to-do. He lives in Denver. His name is Jacob Fuller. There—it
> is the first time I have spoken it since that unforgettable night.
> Think! That name could have been yours if I had not saved you
> that shame and furnished you a cleaner one. You will drive him
> from that place; you will hunt him down and drive him again;
> and yet again, and again, and again, persistently, relentlessly,
> poisoning his life, filling it with mysterious terrors." (p. 293)

Here, the laugh is on those willing to suspend their disbelief about any action as long as it is performed by a Southerner.

The most obvious evidence of the burlesque intent is the description that opens the California half of the story:

> It was a crisp and spicy morning in early October. The lilacs
> and laburnums, lit with the glory-fires of autumn, hung burning
> and flashing in the upper air, a fairy bridge provided by kind
> Nature for the wingless wild things that have their homes in the
> tree-tops and would visit together; the larch and the pome-
> granate flung their purple and yellow flames in brilliant broad
> splashes along the slanting sweep of the woodland; the sensuous
> fragrance of innumerable deciduous flowers rose upon the swoon-
> ing atmosphere; far in the empty sky a solitary esophagus slept
> upon motionless wing; everywhere brooded stillness, serenity,
> and the peace of God. (p. 304)

When the tale was published in book form, Mark Twain in-
terrupted the narration in order to include letters from

readers of the magazine version who were puzzled by references to the "solitary esophagus." In so doing, he was pointing not only to the burlesque element of this description, but
surely also to the possibility that other sections of the story
were written with analogus intent. And, as I have shown,
when evidence of this intent is looked for, it is easy to find.

Mark Twain wrote more than fiction during the Saranac
Lake sojourn. Much of his work derived from his dormant
but still vital reforming impulse, and from his desire to
profit from this impulse, the results being his labors on the
book about the history of lynching in the United States and
the essay "The United States of Lyncherdom." Several critics
have pointed out that Clemens decided to neither proceed
with the project nor publish the essay because he feared that
these works might have a harmful influence on the Southern
market for his books; and these critics have concluded, quite
properly, that there were limits to the writer's reformism.[11]

Other aspects of the episode need to be stressed, however,
in particular that Clemens was very troubled by his decision
and that it was reached with difficulty.[12] A section relating
to his "Gospel" entitled "Moral Courage" and quite possibly written around this time seems to have been influenced
by his reflections on the quandary. The gist of the dialogue
is that only a very few unusual people possess moral courage
at all times and that most people are capable of heroism only
in certain, inexplicable areas and situations.[13] It should also
be emphasized that his concern for sales was not the only
reason he decided against publication. He asserted on several occasions, for example, that to make an issue of certain

11. See, for example, the discussion of this episode in *Mr. Clemens and Mark Twain*, pp. 364–65.

12. Two letters to Frank Bliss convey Clemens's reluctance to
relinquish the project, even while he is deciding that he should do
so, because of the possible effect on book sales in the South. On 29
August 1901 he asserted that someone should write the book immediately and complained about his inability to think of the right
man (TS, MTP). Then, on 8 September, he mentioned still being
haunted by the lynching book and speculated that perhaps George
Kennan could be persuaded to collaborate with him on the project
(MTP).

13. *What Is Man?*, pp. 495–99.

kinds of spectacular acts was often a means of increasing rather than of diminishing their incidence.[14] Moreover, an essay entitled "The Dervish and the Offensive Stranger" written around this period makes the point that, not only is it difficult to predict the results of any action, but frequently good and bad results tend to negate each other.[15]

Still another facet of Mark Twain's attitude toward reform issues can be observed in "The United States of Lyncherdom": his desire to synthesize whenever possible. Here, he suggests seriously that missionaries should be moved from foreign lands to American cities where their good qualities —particularly their courage and ability to endure abuse— could be used to prevent atrocities like lynchings.[16] When Mark Twain attacked publicly, or at least was contemplating publication, he usually tried to suggest ways of eradicating the evils that he described or of using forces that were harmful in one environment for salutary effect in another. It is true that in private his vitriol sometimes spewed forth for unfair or inappropriate reasons—pettiness, sheer bellicosity, the urge to scratch viciously where it itched—but it is also true that as a public man during these years he was almost always responsible, positive, and fair.

Upon settling in Riverdale, New York, in the fall of 1901, Clemens immediately involved himself with the Society of Acorns, a group dedicated to defeating the Tammany Hall ticket in the impending elections. The victory of their cause was significantly assisted by Mark Twain's vigorous contributions: his marching in parades; his essay entitled "Edmund Burke on Croker and Tammany," which he delivered as a speech and allowed to be distributed as a pamphlet when he discovered that he could not publish it in the *North American Review* before the elections.[17] The essay is made up

14. See, for example, his comments in his 10 September 1901 letter to Joe Twichell (TS, MTP).

15. See "The Dervish and the Offensive Stranger" in Frederick Anderson, ed., *A Pen Warmed-up in Hell*, pp. 170–73.

16. See Anderson, ed., *A Pen Warmed-up in Hell*, pp. 157–59.

17. An account of Mark Twain's election activities may be found in *God's Fool*, p. 39. Louis Budd, who is editing the Mark Twain Papers volume of the political writings, was kind enough to inform me of another of the humorist's anti-Tammany actions, not mentioned in *God's Fool*. Information about this activity is given in an

primarily of Edmund Burke's arguments supporting the impeachment of Warren Hastings and is related directly to the supposed crimes of Richard Croker. Here, the writer's favorite technique of employing the past to illuminate the present is used with a devastating directness, simplicity, and seriousness.[18] From reading the essay, one gains the impression that Mark Twain did not dare to risk irony or humor—any technique, in fact, that might render in the slightest way oblique a message that had to be stentorian and clear. Clemens understandably was elated at the Tammany defeat and proud of his own contributions, although concurrent with his effusions about the coming of the dawn in New York City are several disturbed and skeptical notebook entries:

> The entire press, the entire pulpit, the women's organizations—every single moral influence existent in this vast city and in the nation, was arrayed against this criminal and infamous government, in the fight, yet the victory was won by a margin so small that it may rightly be called contemptible. [It is a tremendous arraignment of the character of the people of New York.] * It seems to be proof that of every two men in New York the bread and butter of one was in the grip of Tammany. It is not believable nor conceivable that any entirely free man voted for any person on that ticket except its can. for Mayor.[19] (Mark Twain's brackets)

The election had been won, however; and as a result he was now free to pursue other interests: work on "Which Was It?," negotiations over dramatic rights to several of his novels, his own dramatization of "The Death Disk"—a Mark Twain short story published in the December 1901

---

31 October 1901 article in the *New York Tribune* (p. 31) entitled "Twain Would Be A Bill Poster." According to the article, the humorist had appeared at the headquarters of the Citizens Union on 30 October and volunteered to paint over Tammany propaganda that was hanging on the boards along the route of the rapid-transit tunnel. He was prevented from participating only because the man on duty at the Union couldn't find any paste.

18. A text of the essay may be found in the 19 October 1901 edition of *Harper's Weekly*.

19. See Notebook 34, TS, p. 14, MTP. Quoted in *God's Fool*, p. 39. A good example of Clemens's pride in his political accomplishments may be found in Notebook 34, p. 12.

Harper's—attempts to sell the Hartford house, investments (particularly in Plasmon), efforts to persuade Ida Tarbell that in writing her muckraking history of Standard Oil she should not be one-sided, banquets, other reform ideas.[20] Clemens still was very much concerned about American foreign affairs, but during late 1901 and 1902 he decided to attack his multifarious other interests.

Judging from his letter to Thomas Bailey Aldrich on 30 December he had never been more happy or alive:

> I am having a noble good time—the best I have ever had. All my days are my own—all of them: & I spend them in my study. It comes of wisdom; of establishing a rational rule & then sticking to it: to take no engagement outside the city, & not more than 2 per month *in* it. They can't improve on this happiness in heaven.[21]

One reason for his sense of well-being was that his family was temporarily in good health. Although in January, Jean's condition again deteriorated, this is something that he was getting reconciled to; certainly neither his nonliterary nor his literary activity seems to have been affected much. Notebook entries suggest that by early January he was thinking about both his autobiography and a new Huckleberry Finn/Tom Sawyer book in which the two would return to St. Petersburg after an absence of fifty years.[22] In late January and February his reading of Jonathan Edwards's *Freedom of the Will* inspired him to write some more pages for his "Gospel" and a still unpublished dialogue, "If I Could Be There."[23] As well, in mid-January he started working

20. A further example of his reformism is a "letter" to Jules Hart assaulting the Infants' Home the city of New York ran on Blackwell's Island, which had, according to Hart, a mortality rate of 90 percent; Mark Twain decided not to push the issue when Hart declined to publish the "letter." See *God's Fool*, pp. 39–40. A copy of this letter may be found in Anderson, ed., *A Pen Warmed-up in Hell*, pp. 162–63.

21. SLC to Thomas Bailey Aldrich, 30 December 1901, MTP.

22. See, for example, Notebook 35, TS, pp. 1a (3 January) and 2 (5, 7 January), MTP.

23. The dialogue, which trails off after thirteen manuscript pages (DV 10, MTP), concerns a stranger's request that the Lord punish a man for a sin committed eleven million years ago. The Lord is indifferent to the request because of man's insignificance, his chief function being to provide food for microbes.

again on the Eddypus manuscript he had begun the previous year, writing to Frederick Duneka on 16 February that it was "a mine of learning, well it *is*—a little bit distorted, a trifle out of focus, recognizably drunk." [24] Such a manuscript would have been a congenial project for a writer temporarily indifferent to the proprieties of conventional fiction.

When he had set aside "The Secret History of Eddypus" in 1901, he had been immersed in the burlesque history of science during the nineteenth century; when he begins again, the manuscript focuses for several pages on a distorted history of evolutionary theory in which Martin Luther becomes the father of geology and the narrator's pedanticism a source of comedy; then there begins a discussion of Herbert Spencer's ideas in which the narrator becomes the author's spokesman. The shifts in narrative voice and function are not prepared for, but the writer does not seem to care. The consideration of Spencer culminates with a concept that was also one of the principles in Mark Twain's "Gospel"—the snowballing effects that can be caused by minute changes in circumstances. In the next chapter, the narrator begins to explain that one of the social consequences of scientific discoveries is the resumed importance of the institution of slavery. The analysis halts with the following paragraph:

> Defeated, not by thought-out plan and purpose, but by natural and logical and blind Evolution, each stage a circumstance whose part in a vast revolution was unforeseen and unpremeditated, the linked march a progress which no man planned nor was able to plan, the resulting compact and connected achievement the work of the miracle-accomplishing unintelligent forces that lay hidden from sight in the little drops that made up that irresistible tidal-wave of accumulated accidents. (p. 382)

The future, says the narrator, is impossible to predict. Given Mark Twain's frequent although inconsistent belief in this idea, it is understandable that he was unable to complete the manuscript, since its next section would have concerned the twentieth century.

Before we leave this short consideration of "Eddypus," two other aspects of it should be mentioned. First, it should

24. Quoted in *F of M*, p. 379. Henceforth, references to "The Secret History of Eddypus" are to this volume and will be made in the text.

be observed that, although its tone is occasionally bleak, it is far more frequently playful and wondering, even when the topic is blind force:

> The vast discoveries which have been listed above created an intellectual upheaval in the world such as had never been experienced in it before from the beginning of time, nor indeed anything even remotely resembling it. The effects resulting were wholly new. Men's minds were free, now; the chains of thought lay broken; for the first time in the history of the race, men were free to think their own thoughts instead of other people's, and utter their conclusions without peril to body or estate. This marked an epoch and a revolution; a revolution which was the first of its kind, a revolution which emancipated the mind and the soul.
>
> It opened the gates and threw wide the road to a gigantic material revolution—also the first of its kind. The factors of it followed upon each other's heels with bewildering energy and swiftness, each a surprise and a marvel, and each in its turn breeding other surprises, other marvels, by the natural law of Evolution, automatically directed and executed by the forces inherent in massed circumstances. (p. 380)

It also should be observed how the free-associational structure of the fantasy seems to prefigure the method of the autobiography. Clemens was not consciously to discover this method for almost two years; yet experiments like "The Secret History of Eddypus" were moving him closer to it.

Mark Twain's next significant public political statement, the last important one that he was to make until 1905, was his "A Defence of General Funston," begun in late February and published in the May issue of the *North American Review*.[25] Funston was the brigadier general of the American volunteers who, in the fall of 1901, had captured the Philippine rebel leader, Emilio Aguinaldo, as well as the hearts of many Americans because of his derring-do. Mark Twain's unpublished review of a book about Aguinaldo demonstrates his admiration for the rebel;[26] all of the writer's references to Funston, on the other hand, show how much he

25. The slightly abridged version of this essay that is referred to in this chapter may be found in *damned human race*, pp. 82–94. Henceforth, references to "A Defence of General Funston" will be made in the text.

26. See Paine 89 aa, MTP.

despised him, the public response to him, and the kind of mindless patriotism he seemed to represent. Mark Twain's "defence," rather than being just a tired example of the writer ineffectually applying his deterministic principles to politics, as some critics believe, is in many ways a skillful, courageous performance.[27] Modern readers tend to forget that in the essay Mark Twain was neither pummeling a dead horse nor taking a firm stand on behalf of motherhood. The general was a hero to many people in the United States, as the enthusiastic response to his March speech to New York's Lotus Club emphasized again; so, in trying to reveal the tawdry aspects of Funston's character, Mark Twain was attempting something that many Americans would and did resent.[28]

Most impressive about this essay is the narrator's success in creating a feeling of intimacy between himself and his reader—a sense of shared values and attitudes—so that even while he is revealing unpleasant truths, he is operating from a position of strength. He does this in several ways. His use of dates is one example: as I start to write it is 22 February; now it is 14 April, and I'm back from a little holiday; now it is 16 April, and I've been reading the newspapers. The scrawled, seemingly carelessly written 16 April postscript conveys clearly the impression that the narrator subtly has been trying to create throughout: that he is writing a "letter to a close and understanding friend."[29]

The reader is taken almost into the writer's home, observing him as he prepares a letter that is a sustained commentary on General Funston. The first section is extremely helpful in creating this amicable impression: Mark Twain seems to be saying, let's talk about George Washington, his magnificent influence, our proud heritage; all these things we know, but isn't it pleasant to speak of them again? Another method through which the narrator signals his oneness with his audience is by his use of a language that is "elevated" in a conventional way. In the peroration on

27. For example, *God's Fool*, p. 48.
28. See *damned human race*, pp. 82–84. Arthur Scott refers to the "Funston" essay as a "savage and courageous" performance (see *Mark Twain at Large*, p. 261).
29. *damned human race*, p. 84.

Washington's patriotic influence, for example, the narrator concludes:

> We shall let go our obsequious hold on the rear-skirts of the sceptred land-thieves of Europe, and be what we were before, a *real* world power, and the chiefest of them all, by right of the only clean hands in Christendom, the only hands guiltless of the sordid plunder of any helpless people's stolen liberties, hands recleansed in the patriotism of Washington, and once more fit to touch the hem of the revered Shade's garment and stand in its presence unashamed. It was Washington's influence that made Lincoln and all other real patriots the Republic has known; it was Washington's influence that made the soldiers who saved the Union; and that influence will save us always, and bring us back to the fold when we stray. (p. 85)

The diction is formal and heavily figurative with only the image of "obsequious" America tugging on Europe's "rear-skirts" being fresh and vividly picturesque. In the rest of the passage, the figures verge on the clichéd: "hands" are "guiltless" of "sordid plunder"; Washington's ghost is a revered "Shade." The final image of Washington "saving" America and returning her to the "fold" is conventionally biblical. The diction combines with sentence cadences dependent upon repetitive and balanced phrasing to create a sequence of language squarely within the genteel tradition. And passages such as this are a particularly appropriate way for the writer to suggest that his beliefs are the same as those held by his educated audience.

When he decides to include an unconventional interpretation of Funston's capture of Aguinaldo, Mark Twain begins comfortably, by using irony as a shield against too abrupt and strident an introduction of unpleasant truths:

> It seems to me that General Funston's appreciation of the capture needs editing. It seems to me that, in his after-dinner speeches, he spreads out the heroisms of it—I say it with deference, and subject to correction—with an almost too generous hand. He is a brave man; his dearest enemy will cordially grant him that credit. For his sake it is a pity that somewhat of that quality was not needed in the episode under consideration; that he would have furnished it no one doubts. (p. 89)

The narrator is humble. The hero is not called a coward; it is merely suggested that his reputation for courage is undeserved. But then the narrator drops the euphemisms: Funston, he remarks, defeated his enemy by dressing in "dis-honored" uniforms and by using "forgeries and falsehoods." "Hospitable heads" were greeted with savage bullets. The passage ends with an ironic, not at all genial reflection upon the events: "It was hospitality repaid in a brand-new, up-to-date, modern civilization fashion, and would be admired by many" (p. 90). The reader finishes the passage with the impression that he himself has discovered something about Funston, rather than with the impression that he has been told something by Mark Twain.

Later in the essay, Funston is not blamed for his actions; instead the blame is placed on an "It"—which is shorthand for the concept of disposition, which is personified in such a dryly humorous fashion that the reader can never be quite certain how seriously he is to regard the idea:

> He did not make his own disposition, It was born with him. It chose his ideals for him, he did not choose them. It chose the kind of society It liked, the kind of comrades It preferred, . . . It admired everything that Washington did not admire, and hospitably received and coddled everything that Washington would have turned out of doors—but It, and It only, was to blame, not Funston; . . . It had a native predilection for un-savory conduct, but it would be in the last degree unfair to hold Funston to blame for the outcome of his infirmity; as clearly unfair as it would be to blame him because his conscience leaked out through one of his pores when he was little—a thing which he could not help, but he couldn't have raised it, any-way. (p. 91)

What is certain, however, is that specific actions are being condemned. In contrast to something like "Edmund Burke on Croker and Tammany," in this essay there is no pressure on the writer to produce rapid political results. Here he is hoping to change attitudes and such changes take time. "A Defence of General Funston" contains enough clear, blunt, impassioned statements to inform the reader that Mark Twain is sincere in his criticisms; yet its work is done primarily in a quiet, humorous, understated manner, through a process of friendly persuasion.

9

An Ecstatic Return and Its Aftermath
June 1902 to June 1904

With the publication of the Funston "defence," Clemens's activities as a polemicist ceased until 1905. The major reason for this inactivity was undoubtedly Livy's illness, which became acute in the late summer of 1902 and which had a circumscribing effect upon most of Clemens's activities until her death in June 1904. In the spring of 1902, however, his life was in most ways enjoyable: his family was relatively happy,[1] he was a political force in his country, his reputation not merely as a humorist but also as a writer of American classics was building steadily, he was about to receive an honorary doctoral degree from the major university in his home state, and he anticipated a revisit to Hannibal. He was, moreover, immersed in a new Huckleberry Finn/Tom Sawyer book; and his enthusiastic involvement with it had vanquished for a period of several months his tendency toward impatience with long fiction. We know from notebook entries and letters written during the summer and early autumn of 1902 that his interest in "Huckleberry Finn Fifty Years Later" continued at least into October; it was buoyed by his evocative and triumphant return to Hannibal, and it survived yachting excursions with H. H. Rogers and fears regarding Livy's illness.[2] Yet, surprisingly, even shockingly, nothing survives from this lengthy, seemingly monumental attempt to resuscitate his world-famous rural

1. The qualifying word *relatively* is important. In *God's Fool*, Hamlin Hill talks about Livy's worries over the unsold Hartford house and over the complications created by Clara's friendship with Ossip Gabrilowitsch. And Livy, of course, was not well; although certainly she was in much better health than she would be in the late summer and after. See *God's Fool*, pp. 43–45. For abbreviations used in the footnotes, see "Short References," pp. ix–x.

2. See Walter Blair's comments about these months in *HH and T*, pp. 15–19.

boys as mature adults, other than the numerous notebook references to the developing story.

The premise sound fascinating: Tom and Huck return to St. Petersburg fifty years after their boyhoods; they exchange memories of old adventures and old friends, even meet a few of these friends; and they discover contrasts between the old and the new. Several of the anecdotes mentioned in the notebook were ones that Mark Twain often yearned to use somehow (doughface, Jim Wolf and the cats); one reference also suggests that the writer wanted to incorporate material from "Tom Sawyer's Conspiracy." [3] And a few notes prefigure the author lighting out for territory he had not traveled in many years, by writing about his heroes' relationships with girls, for example.[4] Given the basic idea of the book, the plot and character suggestions, Mark Twain's relatively long and eager involvement with the writing of this seemingly substantial manuscript, and the impetus he was provided by the return to Hannibal, it is unfortunate that the manuscript was not finished and lamentable that it does not seem to have survived. The entries in the notebook suggest an associational structure: Tom and Huck (and probably others) engage in reminiscences—some brief, some lengthy—describe memories evoked by sights of the present, and compare the past with the present. Although the reader only can guess about the manuscript itself on the basis of notebook jottings, the entries suggest a book lacking a conventional plot or structure, a possibility helping to explain why Mark Twain enthused about the project for so many months. What the entries actually suggest is a book containing material and embodying a structure that may have come to seem more potentially appropriate to the writer's embryonic autobiography than to a novel.[5] It is also understandable that such a book would have been almost impossible to complete, because it would have continued to grow as long as its creator had memories of, or reflections upon, the past.

While he was involved with the Tom Sawyer/Huckleberry

3. Notebook 35, TS, p. 20, MTP.
4. Ibid., p. 13, talks of "kissing parties," for example.
5. If Mark Twain abandoned the manuscript for this reason, the irony is that comparatively little of his subsequent autobiographical dictations focused on Hannibal.

Finn material, Mark Twain took another look at "Tom Sawyer's Conspiracy." Evidence indicates that the last few pages of "Tom Sawyer's Conspiracy" were probably added some time in 1902.[6] With the addition of the courtroom scene in which Jim is tried for murder and Tom is on the point of saving him when he recognizes the Duke and the King as the real murderers, the story is almost completed; certainly from one point of view it would have been easy to complete. When Clemens was living in Europe after Susy's death and working on the manuscript, he did not finish and publish the story because it was well short of the desired subscription-book length. In 1902 and after, however, the length was not the primary problem; and Mark Twain's decision to finally discard the manuscript is suggestive of a motive different and more profound—one relevant as well to "Huckleberry Finn Fifty Years Later."[7] The joking reference in "The Secret History of Eddypus" to Tom and Huck as Mark Twain's bastard children may provide the clue; this remark suggests that the disreputable boys have become to a significant extent Clemens's progeny.[8] During his last years, Clemens was naturally concerned about his posterity, particularly in view of Jean's health and his exasperation with Clara and her desires for a "career"; in this connection, two books—the "Gospel" and the "autobiography"—and two characters—Tom and Huck—took on great importance.[9] The books were yet to be completed; the boys, on the other hand, were vigorously alive; and their creator may not have wanted to damage their vitality, as he probably felt he had when he published his two 1890s potboilers, *Tom Sawyer Abroad* and

6. See *God's Fool*, p. 50.

7. Mark Twain says in his 30 August 1906 autobiographical dictations that he destroyed the manuscript. I stubbornly cannot believe that he could have done this, and still expect that someday, like the Lyon-Ashcroft manuscript, "Huckleberry Finn Fifty Years Later" will turn up.

8. Isabel Lyon said that in one presentation copy of *Huckleberry Finn* "Mr. Clemens wrote: 'This is Huck Finn, a child of mine of shady reputation. Be good to him for his parents' sake'" (Box 9, MTP).

9. Whenever he was asked by his admirers during these years to name his favorite books, he almost always referred to *Huckleberry Finn* (although *Joan of Arc* topped the list). See, for example, SLC to Hélène Picard, 22 February 1902, TS, MTP.

Tom Sawyer, Detective. It may have come to seem to Mark Twain almost a sacrilege, therefore, to consider compelling his boys to risk further public adventures.

It is impossible to decide exactly when or how the writer finally came to recognize the value of Tom and Huck and of the books in which they appeared. Certainly one reason was the encomiums—particularly those praising *Adventures of Huckleberry Finn*—that continually were mailed to Mark Twain from every type of admirer. A cogent example is a lengthy letter from a minor writer, Samuel Merwin, sent in 1903. An excerpt from the letter appears below:

> I hope this letter is not an impertinence. I have just been turning about, with my head full of Spenser and Shakespeare and "Gil Blas," looking for something in our own present day literature to which I could surrender myself as to those fine, gripping old writings. And nothing could I find until I took up "Life on the Mississippi," and "Huckleberry Finn," and, just now, the "Connecticut Yankee". It isn't the first time I have read any of these three, and it's because I know it won't be the last, because these books are the only ones written in my life time that claim my unreserved interest and admiration and, above all, my *feelings*, that I've felt I had to write this letter.
>
> I like to think that "Tom Sawyer" and "Huckleberry Finn" will be looked upon, fifty or a hundred years from now as the picture of buoyant, dramatic, *human* American life. I feel, deep in my own heart, pretty sure that they will be. They won't be looked on then as the work of a "humorist," any more than we think of Shakespeare as a humorist now. I don't mean by this to set up a comparison between Mark Twain and Shakespeare: I don't feel competent to do it; and I'm not at all sure that it could be done until Mark Twain's work shall have had its fair share of historical perspective. But Shakespeare was a humorist and so, thank Heaven! is Mark Twain. And Shakespeare plunged deep into the deep, sad things of life; and so, in a different way (but in a way that has more than once brought tears to my eyes) has Mark Twain. But after all, it isn't because of any resemblance for anything that was ever before written that Mark Twain's books strike in so deep: it's rather because they've brought something really new into our literature—new, yet old as Adam and Eve and the Apple. And this achievement, the achievement of putting something into literature that was not there before, is, I should think, the most that any writer can ever hope to do. It is the one mark of distinction between the

"lonesome" little group of big men and the vast herd of medium and small ones. Anyhow, this much I am sure of—to the young man who hopes, however feebly, to accomplish a little something, some day, as a writer, the one inspiring example of our time is Mark Twain.

Very truly yours,
Samuel Merwin [10]

At some point, Mark Twain must have listened to words like these and concluded: the boys and the books are immortal; nothing more should be written about them.

In October 1902, however, "Huckleberry Finn Fifty Years Later" was still a manuscript being considered for publication, as was "Which Was It?," as is evidenced by an August notebook entry that talks of serializing the almost completed novel before bringing it out as a book. [11] In addition to these projects, Clemens also considered publishing a smorgasbord volume consisting of Christian Science material, a recently written story entitled "Was It Heaven or Hell?" whose plot eerily anticipated conditions in the writer's home in December and January, and the best responses to an "amended obituaries" idea in which fans of Mark Twain would be asked to contribute humorous antemortem obituaries of the writer. [12] There were, moreover, still other possibilities for publication: the "Eddypus" manuscript, or "1000 Years Hence" as he referred to it in a July notebook entry; possibly even his "Gospel"; and *Captain Stormfield's Visit to Heaven*, the manuscript of which he had asked his Hartford friend and business agent, Frank Whitmore, to mail to him in mid-October. [13]

The major reason book publication was so much on

10. *MTL*, 2:742–44.

11. Notebook 35, TS, p. 24, MTP.

12. Information concerning his publication plans may also be found in Notebook 35, TS, p. 24, MTP. It is possible as well that sometime during these months he began two still-unpublished fragments entitled "St. Pierre or an Impression of Pelée" (Paine 208) and "Telegraph Dog" (DV 361). The latter story is almost complete.

13. "Eddypus" is referred to on p. 22 of Notebook 35. According to another July notebook entry, Mr. Doubleday had suggested that the "Gospel" be sold and published (p. 22). The request regarding "Stormfield" is contained in SLC to Frank Whitmore, 18 October 1902, TS, MTP.

Clemens's mind during these months was that he was again extremely anxious about money: Livy had become terribly ill in August, the medical expenses were rising, the Hartford house had not been sold, and Livy wanted to make costly additions to the Tarryton estate; moreover, Plasmon investments were draining finances.[14] In a 23 September letter Clemens asked that the "amended obituaries" advertisement be withdrawn from *Harper's Weekly* because of its potential inappropriateness; Livy had almost died the previous evening. On 18 October, however, the advertisement was returned; Livy was improving, and the writer probably did not want to reject a scheme that might be profitable. To F. A. Duneka on 6 October he complained about the medical expenses caused by Livy's illness and about Duneka's failure to pay him quickly enough for accepted articles. In November he took the trouble to count the words in his Christian Science articles submitted to the *North American Review* to discover that he had been correct in believing he had been shortchanged.[15] Some observers might conclude that Clemens's financial "needs" were illusory; an observer might also point out that these needs might have been alleviated if Clemens had not lost so much money in investments (particularly Plasmon). The fact is, however, that he did invest; did—as an aging former bankrupt—feel genuine need; and did, as he had in Europe on several occasions after Susy's death, for a brief period think of almost any manuscript as potentially completable, publishable, and salable.

During the summer, Mark Twain brought the manuscript of "Which Was It?" very close to completion by moving away from the subplots involving the search for the fictitious widow of George Harrison's uncle and by focusing again on Harrison.[16] A freed slave, Jasper, embittered because of his treatment by whites (particularly Templeton Gunning's mother), threatens the protagonist by asserting

14. See Hamlin Hill's account of these months in *God's Fool*, pp. 44–51.

15. SLC to John MacAlister, 23 September 1902, TS, MTP; SLC to John MacAlister, 18 October 1902, TS, MTP; SLC to F. A. Duneka, 6 October 1902, TS, MTP; see David Munro to SLC, 21 November 1902, MTP.

16. See John Tuckey's comments on the dating of this part of the manuscript in *WWD?*, p. 22.

that he and an unnamed white man had observed Harrison's murder of Jake Bleeker; the freed slave will reveal all unless Harrison treats him well by, in effect, acting as the black man's slave when they are in private. Having inserted into the book by far the best section in it—a powerful, memorable scene in which Jasper luxuriates in the benefits of the situation while Harrison fearfully abases himself—Mark Twain left the novel unfinished.[17] Thus, by the summer of 1902 the writer had made two significant fictional attempts to dramatize the condition of the freed slave, but at this point had been either unwilling or unable to complete "Tom Sawyer's Conspiracy" or "Which Was It?" In notes housed at the Mark Twain Papers, Bernard De Voto refers to several possible endings that the writer had considered for the latter manuscript: because Squire Fairfax had treated him well, Jasper saves the squire's life by revealing George as the murderer, and Jasper is then lynched for planning a slave insurrection; George's identity is revealed at a magic-lantern show; George serves on the jury, and his obdurate defense of the squire during the trial results in a hung jury, but George commits suicide because he can neither accept the squire's gratitude nor reveal his own cowardice and culpability.[18] Given these possibilities and given the difficulties involved in tying together the strands of subplots and linking them with the ending, it is understandable that at this point Mark Twain again pushed the manuscript aside. The narrative remained unfinished, although he apparently came back to it again before abandoning it permanently. It would be pleasant to think that the writer finally gave up on the novel because he realized how ineffectual it was, but the ex-

17. Bernard De Voto surmises that the relationship between Pomp (or Jasper) and George Harrison was created in autumn 1899, because on the back of p. 8 there are notes relating to Mark Twain's piece about Joan of Arc. See "Notes on the George Harrison Series," TS, p. 2a, DV 302, MTP. Arthur Pettit's discussion of the Jasper-Harrison relationship in his *Mark Twain & the South*, pp. 168–73, is sensitively written and well worth reading, particularly his analysis of Jasper as "Mulatto Superman."

18. See "Notes on the George Harrison Series," TS, DV 302, MTP, in particular pp. 9, 16. Primarily because of exigencies of space and time, none of these possibilities were referred to by John Tuckey in *WWD?*

planation that he offers in his 30 August 1906 autobiographical dictation is probably true: "The pen is irksome to me."[19] So ends the writer's involvement with a basic idea—the dream as disaster—that, for the numerous reasons already discussed, led to more false starts, literarily unproductive time, and bad writing than any other idea that caught Clemens's fancy during these last years.

One of the reasons he did not persevere with "Which Was It?" in the winter of 1903, either to tie, untie, or cut the knots and thus somehow to finish the book, was that another more cogenial project emerged to occupy him: if he could complete in time a volume centering exclusively on Christian Science, Harper's would publish it in the spring.[20] Since Mark Twain did finish the book, and since it is the only long book that he was able to complete after *Following the Equator*, it is worthwhile to consider the conditions under which it was written. He was, first of all, a "prisoner" because of Livy's illness, his desire for money, and the imposed deadline. For this reason, there existed few of the diversions that often had impeded his momentum on other manuscripts; his only other significant literary project seems to have been the autobiography, which would have served more as a relaxant than as an activity competing for his favors.[21] There were several other factors as well. When he began trying to create a book out of Christian Science materials, he had already written a great many relevant pages, and he knew that there were numerous sources from which he could obtain more material: Mrs. Eddy's published writings, Christian Science bylaws, comments from W. McCrakan (a Christian Science adherent who would be given space to reply to criticisms of the church).[22] The material, in other words, was dependent not upon the author's imagina-

19. *MTE*, p. 198.
20. See F. Duneka to SLC, 28 January 1903, TS, MTP.
21. During this period as well he also made an unsuccessful attempt, at the request of Howells, to write an article about American atrocities in the Philippines. See *Writings*, 22:1196, for a brief account of this situation. It is also possible that he may have worked on "St. Pierre or an Impression of Pelée" and/or "Telegraph Dog" (see Chapter 9, note 12).
22. For some brief comments about the McCrakan involvement, see *God's Fool*, p. 53.

tion, but upon relatively simple research. Length would be a problem only because there might be too many pages; yet he often had dealt with this difficulty in writing his best books, and it undoubtedly would be preferable to the embarrassment of having too little material. The structure would be dictated by polemical, not narrative, exigencies.

The growth of Christian Science influence proved that the subject was important; since he had predicted four years before that the church would become influential, he could quietly brag about his prophetic abilities. Mary Baker Eddy had fascinated him ever since he had begun to appreciate her significance. She possessed enormous power, and the source and exercise of power had always interested him. Her qualities of pride and greed he considered to be the most potent causes of human destructiveness; yet her nerve and organizational ability were qualities that he greatly admired, particularly when her exercise of them helped to illustrate the gullibility of her followers. She was, moreover, an extremely "unpromising hero," a type that according to Robert Regan he had always been drawn to:[23] for many of her years she had been relatively poor, totally unknown, erratically educated; she was, further, a woman, and women who had risen to such spectacular eminence were almost nonexistent in America.

Crucial also to his interest in Mrs. Eddy were the abilities that he himself needed in order to understand her and the process that he was able to follow in order to illuminate her character for his readers: he could begin with premises concerning the importance of heredity and environment and then demonstrate the truth of his premises; he could use as evidence not guesswork, but Mrs. Eddy's own writings and actions; he could then arrive triumphantly at his conclusions like some kind of psychological detective. Moreover, much of the force of his conclusions concerning Mrs. Eddy's hypocrisy would derive from his analyses of a topic that he was peculiarly suited to discuss—her style and the implications of it.

There is one final factor. During these months when his wife was extremely ill due to causes at least some of which

23. Regan makes no reference to Mary Baker Eddy in his book. See *Unpromising Heroes*.

were probably psychological, it may have been subconsciously helpful for Samuel Clemens to involve himself with a religion whose adherents were convinced that mind could conquer illness. He may have felt, as he worked on the book, that there was a force still available to Livy more powerful than, and independent of, the physical, one that they could fall back on if remedies focusing on the physical continued to fail. In sum, the conditions were, in practically every way, propitious; it is therefore completely understandable that this book was finished while so many others were consigned to the scrap heap.

What can be said about the finished product—this book that Mark Twain was almost compelled to write? I should say before beginning my short discussion of *Christian Science* that I have no intention of trying to make a case for it as a neglected masterpiece; on the other hand, I do not find it as tedious or disappointing as do many modern readers. Individual sections are sometimes effective, particularly those deriving from his 1899 articles. Moreover, the writer's comments on Mrs. Eddy's style are often as incisively funny as analogous sections in his essays on James Fenimore Cooper, or as humorous as Hank Morgan's exasperated attempts to fathom Sandy's Malorian prose:

> "If spiritual conclusions are separated from their premises, the nexus is lost, and the argument, with its rightful conclusions, becomes correspondingly obscure." Page 34.
> We shall never know why she put the word "correspondingly" in there. Any fine large word would have answered just as well: psychosuperintangibly—electroincandescently—oligarcheologically—sanchrosynchrostereoptically—any of these would have answered, any of these would have filled the void.
> "His spiritual noumenon and phenomenon, silenced portraiture." Page 34.
> Yet she says she forgot everything she knew, when she discovered Christian Science. I realize that noumenon is a daisy; and I will not deny that I shall use it whenever I am in the company which I think I can embarrass with it; but at the same time I think it is out of place among friends in an autobiography. There, I think a person ought not to have anything up his sleeve. It undermines confidence. But my dissatisfaction with the quoted passage is not on account of noumenon; it is on account of the misuse of the word "silenced". You cannot silence

portraiture with a noumenon; if portraiture should make a noise, a way could be found to silence it, but even then it could not be done with a noumenon. Not even with a brick, some authorities think.[24]

Read as an extended character sketch about a woman of real importance in her time, the volume is at times quite interesting, because it succeeds in conveying a sense of Mrs. Eddy's complexity—both her idiocies and her admirable qualities. Yet one of the barriers in the way of a contemporary reader's appreciation of the book is the tonal variations in the treatment of the central character. Typically, when speaking of Mrs. Eddy the narrator fluctuates between supercilious contempt on the one hand and awestruck wonder and fear on the other. These variations can be explained both in terms of Mark Twain's perception of the woman's complexity and the manner in which she was regarded: she was worshipped by her followers, hence the writer's attempts to make her seem puny and ludicrous; non-Christian Scientists had a lack of respect for, and were ignorant of, her potentialities, hence Mark Twain's almost hyperbolic appreciation of her past and present achievements and his stress on her future capabilities. Unfortunately, since most modern readers probably are unable to grant that the writer's subject justifies such uncomfortable extremes, the repeated sneers and ejaculations may seem intolerable.

But even if the author is allowed his perception of the subject, there are problems with the book. Most crucially, it is too long; and the reader becomes impatient with Mark Twain's unwillingness to drop his analysis of Christian Science bylaws until every implication has been squeezed from them. Even more exasperating is the discussion of miscellaneous material—whether the "Great Idea" was borrowed from Phineas Quimby, for example—after the book's major points have been made repeatedly. By the end, in fact, the polemical structure has disintegrated. The writer actually made his case more convincingly in the essays on Mrs. Eddy that he published while working on the long manuscript; a piece entitled "Mrs. Eddy in Error" is particularly effective

24. *What Is Man?*, pp. 274–75.

as an argument, although it is not as humorous as certain sections of the long work.[25] What seems to have happened is that the subject proved too congenial for Mark Twain; being too close to it he was unable to view it objectively and critically; for this reason, he never recognized that it should have been pruned.

A peculiar aspect of the Christian Science project is that after he had worked so diligently on it, it was not published until 1907. In a letter to an admirer on 20 April 1903, he said that the book was withdrawn by Harper's because the company lacked the courage to publish it over the objections of influential Christian Scientists.[26] Harper's maintained that it did not publish the book because it was not finished in time. More interesting is the seeming equanimity with which the writer accepted the decision. Clearly one reason for his response was that he no longer felt the financial panic that he had experienced for a period after Livy's August collapse. Two other possibilities also suggest themselves. The first is that he was content to imagine that his book was suppressed, because this was more glamorous a reason than that it was not very good, something he may have suspected. A second possibility is that Clemens was pleased that Harper's had decided against publication, because this gave him cause to feel mistreated by Harper's and additional justification either to seek more favorable contract conditions with the company or to break the contract and sign with someone like Robert Collier. Throughout the spring and summer of 1903, the writer schemed continually

25. A text of "Mrs. Eddy in Error" may be found in *What Is Man?*, pp. 382–97.

26. See Clemens's reply to Edwin H. Anderson's 20 April 1903 letter written along the margins of this letter (TS in MTP). He made a similar point in his autobiographical dictation of 17 July 1906. Although Harper's maintained that the real reason was that *Christian Science* was not finished, it is quite possible that the firm did not want to publish the book then because too little of the material in it was new (Mark Twain had of course published several articles on Christian Science in 1903 issues of *North American Review*). Harper's would have been sensitive to this fact because, thus far, in their relationship with the author, every book of his that they had published had depended greatly upon already published material.

about his contract, succeeding finally in negotiating a better one with Harper's only just prior to leaving for Italy in October 1903.[27]

After finishing *Christian Science* in the spring of 1903, he did little writing—"A Dog's Tale,"[28] probably five chapters of "No. 44, The Mysterious Stranger," and a little autobiographical work were his major accomplishments. Worries over the move to Italy, his family, the contracts, and American Plasmon provided ample outlets for his energy.[29]

Late in October the Clemens family and entourage sailed to Italy for the last time. By November they were settled into the Villa Quarto in Florence, where Livy would die in June 1904. Hamlin Hill's biography gives a memorable impression of these Faulknerian months, as do Clemens's own unpublished autobiographical dictations: the huge, ugly mansion (he called it "Calamity House") with the cesspool under the room of the dying woman; the continual squabbles with the garish Italianate American owner, Countess Massiglia; Isabel Lyon—the by now indispensable secretary— prostrate due to the bite of a frenzied donkey; Samuel Clemens alternating between solicitous, brief visits to Livy —the beloved wife who risked being devastated by his company—fights with his landlord and supposedly mendacious medical personnel, and social engagements with Clara on his arm.[30] And all the time Clemens was writing, at times with commendable skill. Although there must have been periods when he knew in this house of horrors that his wife was dying, he seems to have rejected such considerations:

27. Significantly, at almost the same time that he was replying so calmly to Edwin Anderson's request regarding the whereabouts of the Christian Science volume, he was also writing Duneka proposing a reorganization of his contracts. See SLC to F. A. Duneka, 27 April 1903 (TS, MTP). And Clemens's letters to Rogers during this period are full of ideas regarding the author's contractual situation.

28. In dismissing "A Dog's Tale" in such a cavalier fashion, I am being unfair to the story because, judged on its own terms (Mark Twain wrote it in order to make his readers emotionally opposed to vivisection), it is quite effective.

29. See Hill's description of these months in *God's Fool*, pp. 62–71.

30. Ibid., pp. 71–87.

Livy was sick, but she might get well; assuming the best, he would live for the present and plan for the future. And he did, even concluding negotiations for a better summer home a little while before Livy's death.[31]

Early in the fall, Livy was anxious about expenses, particularly those relating to the albatross of the Tarryton estate. Primarily for this reason, her husband wrote several stories and sketches that he believed would bring in $7,500 and allay her fears.[32] Two were sold immediately, and all are competently written, although "Italian with Grammar" is really too long; it was therefore wise for *Harper's* to decide not to publish approximately the last half. "Italian Without a Master" is a meandering sketch, depending upon one comic idea for most of its laughs: the narrator's confident assertions about the meaning of Italian words, phrases, and passages culled from newspapers are juxtaposed against the readers' guesses about their actual meanings. The published version of "Italian With Grammar" is more exuberant and imaginative.[33] It proceeds from the narrator's recognition of the importance of verbs in a language; derives its energy from his ability to vivify the verbs in a series of wild, shifting metaphors; and culminates with a scene where the verb *to have*

31. In a letter to Muriel Pears, however, Clemens mentioned that Livy was too sick to move. The negotiations were primarily a form of subterfuge to make Livy think that she would be leaving the hated villa; they were a means, therefore, of cheering her up. See SLC to Muriel Pears, 9 May 1904, TS, MTP.

32. See SLC to Joseph Twichell, 7 January 1904, TS, MTP. During these weeks he also wrote a political sketch entitled "Major General Wood, M.D." At first, he planned to send it to Colonel Harvey and ask him to use his judgment concerning the timing of publication (see SLC to Colonel Harvey, 28 December 1903 in DV 352, MTP). Then he seems to have reconsidered; in a letter to Duneka on 30 December he said that he had pigeonholed the manuscript. Now that he had signed the renegotiated contract with Harper's, he felt, he must be very careful about making enemies. Only his duties as a citizen would compel him to take this risk, "the lousy Wood Case" was not sufficiently important (PS, MTP).

33. "Italian Without a Master" may be found in Mark Twain, *The $30,000 Bequest and Other Stories* (New York and London: Harper & Brothers, 1903), pp. 171–85. This is volume 24 of The Author's National Edition of Mark Twain's Works. "Italian With Grammar" may be found in *The $30,000 Bequest*, pp. 186–96.

becomes an army battalion that the language tutor has willed to march past for the benefit of his eager pupil. Both pieces are slight, but high-spirited and often amusing.

Three other sketches—"The $30,000 Bequest"; "You've Been a Dam Fool, Mary. You Always Was!"; and "Sold to Satan"—are related thematically, since all focus on the uses and abuses of money and the desire for gain. In "Sold to Satan," because his investments have shrunk considerably, the narrator (called Mark Twain) decides to sell his soul to the devil, who appears not conventionally garbed, but clothed in radium: "But he was not a fire coal; he was not red, no! On the contrary. He was a softly glowing, richly smoldering torch, column, statue of pallid light, faintly tinted with a spiritual green, and out from him a lunar splendor flowed as one sees glinting from the crinkled waves of tropic seas when the moon rides high in cloudless skies."[34] After discussing radium as a potential twentieth-century source of energy, Satan accepts Mark Twain's offer in exchange for information about an important source of radium. As the conversation ends, the narrator looks forward to further discoveries by Madame Curie, because these will help him to control radium's deleterious effects, thereby enabling him to use his private knowledge for prodigious financial gain. Even at the end, he does not realize he has been "sold" in more ways than one: in exchange for his soul he has been told to search for radium in a firefly burial ground. "Sold to Satan" is a weird, subtle little piece, notable both for the manner in which it suggests and predicts how the wonderful properties of the physical universe will come to subserve human greed and for the ironic light that it sheds on its author's own foolishness.

"You've Been a Dam Fool, Mary" is the weakest of the three, being a fairly long, sentimental, moralistic story, based upon a true incident about a Southern man's attempts, after the Civil War, to locate a prewar Northern friend in order to pay back a debt incurred while they had been business partners.[35] In the tale the Northerner is found, is discovered to be in bad financial shape because of his kindness to those

34. *Writings*, 29:327.
35. The story has only recently been published in *F of M*, pp. 251–78.

indebted to him, and then is rescued in a Tom Sawyerish auction scene in which his Southern friend rewards his patience with $600,000. When this happens, the uncle of the Northerner's former fiancée, who has left him because of his poverty, says, "You've been a dam fool, Mary. You always was!" The story is pleasant, but noteworthy only because of the way in which its themes—money properly used, greed transcended by friendship, desire for gain thwarted by kindness—contrast with the thematic implications of "Sold to Satan" and "The $30,000 Bequest." Mark Twain probably liked this story primarily because it was based upon fact and for this reason provided a believable counterexample to tendencies that he saw everywhere around him and strongly within himself.

Of the three tales, "The $30,000 Bequest" is unquestionably the most effective. The plot concerns a husband and wife who, deluded by the prospects of a $30,000 inheritance, immerse themselves more and more deeply in a fantasy life of investment, opulence, and spending even while they live their normal routines in a placid way. They are eventually destroyed when they discover that their prospects are chimerical and that they have been tantalized by the false promises of a misanthropic uncle who has planned to ruin their lives through his treachery. The story is powerful and intense; its effects derive primarily from Mark Twain's decision to focus almost exclusively upon the singular obsessions of his two characters and from his success in controlling his tendency toward diffusiveness. A few other people are mentioned—the couple's daughters, the real and imaginary suitors of the girls, some acquaintances, the editor of a newspaper who finally reveals to them the truth about the uncle—but all are important only as they relate to the dream lives of the married couple. Everything in the story is done clearly and economically, and the writer's control of tempo is superb. The conditions of the fable are slowly made believable: the background is sketched in so that the subsequent obsessions seem plausible; the uncle's letter arrives, and the couple responds cautiously to the conditions of the will; their dreams start to develop and dominate their lives; then the dreams rapidly snowball and soon are out of control. At the story's climax, time almost halts, as the writer focuses on a scene in which the truth is inflicted upon the couple. Then the story speeds to its denouement—the couple's disillusionment and death—and the reader is moved almost in spite of himself.

Notable also about the tale is its moral toughness: the couple learns too late; they do not live happily ever after. It is also remarkably suggestive, for its meanings resonate beyond the simple essence of the story to touch upon ideas related to the importance of habit, the vulnerability of moral standards never tested, the mystery of human identity, the allure of fantasies, the havoc caused when reality strangles dreams. One final aspect of the story is worthy of observation: its suggested meaning extends beyond the meanings that its characters attempt to impose on their actions. The husband says, "Vast wealth, acquired by sudden and unwholesome means, is a snare. It did us no good, transient were its feverish pleasures; yet for its sake we threw away our sweet and simple and happy life—let others take warning by us."[36] Nowhere in this tritely expressed moral does the man admit the power of the pleasure that he has experienced; nowhere does he recognize that it is not so much the wealth itself, but the dream of it, that has caused the problems; nowhere does he seem aware of how his dreams have harmed others, notably his daughters. Thus, even while the character derives solace by making an exemplum of himself, the reader can see implications that undercut the force of the exemplum. The wife blames everything on the uncle, yet she blames him not so much for tempting them in the first place as for leaving "but thirty thousand. . . . Without added expense he could have left us far above desire of increase, far above the temptation to speculate" (p. 47). So while the husband talks of the "feverish" pleasures derived from the "wealth" and utters dark, hackneyed warnings about the evils of greed, the wife complains that there was not more. For these reasons, while on one level "The $30,000 Bequest" can be construed as a sermon against greed, on another it can be seen as a tale about the potency of greed, the pleasures that can be derived from it, and the impossibility of resisting its allure.

Once Clemens had allayed his wife's financial fears by sell-

36. *Writings*, 24:46. Henceforth, references to "The $30,000 Bequest" will be made in the text.

ing "The $30,000 Bequest," "Italian with Grammar," and "Italian without a Master," he was free to concern himself in a leisurely fashion with more substantial literary projects: the dictation of his autobiography—which he enjoyed immensely and which took up approximately two hours of each morning—and the writing of at least one piece of long fiction. Clemens spoke in several letters of attempting to complete two novels begun two years previously, a dating that suggests that one of them was "Huckleberry Finn Fifty Years Later"; however, the only would-be novel that we can be certain he worked on during these months is "No. 44, the Mysterious Stranger." According to John Tuckey, the first seven chapters of this manuscript were written prior to the Italian sojourn.[37] By the end of chapter 7, "44" has arrived, inadvertently created a conflict among the workers, and evoked the narrator's sympathy and wonderment, which causes problems between the narrator and 44's enemies. Chapters 8 through 25 were written in Italy, as was the "life as a dream" final chapter, which was composed some time around Livy's death.[38] The plot of this section is extremely complicated. It involves a strike threatening the completion of an important printing contract; 44's creation of "duplicates" to perform the work; the magical stranger's supposed death and then reappearance; his entertaining of the narrator with his magic and disturbing him with talk of the vanity of life; entanglements deriving from the meeting of dream selves, work-a-day selves, and souls; and so on.

In an early January letter to F. A. Duneka, Clemens wrote, "I believe I will dig out one of my unfinished novels and finish it—a couple of them, for issue as single books, & not

37. *MTLS*, p. 58. William Gibson is incorrect in *MSM* when he writes, "Between November 1902 and October 1903, while in Florence for his wife's health, Twain wrote chapters 2 through 7 or 8" (p. 9). During these months, Clemens was still living in the United States.

38. For information about the composition of the manuscript during this period, see *MTLS*, pp. 58–65. In his "Anatole France and Mark Twain's Satan," Alan Gribben suggests that the "life as a dream" ending for "No. 44" might have been suggested to Mark Twain by Anatole France's *Le Crime de Sylvestre Bonnard*. The chief resemblances between young Satan and France's character are that both impart knowledge, blend whimsy with mocking cruelty, and assert that everything is only a dream.

serially, but only to be added) to the Complete Subscription Set."[39] The letter suggests that for at least part of the time that he was working on "No. 44, The Mysterious Stranger," he was hoping to publish it, which may explain several things about this section of the manuscript. It may explain, first of all, the care with which certain conventions of fiction are adhered to. Because most of the action takes place in a circumscribed setting, the first-person narrator is able to observe directly most of the important events; if he does not, the writer makes sure that he learns about them plausibly. Because Mark Twain chooses to have his narrator delay revealing the real identity of 44, the story possesses a suspense lacking in the other related manuscripts, in which the stranger does not remain "mysterious" for long. Yet, not all of the results deriving from the author's sporadic desire to publish the narrative are positive. The book's lack of consistent satiric bite, for example, may also be traced to this desire.

There were other motives, however, that influenced the nature of the manuscript. Writing to his young friend, Muriel Pears, on 9 May, Clemens said, "It is nearly noon & no call yet; which means that I am not allowed my 2-minute visit to the sick room today. (This happens, these days, after a bad night.) So I will give up waiting for the call, & get me to the work which sweeps the world away & puts me in one which no one has visited but me—nor will, for this book is not being written for print, & is not going to be published."[40] If the book being referred to is "No. 44, The Mysterious Stranger," then it follows that by this time Mark Twain's desire to write only for himself was either competing with or

39. SLC to F. A. Duneka, 5 January 1904. Copy (not in Clemens's handwriting) at MTP. In his new book on the "Mysterious Stranger" manuscripts, on the other hand, Sholom Kahn writes, "Writing for love and not for money, and with no intention of having the work published in his lifetime, Mark Twain was reaching down to his deepest levels of concern and conviction in 'No. 44'" (Mark Twain's Mysterious Stranger: A Study of the Manuscript Texts, p. 94). Kahn's book contains the lengthiest and most persuasive argument yet published to defend "No. 44" as a piece of literature. After reading his discussion of the story, I reread Mark Twain's work. Unfortunately, I still don't like it and still am convinced that it is an unpalatable potpourri.

40. SLC to Muriel Pears, 9 May 1904, TS, MTP.

had won over his wish for a large audience. Given this change in motivation, it is understandable that certain sections of the manuscript are very different in tone from, and are not well integrated into, the rest of the narrative. For example, there is a sardonic scene involving the burning of a "witch," inspired by a similar episode in "The Chronicle of Young Satan" but here more fully developed, moving, and powerful; there is also the "life as a dream" chapter; and there are the incidents deriving from the writer's fascination with a new theory of identity. In this section of "No. 44, The Mysterious Stranger," Mark Twain's purposes are too confused, the tone and quality of individual sections too inconsistent. In sum, the chapters of the manuscript written during these months are simply too diffuse to reward any but the most tolerant reading.

10

What Is Man?
July 1904 to October 1906

One of the most remarkable and creative periods in Clemens's long career was the approximately two years between the death of Livy, when he returned to America, and the publication of *What Is Man?* in late 1906. To begin to appreciate this period, one should consider, first of all, the problems Clemens had to confront: the death of his wife and its effect upon his two daughters; the health problems of his girls, particularly Jean, whose attacks had become increasingly frequent, savage, and dangerous by the winter of 1906; his own ill health and old age; his investment difficulties; his worries over literary contracts; his loneliness and thoughts of death.[1] Then, one should observe his literary productivity: poems; short pieces for *Harper's Weekly*; writings about copyright; stories written almost on demand, such as "A Horse's Tale"; polemical prose, such as "The Czar's Soliloquy" and "King Leopold's Soliloquy"; a highly idiosyncratic version of the Old Testament based primarily on the words of the first woman; miscellaneous other pieces about religion and politics, such as "A War Prayer"[2] and "The Fable of the Bees"; two fairly lengthy unfinished manuscripts entitled "The Refuge of the Derelicts" and "Three Thousand Years Among the Microbes"; several chapters of "No.

1. See Hamlin Hill's description of this period in *God's Fool*, pp. 93–158. For abbreviations used in the footnotes, see "Short References," pp. ix–x.
2. It is impossible to establish with absolute accuracy the date upon which "The War Prayer" was dictated, although the consensus is that it must have been sometime during these months. (Apparently—see *God's Fool*, p. 100—he read it to Miss Lyon on 10 March.) He submitted the piece to Elizabeth Jordan of *Harper's Bazaar*; but, according to her letter of 22 March 1906, she felt compelled to reject it as "not quite suitable to a woman's magazine" (MTP).

44, The Mysterious Stranger"; autobiographical dictations; small revisions to *Captain Stormfield's Visit to Heaven*; the reworking and publication of *What Is Man?* Much of this material is skillfully written; and some, although unfinished, is memorable and powerful.

Several factors may account for his almost incredible productivity during this period; his enforced seclusion for much of 1904 and 1905 because of his wife's death, his desire to provide well for his living daughters, his attempts to alleviate loneliness. What seems to have been the most important motive in much of this writing, however, was a strong, persistent drive to answer large questions and to confront mammoth problems before his death. A great deal of Clemens's activity during this period suggests a man working furiously against time in order to achieve as much as possible before the debilities connected with old age, or death itself, end his opportunities. His political attacks on two of the most powerful men in the world; his fables centering on large, metaphysical questions; his reworking of the Adam and Eve myth and his seeming attempt to link this with "The Secret History of Eddypus"; his autobiographical outpourings; his decision to publish his "Gospel"; even his energetic attempts to change copyright laws—all suggest a man hard pursuing issues of profound importance to him. Much of the writing, moreover, contains an admirable mixture of the detailed and the general, the immediate and the universal, and is the work of an author whose fascination with the present is made more meaningful by his knowledge and love of the past and whose concern for individuals is strongly influenced by a relatively coherent theory about men in general.

A large portion of his political prose was probably written between the last part of November 1904 and the end of February 1905. The usual critical response to works such as "King Leopold's Soliloquy" is that they are filled with evidence of form overwhelmed by feeling. On the other hand, I find almost all of this writing to be competent and to be notable both for the variety of its formal devices and for the writer's success in using them to further his purposes. The first of these statements to be published was written near the end of January and was incited by the "Bloody Sunday" massacre in Moscow on 22 January of over one thousand people; it was entitled "The Czar's Soliloquy" and published in the March issue of the *North American Review*. If one remembers that the soliloquy form is used here for polemical purposes and not, as in many of Browning's monologues (with which Twain's soliloquy has been compared), primarily to reveal character for its own sake, then it should be possible to appreciate the piece's efficacy.[3] The revelations attributed to the czar seem plausible, given his habit referred to in newspapers of meditating before dressing and given that these particular meditations are supposedly inspired by newspaper clippings regarding his cruelty and the sycophancy of his subjects. In order to create good satire, Mark Twain combines the dramatic situation with his own intuitions regarding the essence of the czar's character: he is a student of human nature with a strong sense of history and with cynical doubts about the wisdom of the Creator of Man. Another way of appreciating Mark Twain's technique here is to recognize that what he has done is to assume that the czar is someone much like himself, although lacking his own capacity for moral outrage; then, the writer reveals this character through the words of his narrator, who in the process manifests not only his fear of violent revolution, but also his understanding of why it could happen and his musings about how it could be accomplished. Mark Twain's audacity is striking, and he is commendably successful in taking some of his own favorite ideas, attributing them to someone else in a reasonable way, and then using them to suggest, support, and justify calmly a desired end—revolution.[4] Everything about the solil-

3. In the course of a brief discussion of Clemens's interest in Robert Browning, Alan Gribben observes similarities between the "self-justifying" speaker of "My Last Duchess" and the speakers in "The Czar's Solioquy" and "King Leopold's Soliloquy." Then, Gribben asserts, "Mark Twain tried to emulate Browning's method of allowing his narrators to condemn themselves by introducing evidence of their own hypocrisy and cruelty, but Mark Twain's efforts are far less effective because his moral indignation at their crimes shows through so noticeably" (" 'It Is Unsatisfactory to Read to One's Self': Mark Twain's Informal Readings," n. 8, p. 50).

4. Mark Twain continued to support publicly the revolutionary cause in Russia until April 1906, when "he withdrew his support of the fund-raising revolutionary Maxim Gorki because the visitor to the United States had violated custom by arriving with a mistress rather than his wife" (*God's Fool*, p. 131). The writer explained

oquy points to the writer's control, and the piece ends where it began, with the speaker deliberating about clothes. Noteworthy as well about "The Czar's Soliloquy" is the natural, unstrained manner in which so much material is compressed into such a short space.

It seems, judging from the opening stage directions of a sketch called "Flies and Russians," from its manuscript pagination, its soliloquy form, and its contemptuous references to the Russian people, that this sketch was originally conceived as a continuation of "The Czar's Soliloquy."[5] The piece is interesting because it points to the extremely close links between Clemens's political, metaphysical, and historical ideas. Here, the narrator thinks in a seriocomic way about nature's many blunders and speculates about possible uses for the house fly and the Russian people, phenomena that for the present seem valueless. The fact that the sketch is not a part of "The Czar's Soliloquy" is indicative of the writer's good judgment, because if it had been allowed to stand as a continuation of the published soliloquy, the latter's unity and delicate plausibility balance would have been destroyed and the political points would have been less forceful. In "The Czar's Soliloquy" the reader accepts the pretense that the narrator is a created character, despite the resemblances between the ideas he expresses and those of Mark Twain. Contributing to the success of this illusion are not only those techniques mentioned previously but also the

this withdrawal of support primarily by complaining about Gorki's stupid strategy in violating the customs of a country from which he wanted help. Writing of the episode, Hill asserts "he soothed himself with alibis that sounded shallow and contrived" (*God's Fool*, p. 131). From one point of view, perhaps. But Mark Twain meant what he said, it seems to me: he did feel that after Gorki had committed his social blunder, his chances of financial support had been minimized. Since Mark Twain was feeling progressively older and more tired, and yet still felt that there were several causes that he wished to champion, he probably believed that he could not afford to have his name linked too closely to a cause that, for the time at least, he could not help. It is possible also that his decision was influenced by his frustration over his failure, in January, to influence the U.S. State Department concerning its attitude toward the Belgian Congo.

5. See *F of M*, p. 420. Henceforth, references to "The Czar's Soliloquy" and "Flies and Russians" will be made in the text.

fact that the narrator's formal, slightly pompous, and pedantic language seems appropriate to him; seldom does it threaten the illusion by reminding the reader unequivocally of the well-known voice of the author.

In "Flies and Russians," on the other hand, the distance between the character and the writer disappears; the dignified prose of the czar is overwhelmed by the bumptious imagination of the creator, and the Mark Twain voice insists upon being heard in passages such as the following:

> There is also another hope, and a pleasanter one. The first time Nature tried to make a horse, the result was pathetic. A stranger would have supposed it was a dog. But she worked at it a million years and enlarged it to the dimensions of a calf, removed a toe or two from its feet, and in other ways improved it. She worked at it another million, then another and another and still another million, and at last after nine or ten million years of thought and labor and worry and cussing she turned out for the grateful and cordial admiration of the world the horse as we see him today, that noble creature, that beautiful creature, that matchless darling of our love and worship. Ten million years are soon passed: what may not the fly and the Russian become? (p. 424)

In the following passage, the created character disappears altogether:

> And yet, when we reflect! Even in our own day Russians could be made useful if only a way could be found to inject some intelligence into them. How magnificently they fight in Manchuria! with what indestructible pluck they rise up after the daily defeat, and sternly strike, and strike again! how gallant they are, how devoted, how superbly unconquerable! If they would only reflect! if they could only reflect! if they only had something to reflect with! Then these humble and lovable slaves would perceive that the splendid fighting-energy which they are wasting to keep their chipmunk on the throne would abolish both him and it if intelligently applied. (p. 424)

One of the reasons "The Czar's Soliloquy" is successful, therefore, is that the writer was able to eliminate cherished but also gratuitous material such as the above.

The protagonist of his next important soliloquy was King Leopold of Belgium, the monarch who, since the mid 1880s, had been in charge of a million miles of territory and twenty million blacks in the Congo Free State.[6] The United States in 1884 had been the first country to recognize officially Leopold's authority in the area; since that time America had continued to give either open or tacit support to Leopold, despite the stories of horrible mismanagement of authority emanating from the Congo.[7] When critics discuss Mark Twain's political writings, "The Czar's Soliloquy" and "King Leopold's Soliloquy" usually are grouped together because of their similar form, the fact that they were written around the same time, and the supposition that they are both undisciplined.[8]

Another legitimate reason for grouping them together is that in each case Mark Twain tried to use the medium of print to shake the power of one of the world's most powerful men. In another sense, however, conjoining these two works diminishes our appreciation of the uniqueness of each and of the variety of ways in which the writer could use the soliloquy form. Mark Twain's portrait of the czar is restrained, generally somber in tone; it is a damning meditation by a cruel and intelligent cynic. Leopold's words are equally damning; but the tone of the piece, the writer's handling of the dramatic situation, and his conception of the character are totally different.

The historical Leopold is recognizable in Mark Twain's picture of him; in fact, the author uses more known facts about the king than he does about the czar, whose sketch is quite generalized; Mark Twain refers to Leopold's religiosity, his love of art, his family troubles, and his involvement in the Belgian Congo situation. There are as well the plausible speculations about his motives: his greed; his condoning of punishments as an example to the blacks; his regard for them as barely human creatures; his notion that the saving

6. The scholarly consensus has been that "A Thanksgiving Sentiment on the Congo" was Mark Twain's first statement about this situation and that it was written in the fall of 1904, after he had returned to America from Italy. Louis Budd has informed me, however, that the piece should be dated either 1905 or 1906.

7. See Janet Smith's introduction to "King Leopold's Soliliquy" in *damned human race*, pp. 181–83.

8. See *God's Fool*, for example: "Both monologues exposed a Mark Twain who was too angry at the facts in his indictment to contemplate the method of expressing them" (p. 100).

of their souls is more important than the preservation of their bodies, or parts thereof, such as their hands. Yet, while there is definite restraint in the writer's handling of the czar, in his treatment of Leopold he relys on exaggeration. The narrator is a comic monster, a caricature of Leopold, who says that he has never been caricatured. He is a cartoon figure brought to life as he alternates between slamming down books critical of him and caressing the pages of the books with obscene pleasure, between fumbling with and slobbering over his crucifix; as he schemes to "buy" Andrew Carnegie so as to prevent the financier from paying for a monument to his memory composed of fifteen million skulls; as he balances the munificent pluses of his artistic generosity and religious concern against the pecadilloes of ten million dead; and as he chuckles evilly over his success in "buncoing" the Americans. The writer effectively and prodigiously exaggerates practically everything about this maniacal religious hypocrite—a nightmare Tartuffe—in an effort to compel his readers to visualize the grossness of Leopold. In this connection, the king's exasperation with the power of the Kodak camera is significant, as are the photographs of mutilated Congolese that were included in the Congo Reform League edition of the "Soliloquy." The czar's monologue is short, tightly controlled; the king's is long, repetitious, overflowing with reiterated examples of his atrocities—examples, moreover, culled from eyewitness reports by Congo visitors. Throughout the soliloquy there is actually a mélange of voices: Leopold's, whining and shrill—alternating between maudlin defenses of himself and brutally honest admissions of his offenses—contrasts with quiet, horrible statements of Congolese fact. The most important effect of this mixture is that toward the end of the piece the reader becomes convinced that, in its essentials, Mark Twain's cartoon is real: the king *is* a monstrous madman who, on the one hand, can mutter platitudes about Christian forbearance and brag about his contributions to the world of art and, on the other, can encourage the most relentless and vicious genocide.

It is at this point that the utter appropriateness of the writer's decision to include a series of worthy adversaries for the king becomes evident. There are those, for example, who "picture me in my robes of state, with my crown on my head, munching human flesh, saying grace, mumbling thanks to Him from whom all good things come."[9] And there are the statisticians who blame Leopold not only for the actual dead, but also for the demise of those who were prevented from being born:

> They remark that twice in a generation in India, the Great Famine destroys 2,000,000 out of a population of 320,000,000, and the whole world holds up its hands in pity and horror; then they fall to wondering where the world would find room for its emotions if I had a chance to trade places with the Great Famine for twenty years! The idea fires their fancy, and they go on and imagine the Famine coming in state at the end of the twenty years and prostrating itself before me, saying: "Teach me, Lord, I am but an apprentice." (pp. 52–53)

Then there is the man, "full of vindictive enthusiasm over his strange project," who wishes to memorialize Leopold's name by building a monument of 15 million skulls and skeletons:

> He has it all ciphered out and drawn to scale. Out of the skulls he will build a combined monument and mausoleum to me which shall exactly duplicate the Great Pyramid of Cheops, whose base covers thirteen acres, and whose apex is 451 feet above ground. He desires to stuff me and stand me up in the sky on that apex, robed and crowned, with my "pirate flag" in one hand and a butcher-knife and pendant handcuffs in the other. He will build a pyramid in the centre of a depopulated tract, a brooding solitude covered with weeds and the mouldering ruins of burned villages, where the spirits of the starved and murdered dead will voice their laments forever in the whispers of the wandering winds. Radiating from the pyramid, like the spokes of a wheel, there are to be forty grand avenues of approach, each thirty-five miles long, and each fenced on both sides by skulless skeletons standing a yard and a half apart and festooned together in line by short chains stretching from wrist to wrist and attached to tried and true old handcuffs stamped with my private trade-mark, a crucifix and butcher-knife crossed, with motto, "By this sign we prosper"; each osseous fence to

9. Mark Twain, *King Leopold's Soliloquy*, ed. Stefan Heym. Henceforth, references to "King Leopold's Soliloquy" will be made in the text.

consist of 200,000 skeletons on a side, which is 400,000 to each avenue. (pp. 54–55) [10]

Although the "project" described in this passage is bizarre, Mark Twain implies that it is no more bizarre than the Congolese reality.

Another remarkable aspect of the soliloquy is the skill with which the writer makes his appeals to, and his frontal attacks on, the reader seem to grow out of the character of Leopold—not to mention the courage he displays while doing this: he has never before assaulted the reader so directly. One of the ways in which the king often cheers himself up after he has bemoaned his failure to be appreciated is by savoring and salivating over the fact that it was American recognition that helped him gain power in the Congo and that it is American unwillingness to admit an error that is helping to keep him there:

> Yes, I certainly was a shade too clever for the Yankees. It hurts; it grovels them. They can't get over it! Puts a shame upon them in another way, too, and a graver way, for they never can rid their records of the reproachful fact that their vain Republic, self-appointed Champion and Promoter of the Liberties of the World, is the only democracy in history that has lent its power and influence to the establishing of an *absolute monarchy*! (pp. 38–39)

Then, toward the end of the soliloquy when Leopold's real cynicism finally breaks through the mask of wounded innocence that he wears even in private and when he begins to admit his atrocities openly, he says, of his officers' decision to crucify blacks: "How stupid, how tactless! Christendom's goose flesh will rise with horror at the news. 'Profanation of the sacred emblem!' That is what Christendom will shout. Yes, Christendom will buzz. It can hear me charged with half a million murders a year for twenty years and keep its composure, but to profane the Symbol is quite another matter" (pp. 60–61).

In the last few sections of Leopold's monologue the taunting of the reader continues practically without abatement: the human race does not throw bricks, "it heaves a poem! Lord, what a race it is!" (p. 63); he and the czar could not

10. This particular description continues, unfortunately, and in the process begins to lose its force.

exist save for the disgusting servility of all people when confronted with such power; "The only witness I have encountered in my long experience that I couldn't bribe" is the Kodak camera (p. 68); the public's unwillingness to act against evil derives from its reluctance to look directly at it, "and you will continue to do it. I know the human race" (p. 71). Through both the facts and the almost mythically conceived characterization, Mark Twain seems to be saying, "Here is a force which you pretend to despise. Here is a monster that you have allowed to thrive. What are you going to do about it?"

Unfortunately, Americans were not willing to do anything, probably because of American investments in the Congo rubber industry.[11] This fact Clemens came to realize after an unsuccessful attempt to find an American publisher for his work, after he had permitted the Congo Reform Association to issue it as a pamphlet—offering to pay for distribution himself—and, finally, after talking personally with members of the U.S. State Department in late 1905 and early 1906.[12] Writing to Thomas Barbour on 8 January 1906, while explaining his unwillingness to undertake a nationwide lecture tour, he asserted,

> I have retired from the Congo. I shall not make a second step in the Congo matter, because that would compel a third, in spite of one—& a fourth & a fifth, & so on. I mean a *deliberate* second step; what I may do upon sudden *impulse* is another matter—*they* are out of my control.
>
> If I had Morel's splendid equipment of energy, brains, diligence, concentration, persistence—but I haven't; he is a "mobile," I am a "wheelbarrow."[13]

And yet he continued to fight—and lose—as he indicated in another letter to Barbour, written a month later, describing

11. See Heym's comments in his introduction to *King Leopold's Soliloquy*.

12. See DV 370 and 370A, MTP. Included as well in this miscellany relating to Leopold (some of it still unpublished) is a statement by Mark Twain predicting that the Belgian Congo would eventually become a political issue in the United States, once the Protestants realized that information has been suppressed because of Catholic influence.

13. Quoted in Philip Foner, *Mark Twain: Social Critic*, p. 302.

a visit to Washington and a conversation with members of the State Department about America's responsibilities in the Congo.[14] These dedicated attempts and eventual failures were, however, about a year in the future. In the meantime, he had still a great deal of writing to do.

In particular, for the sake of health and sanity, and as a kind of recoil from misanthropy after his imaginative involvement with examples of human depravity, it was almost mandatory for him to provide as counterexamples figures who were recognizably human and significantly different from his purveyors of death. Thus Mark Twain wrote "Adam's Soliloquy," in which the ghost of the first man visits New York, observes the same dinosaur referred to by King Leopold and called Leopold the Second by one of his enemies, reflects upon Noah's failure to include the beast in the ark, chats with a young mother, and muses about her resemblance to Eve.[15] Despite the reference in "Adam's Soliloquy" to a symbol of evolution—the brontosaur—there is a haunting sense throughout the sketch of human continuity through the ages. And the continuity is not of weakness or evil, but of goodness; it is illustrated by a woman's love for her young child and her friendly willingness to converse with a peculiar stranger.

As another counterexample, Mark Twain wrote "The Refuge of the Derelicts," a would-be novel that he worked on during most of March and April about a young man's attempt to finance a monument to Adam, a figure very different from King Leopold of Belgium, although Adam also had been the cause of many deaths.[16] The plot concerns a young idealistic artist, George Sterling, who, in order to

14. SLC to Thomas Barbour, 10 February 1906, TS, MTP. In his discussion of this anti-Leopold involvement, Arthur Scott suggests that after discovering that the United States was not one of the nations pledged to oversee Leopold's activities, Mark Twain felt sorry for mistakenly charging his country "with unfaithfulness to duty. His government was right in refusing to act" (see *Mark Twain at Large*, p. 283 and n. 61, p. 332). In my own examination of the relevant documents at the Mark Twain Papers, I was unable to discover evidence of such contrition. It is possible, however, that I may have overlooked pertinent documents.

15. "Adam's Soliloquy" may be found in *Writings*, 29:377–86.

16. For information about the composition of the story, see *F of*

finance the monument to Adam, approaches the relatively wealthy, unpredictable Admiral Stormfield. Using the strategy suggested by his friend, David Shipman, in the story's frame George ingratiates himself with the old sailor, is taken on as a boarder, and becomes familiar with the collection of derelicts for whom the admiral's home has become a haven. Most of the story proper is devoted to descriptions of dinner pronouncements made by Stromfield and to conversations between George and the derelicts, through which the artist learns to empathize with suffering. The uncompleted tale ends after the group has been treated to a lecture by the Reverend Caleb Williams on the goodness of nature and nature's God; during the lecture the minister's naivety is revealed by the contrast between his words and the slide accompaniments depicting a variety of gruesome natural scenes.

Once the frame has been established, "The Refuge of the Derelicts" is primarily a series of short stories and anecdotes linked by their common focus on suffering and failure and justified because each is about a person somehow connected with the refuge. In between the stories, which are told to George either by the person involved or by a sailor-butler named the "Bos'n," are dinner-table conversations dominated by the admiral upon such topics as Satan and Adam or the narrator's plan for the monument. Much of the material is old, in the sense that Mark Twain had either used or considered using it before: the admiral's embittering experience of swearing off grog for three years while at sea only to discover upon his return to land that he had been rejected by the temperance society to which he had applied; a character based upon Clemens's servant John Lewis who miraculously saves a child, is rewarded with one thousand dollars, buys a home, then is inundated with mortgage payments; an Orion Clemens character who loses his chance to become governor of a new state because of his political innocence (which he calls principle), who darts lightly from interest to interest, and who was in his youth engaged to two girls simultaneously.

M, pp. 157–61. Henceforth, references to "The Refuge of the Derelicts" will be made in the text.

Up to this point, what I have written about "The Refuge of the Derelicts" probably suggests a mechanically structured, trite narrative that is either pessimistic or maudlin. Yet "Refuge" is none of these things.

Although the structural principle is rudimentary, it does not seem mechanical because the writer varies the length of the stories—some are only briefly mentioned, a few are well developed—and the means by which they are told: some are in scenes, others are summarized narrative, some are told by the person involved or by the Bos'n, others are epitomized by the artist-narrator. Moreover, the monologues of the admiral help to add variety to the novel, and the plot of the frame story—George's success in arousing support for his project—adds interest. Many of the characters and some of the material are "old," but Sterling's responses are fresh, and his perspective fills a vitalizing function. The story about the sailor, the temperance society, and the voyage, for example, is one that Mark Twain had often tried to use; and a reader familiar with these attempts might be tempted to skim wearily over the tale. Yet the manner in which it is used is new: Shipman, the artist's friend, says that the experience was tragic for the admiral; George accepts this kind of sentimentality totally, despite the third-person frame-narrator's wry comment, "That far in his talk David was serious; possibly he was serious in the rest of it; most people would have doubted it; George might have doubted it if he had been differently made" (pp. 188–89). Then, George begins to pontificate on the principle of providence, and a hoary anecdote is turned into something almost fresh.

The writer's treatment of the Orion character—the "Governor"—is another case in point. Over and over again during this period Clemens attempted to use his brother in his fiction, and for good reason, because Orion should have made good copy. But Mark Twain had yet to publish any of the fiction involving this character, something that readers familiar with the posthumous publications may tend to forget. As well, some of George's references to "old" qualities, such as the governor's flightiness, are newly minted: "Without serious success; for he was shavings, not anthracite" (p. 239); "For a week or two, in the beginning, he had a burning ambition to be a Franklin; so he lived strictly on bread and water, studied by the firelight instead of using candles, and practised swimming on the floor" (p. 240). The last phrase is vintage Mark Twain.

Finally, the cumulative effect of these stories of woe is neither dreary nor maudlin, although George's responses to a few of the tales may seem melodramatic. The overall effect is not created by the way in which Mark Twain punctuates the anecdotes with sections of comic "relief," which allow the reader to laugh at the admiral's talk of Satan, Adam, and the naming of the animals or to laugh at the debate between the two blacks about providence. Some of these sections are funny, although occasionally they are too long. Yet they do not provide "relief" from the tragic stories in the narrow and pejorative literary sense. The relief that they create is more fundamental, because the writer's paramount purpose throughout "The Refuge of the Derelicts" is to suggest and dramatize ways in which suffering may be alleviated.

One method Mark Twain uses is to have the characters intellectualize, and thereby render relatively painless, experiences and principles that, responded to differently, might have been excruciating. For this reason, Uncle Rastus and Aunt Phyllis debate about providence, thereby sloughing over the possibility that the black man may have been damaged by a cruel fate; the admiral concludes a discussion by deciding that both money and the lack of it may be the roots of evil; and he speculates about the characters of Adam and Eve, rather than dwelling emotionally on the tragic implications of their fall. Through these intellectual discussions, material that could have caused pain is rendered comic for the reader.

Another more obvious and important way in which a potentially pessimistic book is changed into something quite different is through the author's focus on compassion as a means of alleviating sorrow. The admiral is central here because, despite his vanities, his fatuities, and his peculiar biblical interpretations, he is essentially religious; he is another version of the Old Man in Mark Twain's "Gospel," who is willing to accept all people as they are, not to patronize them with his pity, but to argue with them, to become angry with them, to help them in practical ways if they need aid—to help them both through the force of his personality and the beneficent use of his possessions.

Mark Twain also uses the responses of his artist-narrator to create the mellow, accepting tone of his book. Somewhat like the Young Man in the writer's "Gospel," George Sterling is an inexperienced, idealistic individual who tends to over-react when confronting new experiences, a response that is sometimes a source of amusement for the reader. But George often speaks forcefully and infectiously, as when he talks of the tragedy of common people without conventions (p. 198), or when he responds vibrantly to his new, direct, nontheoretical involvement with those around him:

> Every day the feeling of the day before is renewed to me—the feeling of having been in a half-trance all my life before—numb, sluggish-blooded, sluggish-minded—a feeling which is followed at once by a brisk sense of being out of that syncope and awake! awake and alive; alive to my finger-ends. I realize that I am a veteran trader in shadows who has struck the substance. I have found the human race. It was all around me before, but vague and spectral; I have found it now, with the blood in it, and the bones; and am getting acquainted with it. (pp. 205–6)

It is difficult for the reader to feel depressed when the narrator is so thoroughly alive.

There is an attractive subtlety and a kind of warm resonance to the book. The story's donnée, of course, is George's desire to raise money for a monument to Adam. The conversation frequently circles about the first man, the essence of Mark Twain's attitude seemingly being that,

> "Suppose you ordered a Man at the start, and had a chance to look over the plans and specifications—which would you take, Adam or the germ? Naturally you would say Adam is business, the germ ain't; one is immediate and sure, the other is speculative and uncertain. Well, I have thought these things all over, and my sympathies are with Adam. Adam was like *us*, and so he seems near to us, and dear. He is kin, blood kin, and my heart goes out to him in affection. But I don't feel that way about that germ. The germ is too far away—and not only that, but such a wilderness of reptiles between. You can't skip the reptiles and set your love on the germ; no, if they are ancestors, it is your duty to include them and love them. Well, you can't do that. You would come up against the dinosaur and your affections

would cool off. You couldn't love a dinosaur the way you would another relative. There would always be a gap. Nothing could ever bridge it. Why, it gives a person the dry gripes just to look at him!"

"Very well, then, where do we arrive? Where do we arrive with our respect, our homage, our filial affection? At Adam! At Adam, every time. We can't build a monument to a germ, but we can build one to Adam, who is in the way to turn myth in fifty years and be entirely forgotten in two hundred. We can build a monument and save his name to the world forever, and we'll do it! What do you say?" (p. 221)

Adam as poetic symbol, as myth, as the unfortunate cause of man's suffering, Adam as all of these is much more affecting than anything associated with evolutionary theory—like New York City's brontosaur. This is why the admiral—and his creator—make Adam a focal point of their interests. The implications of the Adamic story are at the heart of this story as well, because it is about suffering, its causes, and the means to endure it. When George begins his project, Adam has no experiential meaning for him; but as he lives in the refuge, he begins to feel the import of the character. What he never seems to realize, however, is that while he has been scheming to gain support for his monument, the admiral—through his personality and his home—has already created a memorial to the father of the human race.

Ever since he returned to America in 1900, Mark Twain was preoccupied, in his efforts at reform, with hacking at the branches of suffering. While writing this manuscript, he seems to have temporarily concluded that the roots of suffering reached throughout the human condition and that, although it is impossible to prevent suffering, it is crucial that it be alleviated when it occurs.

"The Refuge of the Derelicts" is a good story, well begun, and with many possibilities for extension: the narrator refers to a number of characters—the "drifters"—who visit the home and occasionally offer new stories of their adventures in the outside world (p. 230). It would seem, therefore, that Mark Twain could have continued his narrative almost indefinitely if he had wanted to. Yet it remains unfinished. Perhaps his need to counter the heinous monarchs, Nicholas and Leopold, was sated during the two months he spent focusing on the erratic democrat, Admiral Stormfield. Perhaps, since he was attempting to publish *Captain Stormfield's Visit to Heaven* during this period, he felt no need to finish a second Stormfield manuscript. Perhaps he became impatient with his realistic novel with symbolic overtones and decided to pursue his interest in the "minor Biblical characters" more directly, in a different kind of narrative. Perhaps, when he returned to the manuscript later, he was simply too old and too tired to force the story beyond the episode of the slide show. In any event, Mark Twain never completed "The Refuge of the Derelicts," and the most promising piece of long fiction that he began during these last American years remains an interesting long fragment.

Other than "Eve's Diary" and the revision of "Adam's Diary," which we know Mark Twain wrote while at Dublin, New Hampshire, in the summer of 1905, it is impossible to date exactly the other Adam and Eve manuscripts that were composed some time during these years: "That Day in Eden," "Eve Speaks," and what De Voto in *Letters from the Earth* called "Papers of the Adams Family." Since it seems probable, however, that all this material was composed either in 1905 or 1906, I will discuss it all together.[17] Each piece is interesting and skillfully written. In several, the author who often had thought of himself as a representative man and who, in "Eddypus," had referred to himself facetiously as "the father of history," writes from the perspective of the representative woman, Eve, the mother of history.

The published version of "Eve's Diary" was written for the Christmas 1905 issue of *Harper's Monthly*, and then was issued in book form with numerous delicate illustrations in 1906. It is a delightful, short, popular work, gracefully and clearly written, quietly humorous in its analysis of Adam and Eve's courtship and their subsequent "marriage," and filled with a sense of wonder that derives from the writer's successful attempt to intuit Eve's mystified, joyous responses to the just-created universe. Undoubtedly because he was writing for immediate publication, Mark Twain neither asks for any conjectures from the reader concerning the reasons for the Fall, nor bewails the consequences of it, preferring instead a sentimental ending. The last line of the tale

17. For a discussion of the dating of these sketches, see *LE*, p. 77.

frequently is quoted by readers of Mark Twain and is assumed to somehow epitomize the relationship between Samuel and Livy Clemens: "Wheresoever she was, *there* was Eden."[18] "Eve's Diary" is an entertaining sketch, but because it was written for a particular audience at a particular time, it lacks the depth and the real pathos that are present in the Adam and Eve pieces not published in the writer's lifetime.

Unfortunately, the most impressive of the Eve fragments remains unpublished, only a little less than half of it having appeared in *Letters from the Earth* as "Eve's Autobiography."[19] The entire sketch comprises an admirable unity of plot, character, narrative perspective, and theme. Most of the material derives from Eve's diary entries before the Fall; sometimes, however, comments from the postlapsarian Eve interrupt her youthful observations—lamenting the contrast between Eden and her present, imagining reasons for her changed identity, and in general emphasizing the loss suffered because of that day in Eden. The writer uses this device with restraint; Eve's interjections are neither too frequent nor, usually, too heavy-handed, but come often enough to remind the reader that something of cataclysmic importance has taken place, a fact almost ignored in the *Harper's Monthly* version:

> I still remember that time as if it were yesterday. I was a blithe young thing & all alive with the splendid enthusiasms of youth: travel was my delight; every mile of my journey revealed new things & new aspects to me, & every novelty brought its own special pleasure; every day I moved through a new world, new wonders, new combinations of beauty & majesty & sublimity, & every night I reviewed the day's enchantments & lived them again. (p. 19)

Throughout the diary itself the Fall is occasionally foreshadowed, as in Eve's discovery that the animals are carnivorous, although they now eat strawberries—a reference that also appears in "Eve's Diary"—or as in the references to the plant called deadly nightshade. Allusions to phenomena whose full significance will not be revealed until after the

18. *Writings*, 24:381.

19. Manuscript pages 43–79 were published in *LE*. The first forty-two pages may be found in Box 15, No. 2, MTP. Henceforth, references to "Eve's Autobiography" will be made in the text.

Fall not only add suspense and irony to the sketch, but also help to make a thematic point: that post-Edenic conditions were inherent in Eden itself.

This point is also made in Mark Twain's characterization of Adam and Eve; the qualities that led to the Fall were also inherent in the two humans. Most essentially, they are scientists whose major pleasure in life comes from exploring their magnificent environment. Adam's pride in his discovery of the Law of Fluidic Precipitation indicates this fact, as does Eve's excitement in experimenting about the source of milk in the cow and her joy in being able to conclude that milk comes from the air. These episodes are humorous, as are those in which Adam and Eve decide not to eat the apple because their interest is suddenly transferred to a new kind of animal, which they follow and befriend; this delaying tactic also adds suspense to the story. Significant also is the way in which these examples underline Mark Twain's most important point and help intensify the poignancy of the tragedy: Adam and Eve's end is in their beginning; the qualities that cause their fall—curiosity, the desire to affix names to things—are ones they inherited from God as the first human beings. This curiosity and drive to classify and to touch the essence of unknown things are stressed often throughout the sketch, usually in interesting anecdotes, so that the writer's ontological argument is clearly and entertainingly presented.

Mark Twain's fascination with the paradoxes of identity is evinced continually in "Eve's Autobiography." The young Eve asks, "What am I? Whence came I? What am I for?," and the old one thinks,

> This faded manuscript is blurred by the tears which fell upon it then, & after ten centuries I am crying over it again. Crying over it for pity of that poor child; & from this far distance it seems to be not me, but a child that I have lost—*my* child. Other mothers have felt something akin to this in recalling, not their former selves, (as in my case), but the little figures which represent sons & daughters of theirs which have since grown to the gravity & structure of full age. Sometimes, for a moment, these poor mothers have a vision of those little creatures romping by; & they recognize the voices & the laughter—gone silent long ago! —& they have a pain at the heart, as knowing that *those* chil-

dren are lost to them for always, in the flesh, although their grown-up selves are still present in life & still precious. The loved & the lost! *They* know—the mothers! They know what the grown-ups are, & what they *were*—& that the "are" & the "were" are the same, yet not the same; that the "are" remain, but that the "were" have gone out from their mothers' lives to return no more but in visions. (pp. 27–28)

Although Eve is unable to explain all these mysteries and abstractions, she does give the reader an understanding of her specific character through her diary, particularly those entries leading up to her meeting with Adam, their courtship, and their subsequent relationship, a sequence handled less quickly and more subtly here than in "Eve's Diary." We know from what she says about herself before meeting Adam, for example, that she will remain incomplete until she befriends a creature of her own kind; until then, she will make do poorly with her shadow or with the animals. We know as well that it is partly the example of other animals—the fact that they travel in pairs, that they have children—that intensifies her need for a partner. In a sense, therefore, it is social pressure that creates dissatisfaction; yet her feelings also seem to derive from her kinship with the animals and from her recognition of their pleasure in partnership. Although she is related to them, she is also different and thus cannot be satisfied with their company. In explaining to herself why a conversation with a parrot is unrewarding, she decides that the words lack "high spirituality"; the bird could mimic the form of human discourse, but not the essence. Something is missing in the relationship between her and the beasts. We learn also that she can be frustrated by contrasts between what she is and what she sees; when she catches glimpses of the Happy Valley, she is saddened when she cannot find its entrance. Seemingly unlike the animals, she can be made unhappy by contrasts; she possesses an innate longing for the new and unexplained.

Eve's description of her courtship also tells us about herself; when she finds Adam, she enthusiastically embraces him, then is humiliated when he rejects her:

How could he use me so? What had I done? I had not meant any harm. I was glad to be with him, I only wanted to express it & I knew no other way: I am young & have had no one to teach me, & if I made a mistake was it so great a one that I deserved such humiliation? I could hardly believe it had happened. I had never been treated so before; the animals always gave me love for love, & never thought to hurt my body or shame my pride. It was so strange—this that had happened. (p. 31)[20]

One can conclude that her propensity to feel pain at sexual rejection is also part of her identity, as is the way in which she pursues the man even while pretending to herself that she is engaged in other activities; the tendency to rationalize, therefore, also seems innate. Mark Twain's sketch continually suggests paradoxes of identity: that the "I" cannot be fully a self until it relates intimately to another in a manner that may often bring pain as well as joy; that the Edenic "I" had a curiosity that was magnified by the relationship with another and led eventually to the death of self. In keeping with these ideas, the tone of "Eve's Autobiography" is bittersweet. And the sketch itself is a generally admirable one.

Two of the Adam and Eve pieces published in *Europe and Elsewhere*—"Eve Speaks" and "That Day in Eden"—are linked obviously to "Eve's Autobiography" and contrast radically with the Eve manuscript published in *Harper's Monthly*. In "That Day in Eden," Satan interprets the Fall and refers again to a point made in "Eve's Autobiography": it was impossible for Adam and Eve to know the meaning of abstract terms like death, good, and evil, and God's warning was therefore useless. In "Eve's Autobiography" the narrator cannot bring herself to describe the Fall; and when the sketch halts, she is discussing her children. In "Eve Speaks," on the other hand, the Fall is described with acrid power by the disillusioned matriarch:

> They drove us out. Drove us out into this harsh wilderness, and shut the gates against us. We that had meant no harm. It is three months. We were ignorant then; we are rich in learning now—ah, how rich! We know hunger, thirst, and cold; we know pain, disease, and grief; we know hate, rebellion, and deceit; we know remorse, the conscience that prosecutes guilt and inno-

20. Howard Baetzhold suggests that the writer's memories of the breakup of his youthful love affair with Laura Wright may have influenced his handling of the estrangement of Adam and Eve. See "Found: Mark Twain's 'Lost Sweetheart,'" pp. 425–26.

cence alike, making no distinction; we know weariness of body
and spirit, the unrefreshing sleep, the rest which rests not, the
dreams which restore Eden, and banish it again with the waking;
we know misery; we know torture and the heartbreak; we know
humiliation and insult; we know indecency, immodesty, and the
soiled mind; we know the scorn that attaches to the transmitted
image of God exposed unclothed to the day; we know fear, we
know vanity, folly, envy, hypocrisy; we know irreverence; we
know blasphemy; we know right from wrong, and how to avoid
the one and do the other; we know all the rich product of the
Moral Sense, and it is our possession. Would we could sell it
for one hour of Eden and white purity; would we could de-
grade the animals with it! [21]

In this sketch Adam and Eve discover the existential meaning of death as they attempt, in a very emotional scene, to
awaken their son Abel from a perplexingly long sleep:

I have sat by him all night, being afraid he might wake and
want his food. His face was very white; and it changed, and he
came to look as he had looked when he was a little child in Eden
long ago, so sweet and good and dear. It carried me back over
the abyss of years, and I was lost in dreams and tears—oh, hours,
I think. Then I came to myself; and thinking he stirred, I kissed
his cheek to wake him but he slumbered on and I was disappointed. His cheek was cold. I brought sacks of wool and the
down of birds and covered him, but he was still cold, and I
brought more. Adam has come again, and says he is not yet
warm. I do not understand it.

III

We cannot wake him! With my arms clinging about him I
have looked into his eyes, through the veil of my tears, and
begged for one little word, and he will not answer. Oh, is it
that long sleep—is it death? And will he wake no more?

FROM SATAN'S DIARY

Death has entered the world, the creatures are perishing; one
of The Family is fallen; the product of the Moral Sense is complete. The Family think ill of death—they will change their
minds. (p. 350)

And there is even more Adam and Eve material, some of it
still unpublished: a fragment, for example, that is written
from the point of view of an Eve who has outlived her hus-

21. *Writings*, 29:348. Henceforth, references to "Eve Speaks"
will be made in the text.

band, who has overcome her post-Edenic bitterness, who maintains her zest for life despite her approximately one thousand years, and who now can accept even the death of her daughter with equanimity. In the following passage, Eve remembers the exasperation that her husband came to feel because of condolences sent to them:

> To me he spoke out quite frankly & said that if Gladys had really been as good & gracious & magnanimous & just & liberal & benevolent & unselfish & wise & firm & great & grand & intellectual as these adulations made her out to be, she would have died earlier from pure lonesomeness, & she wouldn't find any society in heaven now that would be suitable for her, neither.[22]

Worth observing in these humorous reminiscences is the probable resemblance between the feelings of Adam and those of his literary creator.

Some of this Adam and Eve material—most of it published in "Papers of the Adams Family"—involves a prophet named Reginald Selkirk who worries about overpopulation; who shows how the problem is related to medical advances made in his generation; and who talks of the beneficial effects of wars, microbes, and floods (at the time he speaks, the Great Flood is being prepared for). Once Mark Twain had taken his narration into the tenth century and had begun to include the Selkirk material, his focus and purpose began to change, particularly in several passages where parallels are drawn between the imagined biblical situation and the contemporary American one. The following passage is typical:

> Only when a republic's life is in danger should a man uphold his government when it is in the wrong. There is no other time.
> This Republic's life is not in peril. The nation has sold its honor for a phrase. It has swung itself loose from its safe anchorage and is drifting, its helm is in pirate hands. The stupid phrase needed help, and it got another one: "Even if the war be wrong we are in it and must fight it out: we cannot retire from it without dishonor." Why, even a burglar could have said it better. We cannot withdraw from this sordid raid because to grant peace to those little people upon their terms—independence—would dishonor us. You have flung away Adam's phrase—

22. Box 15, 10a, MTP.

you should take it up and examine it again. He said, "An in-
glorious peace is better than a dishonorable war."
You have planted a seed, and it will grow.[23]

Here, Mark Twain seems to have wanted to create a manuscript that would have allowed him to be both a reformer and
a metaphysician; as the following note suggests, at one point
he planned to link his biblical and "Eddypus" ideas:

> Discov. of America, yr. 314   Eve dies 972. Decay of civilization
> begins then: spreading of X^n Sci. Religious wars produced. By
> 1200 civ. is dead, & X^nS with it. Savagery till resurrec. of X^nS—
> flood results. No trade for life ins. except insuring the Ins. com-
> panies. Ruined monument to Adam. A savage discourses on it.[24]

There is also evidence in this area, therefore, of Mark
Twain's need to involve himself with large projects dealing
with important themes.

Perhaps surprisingly, there is very little that I wish to say
about the other literary projects with which Clemens involved himself in the summer of 1905 and in 1906: "3000
Years Among the Microbes," "No. 44, The Mysterious
Stranger," the additions to and revisions of the "Gospel" in
preparation for its anonymous publication as *What Is Man?*.
We know how much he enjoyed his work on the first two
manuscripts, particularly his first few weeks of work on the
"Microbes" narrative. Yet, compared with the material of the
previous months, these manuscripts are unequivocally inferior.

"Three Thousand Years Among the Microbes" begins
with a scientist being turned into a microbe by a magician;
after this, the story concerns itself with a series of conversations between the narrator, nicknamed Huck, and residents
of a microbe world that exists within the body of a drunken
tramp called Blitzowski.[25] The manuscript halts as Huck
prepares to leave on a gold-seeking expedition to a far country named Major Molar. The tale begins with an absolute
minimum of preparation; proceeds with practically no pre-

23. *LE*, pp. 97–98.
24. Box 16, 1a, MTP.
25. The text I am using for "Three Thousand Years Among the
Microbes" is *WWD?*, pp. 433–553.

tense of a plot and little attempt to justify the conversations that occur; then, when a possible plot emerges, the narrative stops.

As a satire, the manuscript is eminently forgettable, because it has neither satiric focus nor sting, only a series of random observations about pride, greed, Christian Science, the American love of titles, currency reform, medical butcheries during the Spanish-American War, stock watering, and so on. The notes suggest that the satiric potshotting would have continued if Mark Twain had decided to finish. Another problem is that many of the ideas are treated elsewhere in the writer's work and are handled much more effectively. What passes for satire in "Microbes" is almost without exception tame and really not worth bothering about.

As a vehicle for the exploration of metaphysical ideas, the narrative is more interesting; but one wishes that Mark Twain had not decided to do this in fiction. Using his plot gimmick, he considers several ideas: that everything is organic and that there is no such thing as death, although personal identity would no longer exist after "life" is over; that the entire universe, from its smallest to its largest form, is cannibalistic; that man's relationship to God may be analogous to the microbes' relationship to their tramp; that one person's dream is another person's reality, and so on. Several of these ideas are unusual; given this fact, it is possible to guess why the story trails off so quickly just when a plot begins to appear: by this point, the imaginative daring that had informed some of the earlier sections was gone; if Mark Twain had continued, the plot would have been still another quest providing opportunities for more diatribes against greed and hypocrisy. Gone too, I suspect, would have been the sense of wonder that is present in much of the first part and that makes sections palatable reading, despite the author's indifference to such fictional amenities as plot and character. The narrator, for example, is not terrified by his deductions concerning the principle of universal cannibalism; he is fascinated by them. Moreover, he is happy to discover that all microbes possess a usefulness that outweighs their ability to harass.

The man who makes these discoveries, of course, is not Samuel Clemens; he is a personalized narrator. Yet through his persona, the writer signals his own temporary willingness to consider that the natural phenomena and laws that he often had railed against and used as proof of a malevolent deity were really benevolent. In his recent article, Henry J. Lindborg suggests that, in this work, Mark Twain attempts halfheartedly to balance C. S. Saleby's (*The Cycle of Life: According to Nature*) pessimistic attitude toward the relation of man to the microbe by contrasting it with the optimistic attitude of R. D. Conn (*Life of the Germ*). According to Lindborg, however, "a vision of loathsome parasitism . . . remains more powerful than a positive life cycle," and "the negative side of the adventure with the microbes was more impressive to him."[26] It seems to me, on the other hand, that the tone of "Microbes" is described more accurately by Richard Hauck when he writes, "The vision of life in everything is joyfully celebrated. The vision of life in everything is hilariously satirized. . . . The final irony, comic and deeply serious, is that optimism can be enjoyed by any man willing to forget that he sees only what he can see and that what he can see is always a joke."[27] "Three Thousand Years among the Microbes" is primarily the cheerful work of a man enjoying his imaginings. Although it contains a few misanthropic moments, it is generally the manuscript of Mark Twain in a good mood.

So too is the last section of "No. 44, the Mysterious Stranger," which Mark Twain took up again after "Microbes" was

26. "A Cosmic Tramp: Samuel Clemens' 'Three Thousand Years Among The Microbes,' " p. 654.

27. *A Cheerful Nihilism: Confidence and the Absurd in American Humorous Fiction*, p. 166. It is possible that Mark Twain's attitude toward the relationship between man and his microbes may have been influenced by the following comments made in a letter dated 22 March 1904 by his friend J. Y. W. McAlister, who was recovering from tuberculosis in a sanatorium. McAlister writes of having discovered that his hemorrhage was "a *result* of tuberculosis mischief and that the little devils were making rapid headway with an excavating contract they had got on my lungs. . . . Today the doctors have been hunting microbes in vain—they are as scarce as the Swiss Chamois (large size). They can't even find a corpse of one for which I am rather sorry as I should have liked to celebrate the obsequies with fitting ceremony . . . but the truth is in this palace of disease and death one must try to laugh or go mad or die. We have a death every week" (MTP).

put aside, a fact that explains why the "life as a dream" ending written at the time of Livy's death seems so inappropriate for the chapters written at this time. If we believe his secretary, Isabel Lyon, when he resumed work on the manuscript he again thought of trying to publish it.[28] And even more than is the case with the earlier sections of the book, this possibility helps to explain the relative absence of satire in the last chapters. There are some gibes about Mary Baker Eddy's comments on the Russo-Japanese War, but in general the only real interest for the modern reader probably will derive from the story's continuing metaphysical speculativeness concerning, for example, the nature of identity, and the relationship between the mundane and dream selves and something referred to as "Soul"—a dimension that according to the narrator's dream self is the only condition in which true freedom can exist. Mark Twain also considers the implications of recent inventions like the tape recorder and the camera as they relate to the individual's ability to know himself. Unfortunately, in order to dramatize these ideas, he depends too frequently either on farce, which soon becomes tedious, or on a new romance subplot centering on the sixteen-year-old narrator's infatuation with a girl named Marget; the passion that he displays in his pursuit of her has not even been hinted at in the previous pages.

Approximately a year after he had laid aside the "No. 44" manuscript, Clemens's letter to his friend Thomas Bailey Aldrich suggested that he had at last accepted his limitations and definitely needed a rest:

> I have just returned from another 3 weeks' junketing—& still with a good conscience, for "wasted time" is no longer a matter of concern to me; at least in the summer time. I have worked pretty steadily for 65 years, & I don't care what I do with the 2 or 3 that remain to me so that I get pleasure out of them. I am 300,000 words to the good on the autobiography, & if I add an average of 50,000 a month for the rest of my life I shall be satisfied—especially if I can find ways to put in the rest of the month

28. Referring to "No. 44," Isabel Lyon wrote in her diary entry of 3 July 1905, "He's going to make that book with flavoring enough to suit the palate of the ordinary family" (IVL Diary, 3 July 1905, MTP).

agreeably. If I had you near by I would make you read a chapter of it every day for your sins.[29]

The letter from this now almost seventy-one-year-old man was written at the end of another typically hectic parade of months (during which he earned the name "The Belle of New York") replete with the usual family problems, social engagements, and attempts at social reform.[30] More importantly, it came after the private, anonymous publication of his "Gospel," an event that for a period at least must have served as a kind of symbolic climax to his career as a serious writer and that was an almost inevitable culmination of his activities during these last years, particularly during the years after Livy's death. With her death, of course, he no longer felt the same constraints he had experienced before. Moreover, the types of ideas that he had been considering in other manuscripts and the targets that he had chosen to attack had all been involved either directly or indirectly with the question that became the title for his philosophical dialogue—*What is Man?*.

Another factor influencing his decision to publish his "Gospel" was undoubtedly that much of the work already had been done on the dialogue; all that remained would be the composition of a few more sections and the restructuring necessary to satisfy the writer's sense of form. A further reason may have been the influence of Clemens's admired friend Joe Goodman, who himself had just completed an unremunerative but intellectually impressive study of Mayan culture. A few years before, Goodman had urged his old newspaper cohort to publish his "Gospel," speculating that it could prove to be the capstone to his career.[31] Moreover, by 1905 and 1906, encouraged by the publication of his political prose and by the general respect with which these pieces had been

29. SLC to T. B. Aldrich, 2 October 1906, MS at Houghton Library. In the last part of the letter, Clemens refers to Jean's ill health and his own responsibility to her.

30. See Hill's account of these months on pp. 118–52 of *God's Fool*.

31. See Joseph Goodman to SLC, 18 October 1903: "I see in the idea, as you outlined to me, the possibility of your crowning achievement" (MTP).

greeted, Clemens had gained sufficient confidence in his identity as a thinker to publish a serious, unprofitable work, although he still was not secure enough to publish it under his own name. One final possibility might be considered: he hoped by finishing the manuscript and publishing it to answer, once and for all, the questions concerning the nature of man that periodically had invaded his consciousness for so many years. Perhaps he hoped that if he finally put his ideas into print, he would stop rethinking them.

After devoting this much space to a consideration of his motives in publishing *What Is Man?*, I have little to say about the work itself. I prefer the more modest dialogue with the less prepossessing title of "What Is the Real Character of Conscience?" or "Selfishness," because its ideas are not repeated to the point where they become tedious, because its two characters are more than Mark Twain mouthpieces, and because there is in it a definite freshness and enthusiasm that prevents the deterministic ideas from being depressing or despairing. These qualities are weakened in the later version, as the writer plays with the structure, reiterates points already made ruthlessly, excises inappropriate material such as thoughts about God, and then includes new sections in order to flesh out the manuscript to a length commensurate with the importance suggested by the book's imposing title.

To me, the most annoying aspect of the finished manuscript is the disparity between the structure symbolized by the careful numbering of the various sections and subsections—because the numbers signal that the work has a recognizable and coherent organization—and the structure felt by the reader: the work is incomplete, the organization arbitrary.[32] In *What Is Man?*, Mark Twain seems to have attempted—perhaps unconsciously—to use the numbers to wrestle into shape ideas that could not possibly have coalesced. To understand why they could not, we need recognize two things: first, the dialogue embodies old ideas from sections written earlier about man as a selfish creature, life as an unbroken chain of events, and the mind as a machine; second, the dialogue also reflects—in the more recently written section called "A Difficult Question," for example—new

32. I feel a similar frustration, for an analogous reason, when I read many of Emerson's early essays.

ideas about such topics as dream selves. In general, Mark Twain's mechanistic philosophy cohabits uneasily with his intuitions about the mind's mysterious capabilities and associational tendencies—qualities that he must have noticed in himself as he dictated his autobiography.[33] The result of these problems is a work that is neither as complete as the unfinished early dialogue, nor as dramatic, nor as interesting, in sum that is not as good, although sections still are worth reading. Characteristically, Mark Twain's attempt to fasten his ideas into a large, tidy bundle resulted primarily in something big and disheveled.

33. In his "Mark Twain's Later Dialogue: The 'Me' and the Machine," John Tuckey discusses some of the sources and other evidence of this tension between deterministic and nondeterministic ideas. Tuckey's discussion, however, is only one of the latest and most cogent about a topic that has interested many Mark Twain scholars.

11

The Holiday
November 1906 to April 1910

Mark Twain did not really conclude his activities in the fall of 1906, despite his opinion that after a man has reached his seventieth birthday, his work is done, whatever its quality, and he has earned a vacation.[1] After having expressed this conviction, he continued to publish: *Christian Science* in 1907, excerpts from his autobiography in the *North American Review* in 1908, *Captain Stormfield's Visit to Heaven* in 1909.[2] Almost all this work, however, had been completed before 1906. Of the pages composed during these years, a great many were of mediocre quality: *Is Shakespeare Dead?*, for example, which was written in the spring of 1909 at the suggestion of Mary Lawton and Helen Keller and was stimulated by Mark Twain's desire to once more enter a public argument armed with his theories about training;[3] this time he would embarrass scholars foolish enough to believe that William Shakespeare had created the magnificent plays popularly attributed to him. If, Mark Twain asked on 25 March 1909, the dramatist actually had written the plays, then why did so few Stratfordian anecdotes survive his death? By con-

1. Autobiographical Dictations, 8 October 1906, MTP. For abbreviations used in the footnotes, see "Short References," pp. ix–x.

2. *Captain Stormfield* was published, of course, without the anti-imperialistic chapter, "Journey to an Asterisk" (DV 203, MTP), which at some point during these years, Mark Twain had considered using. For information concerning this unpublished chapter see Arthur Scott, *Mark Twain at Large*, p. 268.

3. For more information concerning the background of "Is Shakespeare Dead?" (particularly its relation to George Greenwood's *The Shakespeare Problem Restated*) and the public responses to it, see *God's Fool*, pp. 216–17. It is Isabel Lyon, however, who mentions in her 8 January 1909 notes (MTP) that her employer was encouraged to undertake the project by Helen Keller and Mary Lawton.

trast, townspeople in Hannibal, Missouri, were bursting with stories about their homegrown genius.[4]

The humorist involved himself with other literary projects in addition to his pamphlet about Shakespeare, but it can be argued that these are less interesting than other projects that he considered but never actually undertook: the completion of his old manuscripts (a task that, in the spring of 1908, he said he lacked the energy to perform); a life of Jesus; an assault on Anatole France's iconoclastic biography of Joan of Arc. Replying to a request from Andrew Lang, on 25 April 1908 Clemens said, "It is long since I touched a pen ($3\frac{1}{2}$ years), and I was intending to continue the happy holidays to the gallows but—there are things that could beguile me to break this blessed Sabbath." The Joan of Arc project, unfortunately, was not one of them. Neither did Mark Twain ever write a continuation of the attacks upon King Leopold of Belgium, a possibility suggested by Sir Arthur Conan Doyle in the fall of 1909 and rejected as being "too enflaming."[5]

In regard to the projects Mark Twain did tackle, his failures are not difficult to explain; neither are they particularly revealing about him as a writer. If, as he remarked in his autobiographical dictation of 7 July 1906, writing in his younger years had been "merely billiards to me," in the last years of his life only billiards was like billiards for him, because he preferred this game to the debilitating task of pushing a pen across a page. He seemed, in fact, to prefer practically any form of amusement to writing: playing cards, attending banquets (although at one point, he vows that he will attend no more banquets "even if it is the Last Supper"), voyaging to England for an honorary doctorate in the summer of 1907, jaunting to Bermuda on many occasions, taking photographs.[6] Moreover, particularly after his home in Connecticut had been built in the summer of 1908, he devoted an

4. See the Autobiographical Dictations, 25 March 1909, MTP.

5. See SLC to Mr. Phillipots, 26 April 1908, MTP; Isabel Lyon Notebook III, 11 October 1907, MTP; SLC to Andrew Lang, 25 April 1908, MTP; Albert Bigelow Paine to Sir Arthur Conan Doyle, 29 October 1909, TS, MTP.

6. The collection of photographs donated in 1976 to the Mark Twain Papers demonstrates how much Clemens enjoyed this activity.

increasing number of hours to pursuing the friendship of substitute grandchildren—an international "Aquarium" of preadolescent girls whom he called his "Angel Fish."[7] Hamlin Hill writes that, after he received his Oxford degree, "Mark Twain was as completely lost to the world . . . as if it had indeed been the funeral he was planning."[8] The man had a "tobacco heart," and he was tired. He had become old.

But his pen was not yet silenced. Only a few months after the "finality" of the writer's Liverpool speech delivered before leaving England, his interest in life was manifesting itself in a series of funny letters written for a variety of audiences. Commenting on the poetry of a man who considered himself worthy of becoming poet laureate, Mark Twain wrote on 21 August, "But he is not a legitimate successor—his poem proves it. It lacks incoherency, it lacks idiocy, it lacks a windy emptiness, it lacks putrid & insistent bastard godliness—indeed it lacks every essential that goes to the making of a real Poet Lariat."[9] Then, on 4 October, in the final page of a letter to Jean, he added,

> P. S. Jean dear it is an outrage the govment is acting so I am sending following complaint to N. Y. Times with Howels name because it will have more weight:
> To the Editor
>   Sir to you, I would like to know what kind of goddam govment this is that discriminates between two common carriers & makes a goddam railroad charge everybody equal & lets a goddam man charge any goddam price he wants to for his goddam operabox.
>   W. D. Howels[10]

His published thanksgiving message in the *New York World* upon the failure of the Knickerbocker Trust Company is neither as pungently crude as the above two letters,

7. As the many letters—both to and from a variety of "Angel Fish"—in the Mark Twain Papers indicate, Clemens was not exaggerating when he wrote on 7 July 1908 that his "Aquarium" was one of his life's chief interests (SLC to Margaret Blackmer, MTP).

8. *God's Fool*, p. 177.

9. SLC's comments on the would-be-poet-laureate Lewis Elmer Truscott appear (in Isabel Lyon's handwriting) in a 21 August 1907 letter to Ospian Lang. See DV 109, No. 3, MTP.

10. SLC to Jean Clemens, 4 October 1907, TS at MTP, MS at Yale. See also *MTHL*, 2:827.

nor as delightfully ungrammatical as the "Howels" example, but it is equally pithy:

> To the Editor of *The World*:
>
> Sir: You ask me for a sentiment which shall state how much I have to be thankful for this time. For years it has been a rule with me not to expose my gratitude in print on Thanksgiving Day, but I wish to break the rule now and pour out my thankfulness; for there is more of it than I can contain without straining myself. I am thankful—thankful beyond words—that I had only $51,000 on deposit in the Knickerbocker Trust, instead of a million; for if I had had a million in that bucket shop, I should be nineteen times as sorry as I am now.
>
> Trusting that his paen of joy will satisfy your requirements, I am
>
> > Yours truly,
> > Mark Twain.[11]

It was not only in letters like these that the writer's continuing interest in life was manifesting itself. From time to time throughout these years his involvement with his autobiographical dictations was creative and rejuvenating, a fact suggested by many selections in Paine's bowdlerized *Mark Twain's Autobiography*, in *Mark Twain in Eruption*, and in Charles Neider's idiosyncratic edition of the autobiographical material, as well as in sketches like the one in which the writer describes the massacre by American soldiers of the Moro tribe in the Philippines (this sketch was entitled "Grief and Mourning for the Night" by Frederick Anderson).[12] Moreover, there are hundreds of pages still unpublished. In sum, there are enough passages of interesting material scattered throughout both the published and unpublished dictations to prove that—at least on occasions—attempts made to bury Mark Twain's genius by the man himself were premature, and those made by subsequent commentators, misleading.

Even in 1909, despite his ill health and his 4 February remark that he was too old and lazy to begin writing again, he did begin to write.[13] His lengthiest involvement (from April

11. TS at MTP.

12. Frederick Anderson, ed., *A Pen Warmed-up in Hell*, pp. 78–87.

13. SLC to Ruth [?], 4 February 1909, MTP.

236 / Mark Twain's Last Years As a Writer

to October) was in the creation of the "Lyon/Ashcroft" manuscript; this was his own peculiar version of the events leading up to the firing of his hitherto trusted secretary, Isabel Lyon, and business adviser, Ralph Ashcroft (a tragifarcical episode treated primarily from an anti-Clemensian viewpoint in *God's Fool*).[14] Mark Twain conceived of the over-four-hundred-page manuscript as an extension of his autobiography and as an improvement over the method of dictation; on 17 April he began the manuscript as a "letter" to Howells, explaining that he intended never to mail it (or others of a similar type that he would write to Rogers and Twichell). Through this innovation he thought that he could circumvent the censorship problem created, in the dictations, by the presence of female and religious auditors; and in this way he could come closer to voicing the truths—unpalatable to his generation and others close to it—that might benefit readers living in the distant future.[15]

Mark Twain begins the letter employing a chapter organization, which suggests that he originally intended the manuscript to be both autobiographical and novelistic. From many of the pages, moreover, the reader receives the impression that, for a time at least, the writer viewed the manuscript as the ultimate in detective stories. The detective is not a mere character in the work, like Tom Sawyer or Pudd'nhead Wilson; this time, he is the writer-narrator himself, delineating and dramatizing the treachery of his unfaithful employees and exposing their perfidy for the edification of unknown future readers. As it proceeds, the manuscript becomes tedious, but it does occasionally suggest that Samuel Clemens's instincts as an artist had not been dulled totally by his intense personal involvement with the events that he brings to light.

What speaks most persuasively of the survival of these instincts is the unfinished "Letters from the Earth" (which he began after he had lost interest in the "Lyon/Ashcroft" manuscript); the stimulus for this new project was at least partly provided by the apparent solution to his family problems: in October, Clara at long last married Ossip Gabrilo-

14. See *God's Fool*, pp. 219–43.
15. The preamble to the "Letter" is quoted in *MTHL*, 2:844–45.

witsch; her thoughts of a "career" were blessedly over for the time being.[16] Perhaps more important, Jean was now living with her father and, according to a 21 June letter by him, was in "perfect health." So, says the writer happily, "I've a family again, you see."[17] Further evidence of Clemens's happiness during this period is a letter that he wrote to the mother of one of his "Angel Fish" on 13 October:

> I wish it could be *now,* while the woods are so beautiful and the hickory-nuts raining on you as you pass along. Jean gathered a harvest of them yesterday—but not from Margaret's trees and mine. I'm *saving* those. Fetch her along as soon as you can. The sooner the better. The woods were never lovelier than they are now.[18]

On 8 November he wrote of the world as being "delightful" and of people as being "entertaining" (attitudes almost certainly manifested in the cynical but high-spirited opening sections of "Letters" in which Satan bemusedly describes the bizarre religious beliefs of God's newest creations).[19] Two

16. Writing to Mrs. Ogden on 13 October 1909, Clemens spoke happily of Clara's wedding; then, in remarking on his daughter's now seemingly dead career aspirations, he said of the career: "I hate the word" (MTP). He said that the idea of a musical career for Clara was so repugnant to him because the concept was linked in his mind with his own platform work.

17. SLC to Frank Whitmore, 21 June 1909, MTP.

18. SLC to Helen K. Blackmer, 13 October 1909, TS, MTP.

19. The letter is to Miss Roberts (MTP). Hamlin Hill for once seems to accept the evidence of Albert Bigelow Paine when he assumes that all of the letters in "Letters from the Earth" were written before Mark Twain left for Bermuda in mid-November (See *God's Fool,* pp. 246–49). It is possible, however (and from my point of view, probable), that the writer worked on at least the last three letters either after returning to Stormfield around Christmas—perhaps during the days between Jean's drowning and his final departure for Bermuda when he was also writing "The Death of Jean"—or even during the months in Bermuda before his last illness. We know he did some work in Bermuda; we may surmise that Paine may not have been aware of all of Mark Twain's projects, since the biographer was not with him for most of the time. Most significantly, we know that a large tonal disparity separates the early letters that satirize man's conception of God from the later diatribe against man and God himself. What I am suggesting is that the acrid power of those last letters may derive from the writer's response to his daughter's death (in contrast to his resigned public remarks about his "happiness" over this death).

days later in a letter to Elizabeth Wallace he referred approvingly to an essay just completed for *Harper's Monthly* entitled "The Turning Point of My Life" and commented contentedly about Clara's marriage and Jean's ability to accept the responsibilities of Stormfield housekeeping.[20] Later in November and in December he left on one of his periodic voyages to Bermuda (this time without his crony, Rogers, who had died earlier that year). Upon returning from his trip, he reported to the manager of the Associated Press, "I hear the newspapers say I am dying. The charge is not true—I would not do such a thing at my time of life. I am behaving as good as I can. Merry Christmas to everybody! Mark Twain."[21]

Unfortunately, at her time of life, Jean Clemens would and did die. Early on Christmas Eve morning she suffered an epileptic seizure and drowned in her bath. Her father, writing to Twichell on 27 December, praised her "fine mind"; then, Clemens spit out a brief, bitter profanity against Ralph Ashcroft, who had called Jean insane. After the funeral and after writing the poignant "The Death of Jean," he was off again for Bermuda, calling himself in a letter superlatively happy. But he was also irrevocably old and irredeemably sick. By the end of April, after he had composed for Albert Bigelow Paine some humorous advice about etiquette in heaven, reports of his own death were—at long last—accurate.[22]

20. SLC to Elizabeth Wallace, 10 November 1909. In connection with "The Turning Point of My Life," the editors of *MTHL* write, "It is notable as the first widely-circulated exposition of Mark Twain's deterministic philosophy" (2:851, n. 1). The analysis of the two manuscript versions of the eassay by Robert Rees and Richard Rust is interesting because it demonstrates again that Mark Twain's self-critical skills continued to exist even this late in his career. Rees and Rust point out that after the writer had sensed the disapproval of A. B. Paine and Jean to the first version of the essay, he made significant improvements in it before submitting it to Howells and Harper's, while he was living in Bermuda in November and December 1909 (see "Mark Twain: 'The Turning Point of My Life' ").

21. SLC to Manager, Associated Press, 24 December 1909, TS at MTP, MS at Meissner Collection, University of Washington. DeLancey Ferguson informs us that Jean phoned the message to the press (see *Mark Twain: Man and Legend*, p. 320).

22. SLC to Joseph Twichell, 27 December 1909, TS, MTP; SLC

----

to Elizabeth Wallace, 26 January 1910, TS, MTP; the "advice" is quoted, in part, in Paine's *Mark Twain: A Biography* (*Writings*, 33:1566–67). The full manuscript is at the Mark Twain Papers. While in Bermuda he also made notes for a manuscript that he hoped to write about one of his "Angel Fish," Helen Allen. For a description of Clemens's somewhat ambiguous relationship with this girl, see *God's Fool*, p. 260.

12

Conclusion

━━━

What can be said in summary about the years 1897–1910? What can be said, for example, about the causes of Mark Twain's many literary failures, about the projects that aborted or the sometimes misshapen creatures that reached the light of day? It should be mentioned first of all that the qualities of the writer's essential personality that survived his bankruptcy and his favorite daughter's death were contributing factors: his moodiness, occasional indolence, and tendency to forsake partly furrowed pastures for the promise of green and unturned fields. Another cause was the persistent influence of personal problems: his own erratic health and that of Livy and Jean, his sporadically acute concern about the ways in which his actions were affecting them. A continuing factor also was the effect of reasons more or less aesthetic, although also related to the writer's personality: his ambivalence about the manner in which his books would be received by the variety of audiences for which he wrote; his discomfort with structures conventionally used to embody long fictions; his alternations between thrusts toward, and withdrawals from, structural innovations; his impatient inability to find techniques through which his naturalistic ideas could be dramatized effectively.

All the factors mentioned above created continual difficulties. Contributing also to these difficulties were influences that were particularly bothersome during certain years.

While living in Europe between 1897 and 1900 and trying to resurrect himself as a writer and as a man, he was assailed by multiple confusions, not the least of which was his perplexity over whether literature should even continue to be his dominant vocation. If he was to be a writer, then many questions remained to be answered: Which would be his most effective medium? What kind of audience should he primarily write for? What subjects should he attempt to treat? What tones should he adopt? What would be the most efficient way of writing a subscription book? What should be the proper relation between his life and his work? What was the truest perspective on his past and on life in general? Near the end of this period, the problems created by these questions were complicated by another factor: homesickness.

Upon returning to America, for several years one reason Mark Twain failed in one area was that he was too successful in another: well written polemics and satisfying social involvement were more enjoyable than fiction written with difficulty and inconsistent skill; the writer's infatuation with subjects that were above all timely, concrete, and treatable in succinct forms blunted his ability to create fiction that was timeless, patterned, and long. Between 1904 and 1906, on the other hand, essentially the reverse was true: enamored of his own answers to the query "what is man?," he lacked interest in the types of particular men whose presence in his fiction would bring it to life. Within this period, moreover, his involvement with his autobiography—a form that might have allowed him to vacillate between the particular and the general, the concrete and the abstract, anarchistic freedom and significant structure—was primarily a force-scattering flirtation, not a fulfilling affair. Finally, between the last part of 1906 and his death in 1910, Mark Twain seldom wrote well or finished what he began because he was old.

A problem with generalizations like the ones I have been making is that they may tend to shift the emphasis of this study away from its truest conclusion about Mark Twain's unfinished projects: individual sections of particular manuscripts fail for specific reasons. A more important problem may be that—invited to remember reasons for failure—a reader may forget the evidence of manifold success: completed, published, and superbly written short stories such as "The Man That Corrupted Hadleyburg" and "The $30,000 Bequest"; essays such as "Stirring Times in Austria"; polemical sketches such as "To the Person Sitting in Darkness"; incomplete manuscripts of varying length but generally high quality such as "The Chronicle of Young Satan"; published long works of uneven but sometimes superior quality like

What Is Man? and *Christian Science*; unfinished, generally bad manuscripts like "Which Was It?" that are occasionally redeemed by sequences of concertedly good writing.

In his 1973 review of *Fables of Man*, George Arms observes, "Each section has manuscripts that strike me as Mark Twain's work at its happiest (even when pessimistic) best, and I can imagine no future selections of Twain's shorter pieces that will not include at least ½ dozen."[1] It has been argued here that many examples of "Mark Twain's work at its happiest" appeared during these years. Also, of course, there were many examples of his work at its unhappiest; enough, some readers might decide, to more than counterbalance the effect of occasional instances of serendipity. Yet, in overall quality, Mark Twain's output between 1897 and 1910—and in particular between 1897 and 1906—is not markedly inferior to the writing that he produced in any comparable period during his career. Impatient readers with rigorous critical standards must often be frustrated with Mark Twain, because his work before 1897 was deplorably bad almost as frequently as it was remarkably good. And in this respect, the manuscripts of these last years are not atypical.

1. See *American Literature* 45 (1973):122.

Selective Bibliography

For abbreviations used in the bibliography, see "Short References," pp. ix-x; works listed in "Short References" are not repeated here.

Archer, William. Review of *The Man That Corrupted Hadleyburg and Other Stories*, by Mark Twain. *London Morning Leader* 22 September 1900.

Anderson, Frederick, ed. *A Pen Warmed-up in Hell*. New York, Evanston, San Francisco, London: Harper & Row, 1972.

Baender, Paul. "The Date of Mark Twain's 'The Lowest Animal.'" *American Literature* 36 (1964):174–79.

Baetzhold, Howard. "The Course of Composition of *A Connecticut Yankee*: A Reinterpretation." *American Literature* 33 (1961): 195–214.

————. "Found: Mark Twain's 'Lost Sweetheart.'" *American Literature* 44 (1972):414–29.

————. *Mark Twain and John Bull: The British Connection*. Bloomington and London: Indiana University Press, 1970.

Beatty, Richard Croom, Sculley Bradley, and Hudson E. Long, eds. *Adventures of Huckleberry Finn*. By Samuel Langhorne Clemens. New York: Norton, 1961.

Bellamy, Gladys. *Mark Twain as a Literary Artist*. Norman: University of Oklahoma Press, 1950.

Blues, Thomas. *Mark Twain & the Community*. Lexington: University of Kentucky Press, 1970.

Bridges, Robert. "Mark Twain Re-discovered." *Life*, 20 August 1896, pp. 134–35.

Brodwin, Stanley. "The Humor of the Absurd: Mark Twain's Adamic Diaries." *Criticism* 14 (1972):49–64.

————. "Mark Twain's Masks of Satan: The Final Phase." *American Literature* 45 (1973):202–27.

Budd, Louis J. *Mark Twain: Social Philosopher.* Bloomington: Indiana University Press, 1962.

———. "Mark Twain Talks Mostly About Humor and Humorists." *Studies in American Humor* 1 (1974):4–22.

Carrington, George. *The Dramatic Unity of Huckleberry Finn.* Columbus: Ohio State University Press, 1976.

Chubb, Edwin Watts. *Stories of Authors British and American.* New York, 1910.

Cox, James. *Mark Twain: The Fate of Humor.* Princeton: Princeton University Press, 1966.

Cummings, Sherwood. "*What Is Man?* The Scientific Sources." In *Essays on Determinism in American Literature,* edited by Sidney J. Krause, pp. 108–16. Kent, Ohio: Kent State University Press, 1964.

Ensor, Allison. *Mark Twain and the Bible.* Lexington: University of Kentucky Press, 1969.

Dennis, Larry. "Mark Twain and the Dark Angel." *Midwest Quarterly* 8 (1967):181–97.

De Voto, Bernard. "Notes on the George Harrison Series." De Voto 302, MTP.

Ferguson, DeLancey. *Mark Twain: Man and Legend.* New York: Russell & Russell, 1943.

Ferri, Enrico. "The Delinquent in Art and Literature." *Atlantic Monthly,* February 1897, pp. 233–40.

Foner, Philip. *Mark Twain: Social Critic.* 2d ed. New York: International Publishers, 1966.

Geismar, Maxwell. *Mark Twain: An American Prophet.* Boston: Houghton Mifflin, 1970.

Gibson, William. *The Art of Mark Twain.* New York: Oxford University Press, 1976.

———. "Mark Twain and Howells: Anti-Imperialists." *New England Quarterly* 20 (1947):435–70.

Grant, Douglas. *Twain.* Edinburgh and London: Oliver and Boyd, 1962.

Gribben, Alan. "Anatole France and Mark Twain's Satan." *American Literature* 47 (1976):634–35.

———. " 'It Is Unsatisfactory to Read to One's Self': Mark Twain's Informal Readings." *Quarterly Journal of Speech* 62 (1976):49–56.

———. "Mark Twain, Phrenology and the Temperaments: A

Study of the Pseudo-Scientific Influence." *American Quarterly* 24 (1972):45–68.

Harrison, Benjamin. "Musings Upon Current Topics." *North American Review* 172 (1901):177–90.

Hauck, Richard. *A Cheerful Nihilism: Confidence and the Absurd in American Humorous Fiction.* Bloomington and London: Indiana University Press, 1971.

Howells, William Dean. "Mark Twain: An Inquiry." *North American Review* 172 (1901):306–21.

———. "The Modern American Mood." *Harper's New Monthly Magazine*, February 1897, pp. 199–204.

Jones, Alexander. "Mark Twain and the Determinism of *What Is Man?*" *American Literature* 29 (1957):1–17.

Jones, Daryl E. "The *Hornet* Disaster: Twain's Adaptation in 'The Great Dark.' " *American Literary Realism, 1870–1910* 9 (1976): 243–47.

Kahn, Sholom J. *Mark Twain's Mysterious Stranger: A Study of The Manuscript Texts.* University of Missouri Press: Columbia & London, 1978.

Kaplan, Justin. *Mark Twain and His World.* London: Michael Joseph, 1974.

Krause, Sidney J. *Mark Twain as Critic.* Baltimore: Johns Hopkins Press, 1967.

Lang, Andrew. "The Art of Mark Twain." *Illustrated News of the World* (London), 14 February 1891, p. 222. In Samuel Langhorne Clemens, *Adventures of Huckleberry Finn*, edited by Sculley Bradley, Richard Croom Beatty, and E. Hudson Long, p. 283. New York: Norton, 1961.

Leary, Lewis Gaston. "The Bankruptcy of Mark Twain." In *Southern Excursions: Essays on Mark Twain and Others*, pp. 75–86. Baton Rouge: Louisiana State University Press, 1971.

Lindborg, Henry J. "A Cosmic Tramp: Samuel Clemens' 'Three Thousand Years Among the Microbes.' " *American Literature* 44 (1973):652–57.

Lyon, Isabel Van Kleek. "Diary." MTP.

———. "Daybook." MTP.

Madigan, Francis, Jr. "Mark Twain's Passage to India: A Genetic Study of *Following the Equator.*" Ph.D. dissertation, New York University, 1974.

Matthews, Brander. "The Penalty of Humor." *Harper's New Monthly Magazine*, May 1896, p. 900.

Mott, Bertram. "The Turn-of-the-Century Mark Twain: A Revisit." *Mark Twain Journal* 18 (January 1976):13–16.

Neider, Charles, ed. *Mark Twain's Autobiography*. New York: Harper, 1959.

Parsons, Coleman O. "Mark Twain: Traveler in South Africa." *Mississippi Quarterly* 29 (1975):3–41.

Pettit, Arthur. *Mark Twain & the South*. Lexington: The University of Kentucky Press, 1974.

Regan, Robert. *Unpromising Heroes: Mark Twain and His Characters*. Berkeley: University of California Press, 1966.

Rees, Robert, and Richard Rust. "Mark Twain: 'The Turning Point of My Life.' " *American Literature* 40 (1969):524–35.

Review of *Celibates*, by George Moore. *Atlantic Monthly* 76 (November 1895):707.

Review of *Jude the Obscure*, by Thomas Hardy. *Atlantic Monthly* 77 (February 1896):279.

Review of *The Man That Corrupted Hadleyburg and Other Stories*, by Mark Twain. *Academy*, 29 September 1900, p. 258.

Rogers, Franklin R., ed. *Mark Twain's Satires and Burlesques*. Berkeley: University of California Press, 1967.

Rucker, Mary E. "Moralism and Determinism in 'The Man That Corrupted Hadleyburg.' " *Studies in Short Fiction* 14 (1977): 49–54.

Schwartz, Thomas D. "Mark Twain and Robert Ingersoll: The Free Thought Connection." *American Literature* 48 (1976):183–93.

Scott, Arthur. *Mark Twain at Large*. Chicago: Henry Regnery Co., 1969.

Smith, Henry Nash. *Mark Twain: The Development of a Writer*. Cambridge, Mass.: Harvard University Press, 1962.

Tanner, Tony. *The Reign of Wonder: Naivety and Reality in American Literature*. Cambridge: At the University Press, 1965.

Tuckey, John. "Hannibal, Weggis and Mark Twain's Eseldorf." *American Literature* 42 (1970):235–40.

————. "Mark Twain's Later Dialogue: The 'Me' and the Machine." *American Literature* 41 (1970):532–42.

Tuckey, John, ed. *Mark Twain's Mysterious Stranger and the Critics*. Belmont: Wadsworth Publishing Co., 1968.

Twain, Mark. "Conversations with Satan." Paine 255. MTP.

————. "Eve's Autobiography." Box 15, no. 2, pp. 1–42. MTP.

————. "Fragment of Prussian History." Paine 212. MTP.

————. "If I Could Be There." De Voto 10. MTP.

————. "Is He Dead?" Play folder. MTP.

————. "Journey to an Asterisk." De Voto 203. MTP.

————. *King Leopold's Soliloquy*. Edited by Stefan Heym. Berlin: Seven Seas Books, 1961.

————. "Lyon-Ashcroft Manuscript." MTP.

————. Materials relating to Mark Twain's "Autobiography." MTP.

————. "The New War Scare." Paine 46. MTP.

————. Notebooks 29 (II), 30 (I), 31 (I), 31 (II), 32a (I), 32a (II), 32b (I), 32b (II), 33, 34, 35. TS. MTP.

————. Photographs. MTP.

————. "Proposition for a Postal Cheque." Paine 211. MTP.

————. "St. Pierre or an Impression of Pelée." Paine 208. MTP.

————. Scrapbooks. MTP.

————. "Shackleford's Ghost." MTP.

————. "Telegraph Dog." De Voto 361. MTP.

————. "What Is the Real Character of Conscience?" MTP.

————. "Travel Scraps." De Voto 82. MTP.

"Twain Would Be A Bill Poster." *New York Tribune*, 31 October 1901, p. 31.

Wagenknecht, Edward. *Mark Twain: The Man and His Work*. Rev. ed. Norman: University of Oklahoma Press, 1961.

Waggoner, Hyatt. "Science in the Thought of Mark Twain." *American Literature* 8 (1937):357–70.

Warner, Charles Dudley. Review of *Equality*, by Edward Bellamy. *Harper's New Monthly Magazine* 95 (October 1897):799.

Index